Black
&Human

*Rediscovering King as a Resource
for Black Theology and Ethics*

Rev. Dr. Don L. Davis

TUMI Press
3701 East 13th Street North
Wichita, Kansas 67208

To my mother and father,

Mary Alice and Theodore Roosevelt Davis,

the two human beings who taught me
more than anyone else
what it means be both black and human,
to affirm my own worth and dignity
in the midst of difficulty, pain, and struggle
while simultaneously affirming
the dignity of all others.

Table of Contents

Foreword

I am the product of the African-American church, the urban multi-ethnic church and prophetic voices for racial reconciliation and righteousness within the body of Christ. Growing up I was inspired and encouraged in my calling to ministry by preachers such as Tom Skinner, John Perkins and Tony Evans. These African-American voices helped me understand that the core of the African-American church is not just a gift for African-American people but also a deep blessing for the broader Church.

The African-American or Black church begins within the tragedy, affliction and great tribulation of American slavery. Who could imagine that slaves stripped of their basic humanity could see themselves as beloved children of God and citizens of the kingdom of Christ in the midst of a dominant Christian framework that led to their lynching, mutilation, rape and treatment beneath even the pet dogs of their masters? Yet within this oppressive reality this slave people became not only Christians, but birthed a new American narrative of what church and missions could be.

Missionaries, church planters, evangelists and an army of spiritual entrepreneurs emerged within this context. One would think that even being Christian, these people would have nothing but utter hatred for their oppressors and would forge a central focus of escaping the matrix created by their oppressors, who also happened to be the sole cultural group framing the social landscape of the American dream. In some cases the hatred of the oppressor and the dream of returning to Africa, the motherland of the enslaved people, did indeed take root. But at the same time an army of African-American Christian ambassadors of reconciliation arose. Years later we would see an initial climax of this reconciling army through a drum major for justice known as the Reverend Dr. Martin Luther King, Jr.

Martin Luther King, Jr. not only served as an advocate and prophetic voice for African-Americans (and more broadly, all poor and marginalized people), but he also was a dreamer and architect of a reconciling future. His vision, which he called the Beloved Community, not only included the liberation and empowerment of the oppressed, but a second conversion and further liberation for the soul of the oppressors. King was able to see the possibility of other-worldly empowerment for the worldly powerful. I believe as other scholars, that King's vision of the Beloved Community was deeply tied to the core elements of the eternal kingdom of God. Yes, salvation, truth, love, grace, repentance, forgiveness and deliverance are members of these core elements of the kingdom of God. But flowing through all these elements, and sitting alongside them, is the mysterious and powerful element of reconciliation. King believed that reconciliation was the true end of the Civil Rights Movement being actualized. Yes, he demanded equality, justice and the dismantling of oppressive systems, but he also promoted harmony and reconciliation between enemies. When I look at the deep divisions that still exist in my nation and around the world across ethnicity, race, political groups, community and police relations, and religious groups, it is obvious to me that the true goals of the Civil Rights Movement are yet to be fulfilled.

Though we have much work to do in realizing the Beloved Community and advancing the kingdom of God, I remain hopeful. Part of my hope is in how God has declared and demonstrated his kingdom through the African-American church and the gift that it can be to the whole body of Christ. The idea of this gift leads me to the importance of this book. The rich theological journey Dr. Davis takes us through in this powerful resource provides a significant introduction to this gift if we are willing to dive in and allow our hearts and minds to unwrap it.

I am so honored to serve on the staff of World Impact with Dr. Davis. He is yet another powerful, determined, and fruitful prophet, scholar and pastor of reconciliation and the missional empowerment of the poor. He is truly a gift to World Impact and also to the broader body of Christ. He is an innovative and deeply biblical voice on church planting, urban ministry, missions and church leadership. In many ways I see my ministry calling and work as building upon what he has preached, taught and developed. Today he is still dreaming, developing, preaching and writing in the tradition of the great reconcilers such as Martin Luther King, Jr. Within this book, Dr. Davis provides sound honor, analysis, and critique of Black theology. He also shows that by the development of a Black theology being more influenced by the Black Power movement outside the Black church than by the liberating and reconciling Black theology of the Black church itself we miss the broader gift of kingdom transformation. This is not to throw the baby out with the bathwater by any means because there are rich elements to be gleaned from the roots of Black and Womanist theologies today. But, without the liberating and reconciling Black theology emphasized by King, we are left with a limited framework for solving the great challenges of individual and systemic injustice and sin today.

Because this resource is based on Dr. Davis' dissertation, we get to enter into his research, wrestling, passion and intellect. I hope you will take advantage of the true spiritual buffet that this book is. I was not only full after I read it, but better equipped for the journey of ministry ahead. Enjoy this book deeply, my brothers and sisters, and be blessed.

Reverend Efrem Smith
President and CEO
World Impact, Inc.

Acknowledgments

I am deeply indebted to many for both the content and form of this thesis. My richest thanks go to the faculty and students of the University of Iowa School of Religion, whose teaching and interaction have forever shaped my understanding of theology and ethics. I am also grateful to my colleagues at World Impact and The Urban Ministry Institute, especially Lorna Rasmussen whose support was key to the completion of this project, and Dan Hennings' technical support helped me immeasurably with formatting. I am also very thankful for the patience that my wife, Beth, and our children have displayed. Their perseverance has been Herculean on my behalf over these belabored days of preparation.

Above all, I owe my deepest heartfelt thanks to Dr. Diana Cates for her mentoring and overseeing of this process. Truly, without the influence of her careful reasoning, clear dialogue, and persistent editing, this project would never have come to completion. Her special assistance was the decisive factor in the preparation of this document, and in the formation of my thinking regarding the possibility of a newer, more open kind of Black theology and ethic.

Introduction

The form and content of this project have been influenced by many factors. The most significant of these are personal. My thinking as an academic has been deeply formed by my lifelong participation in the struggle of African-Americans to develop a sense of their fundamental and equal human dignity and to enjoy the benefits of full citizenship in the American context. I grew up during the social upheaval of the 1960s, during which Blacks, Whites, and others of conscience sought to make our society more just and humane. My father died the year that the federal government guaranteed to him and to other Blacks the right to vote. Like the vast majority of mid-twentieth century African-Americans, he and my mother had grown up in the South, having been subjected to the exclusion, humiliation, and neglect that was so prominent in the lives of most Black people at that time. I continue to live and work in a predominantly Black community in an effort to improve the quality of life for the poorest of the poor, many of whom are Black.

With these historical and personal interests in mind, I have sought in this thesis to recommend some changes in the way that Black theology and ethics is done, so that it might become more effective in fulfilling one of its fundamental aims: to affirm the human dignity of Black people in America and the infinite ground of this dignity in the divine life, within the frame of the Judeo-Christian tradition. The thesis of this thesis is that there is a disabling problem within the discourse of Black theology and ethics – a problem that has undermined the discipline's ability to speak cogently to Black people, as well as to others, many of whom share with Blacks a legacy of intense suffering due to oppression. The problem is the propensity to oversimplify, over-generalize, and romanticize Black experience, and then to absolutize that experience by ascribing it unique and supreme ontological significance. This thesis seeks to identify what I call the problem of absolutized particularism within the writings of prominent Black theologians. It seeks to reveal how some Black theologians and ethicists have noticed the problem and have sought to move beyond it, but have not managed, finally, to transcend it. Finally, this thesis seeks to convince readers who are in principle sympathetic to the Black theology project that a rediscovery of the work of Martin Luther King, Jr. reveals a way to break free from this crippling tendency.

This thesis does not presume to offer the final word on Black theology or the problem that continues to plague it, albeit in increasingly subtle forms. Nor is this thesis a philosophical analysis of the age-old problem of the relationship between the particular and the universal. Nor is it a thoroughgoing historical analysis of the various dimensions of the highly diverse experiences of Blacks in

America. What I attempt here is a modest "first word," which acknowledges the validity of Black theology's central purpose, admits the past tendency to absolutize Black experience and to ignore the disabling effects of this tendency, and proposes a rereading of Dr. King's theological ethics as a way of finally getting beyond this tendency, so that a more compelling Black theology might emerge.

A great theological and ethical divide appears to be present within the academy of religious studies between those who concentrate on the particular, deeply situated religious experiences of specific people (e.g., specific groups of Blacks, women, Latin Americans, Asians, etc.) and those who analyze God and human goodness in universal and trans-cultural terms. The former group is concerned with addressing religious and moral issues that arise in specific forms within particular socio-cultural, linguistic contexts, while the latter concentrates on interpreting ultimate reality and the requirements of morality in light of what are thought to be common human experiences. Most Black theologians and ethicists belong to the former group. I hope to engage these Black theologians and ethicists in this thesis. I openly sympathize with the Black theological and ethical enterprise and hope to engage in various kinds of future intellectual projects which demonstrate that reflection on Black life, particularly Black Christian life, is tremendously interesting and valuable. Yet I want, at the same time, to show that such reflection is interesting and valuable, not only for Black people, but for a wide variety of other people, many of whom might learn something about their own situations and their own lives from their engagement with the problems and promises of Black life in America – and from whom

Blacks might, in turn, learn a great deal. In other words, I want to connect Black concerns with the concerns of other human beings and to locate them, to some extent, on common human ground.

Certain definitions will play an important role in the argument of this thesis, and are best stipulated at the start. Black theology and ethics as a discourse is based upon a racial categorization, the meaning of which seems clear enough at first glance, but is regarded by some as ambiguous and difficult to define. In this thesis, I refer to a group of people as "Blacks" or "African-Americans" (interchangeably) and I refer to other things as being "Black," including Black theology, Black life, and Black history. In doing so, I mean to denote the people, and the life experiences of people, who are the descendants of African slaves in America, who live more or less reflectively in light of this legacy, and seek to this day to find a way to live well in a society that is characterized by racism.

There is, of course, no such thing as a single, monolithic "Black" or "African-American" experience. The life struggles and possibilities of Blacks are affected by the same variables that affect other social groupings, including age, gender, and socioeconomic background. Furthermore, Blacks in America have had different encounters with different forms of racial animus in different places, with different results. There is no one way of drawing and labeling boundaries that can do justice to the nuances of all these diverse conditions, characters, and situations. Nevertheless, phenomenological and phenotypical classifications of Black people have been used throughout the history of America to exclude and discriminate on the basis of skin tone, phenotype, and genetic background. In light of the pervasive *de facto* and *de jure* discrimination that has shaped the lives of African-Americans, it seems clear that a common thread binds the lives of these people together: they all seek to function well as human beings and as full citizens in a context where they and their ancestors have been historically excluded, neglected, and demeaned, based on racial and ethnic qualifications. The great social gains won by the Civil Rights movement have yet to fully transform our society into a haven of harmonious relationships characterized by equal civic and human rights and responsibilities.

Commentators tend to stipulate their own meanings of the terms "Black" and "African-American," in addition to terms like "colored people" and "Negroes." In this thesis, I allow each author to employ these terms as they choose within the context of their own discussions. There are situations in which particular uses of "Black" and "Blackness" become highly problematic, however, because they involve equivocation. I will consider these situations as they arise.

In addition to the terms like "Black" and "Black experiences," another term will be used often in this thesis, and is worth an initial comment. As I have already hinted, "absolutized particularism" refers to the inclination of a group, culture, or people to treat its own culture, social grouping, or racial identity as a *sui generis* reality, even a sacred reality, which bears special ontological significance. I am most interested in the problem of absolutized particularism within Black theology and ethics, but I want to note that this is a propensity that one would expect to find in other communities of discourse as well. Any racial, ethnic, or cultural group can fall into the trap of romanticizing its own history and legacy, and can be tempted to attribute a kind of ultimacy to its way of being human. Any group can succumb to the temptation to view itself as *the* definitive or superior culture or grouping by which others must be measured or understood. Often such tendencies arise within oppressed groups whose members struggle to define themselves as worthwhile human beings in the face of overwhelming messages to the contrary.

The argument of the thesis is straightforward. In *chapter one* I provide some selective historical background to the origin of Black theology and ethics, and I seek to display the emergence of the problem of absolutized particularism against that background. *Chapter two* reveals the full flowering of this problem in the early thought of James Cone, who is arguably the father and progenitor of modern Black theology and ethics. Cone's argument that "Blackness" is best construed as a symbol for ultimate reality is paradigmatic of the problem with which I am concerned. *Chapter three* focuses on the attempts of various thinkers within the discipline's brief history to address and transcend this absolutizing tendency. I include three types of respondents: those early respondents who accepted the basic terms of Cone's analysis, but insisted on the importance of forgiveness and reconciliation between Blacks and Whites (e.g., J. Deotis Roberts), those scholars who are presently focusing sharply on Black religion and its African roots (e.g., Dwight Hopkins), and key womanist scholars (e.g., Katie Cannon). Much progress has been made by these respondents toward transcending the problem of absolutizing Black experience, but I will argue that these attempts nevertheless come up short.

Chapters four and five point to an alternative trajectory for Black theology and ethics. Using the thought of Martin King, I seek in *chapter four* to show how Black life needs to be understood, fundamentally, as a form of human life. Black people, like all other people, are children of God who are created in the image of God, with equal dignity. Black people, and all other people, are connected to each other in their dignity, and in their responsibility to acknowledge each other's dignity. They have a common destiny, and are dependent on each other for realizing that destiny. It is only within some such theological framework that it is truly profitable, in my view, to explore the particularities of Black lives, and other diverse lives, for it is only against such a theological horizon that these particularities appear as intriguing dimensions of our common human life, rather than as things about us that threaten to divide us and leave us mutually unintelligible.

I close the dissertation with *chapter five*, which is an attempt to show how once the problem of absolutized particularism is transcended, Black theology and ethics is freed to rediscover within traditional theological and ethical sources new resources for illuminating the Black struggle for dignity, freedom, and justice in the American context. King's use of sources was dynamic and pragmatic; he never treated sources systematically. Yet his writings are suggestive of how Black theologians and ethicists today could possibly find, in critical conversation with traditional sources, new insights into Black lives and the problem of Black suffering. As a case in point, I show how King and other Black theologians have alluded profitably to Tillich's concept of "the courage to be" to clarify the meaning of Black self-affirmation in spite of the threats of death, meaninglessness, and moral impotence. This chapter is not a full-blown analysis of Tillich's notion of courage, nor a final answer to all of the questions associated with employing traditional theological sources in Black particularistic religious reflection. I hope only to provide reasons for renewing the dialogue between Black experience and traditional theological and ethical construals. The problem of absolutized particularism has made such dialogue difficult, if not impossible.

Finally by attempting to renew interest in the theological ethics of Martin Luther King, Jr., I am not suggesting a simplistic return to a traditional reading of King, but rather a reading that reveals some of the quiet genius with which King held together both a concern for the struggle of Black Americans for dignity and justice *and* a concern for human beings and the human community as such. While Black life in America is the historical outworking of the experience of the descendants of African slaves on this continent, it is also and simultaneously the experience of human beings who are seeking to affirm their worth in contexts that make this extremely difficult. A fresh and critical rediscovery of King's thought can provide Black theologians and ethicists with the outlines of a model for integrating a particularistic view with a universalistic and global perspective.

CHAPTER 1
Black Theology and Ethics, and the Emergence of Absolutized Particularism

The kinds of writing and thinking that are now included under the rubric of Black theology and ethics exhibit considerable diversity in subject matter and method. Virtually all of the literature that goes by this name, however, seeks to fulfill the original purpose of Black theology and ethics, which was to explicate the significance of God and the moral life within the context of the Black struggle for freedom, wholeness, and justice, primarily within the American context. As a theology and ethic of liberation, Black theology and ethics is dedicated to finding ways in which God's saving activity in the world can be correlated with both the utter devastation and the transformation of Black people.

Given its intention to engage in discourse that exposes the problem of racial oppression and contributes to the liberation of Black people from forces of dehumanization and exploitation, Black ethics and theology is particularistic. It is a discourse that is rooted particularly in Black people's experiences, including the experiences of Africans in their

homeland before slavery and *en route* to the Americas, and
the experiences of African-Americans during the slavery
period, through the periods of Reconstruction, "Jim Crow"
segregation, the civil rights and Black Consciousness
movements, and into our current post-civil rights era. Black
theology and ethics is rooted in these experiences in that
it seeks to make sense of them; it seeks to discern the good
and the evil in them, to illuminate what is truthful in them
and what is distorting. Black theology and ethics is rooted
in the experiences of Black people in that it seeks to
interpret the gospel in a way that answers the questions
that are raised by those experiences.

There is nothing inherently problematic in seeking to
articulate a theology and ethic that is particularistic in this
sense. It is hard to imagine, at this juncture in history,
articulating a theology and ethic that is not to some degree
particularistic. It is untenable to hold that one can speak
about matters divine and human from a vantage point that
is not socially and historically situated and thus limited in
perspective. It is also difficult to imagine a single discourse
gripping every possible human being who might hear that
discourse. A variety of theologies and ethics seem to be
needed to reach a variety of persons. There are, however,
perils associated with the construction of particularistic
theologies and ethics. This thesis concerns two related
perils that threaten Black theology and ethics.

There is first the tendency to repeat the mistake of many
White theologians and ethicists by (implicitly, if not explicitly)
construing one's own experience, or the experiences of
one's group, as absolute in the sense of being uniquely and
finally definitive of normative humanity. There is, associated
with this, a tendency to construct one's own group's

experiences negatively, over and against the experiences of others. There is, second, the tendency to focus so intently on one's own group and its concerns that one fails to attend to the larger project of theology and ethics, which is to speak the truth about God and the human good in a way that promises to improve the lives of as many human beings as possible – those outside, as well as inside, one's group. Even though theological and ethical reflection is situated reflection, and Black theology and ethics probably cannot hope to speak to everyone, still it is important for its practitioners to try to make meaningful connections with people outside the Black community. Sympathetic and critical reflection on some of the particularities of Black experience is capable of shedding light on dimensions of human life that most, if not all, persons share.

In this chapter and the next, I argue that there is a tendency within Black theology and ethics to absolutize Black experience and, at the same time, to neglect the work of understanding and transforming elements of our common humanity. There is a tendency for Black scholars to romanticize the historical and cultural legacy of African-Americans, to attribute a sense of ultimacy to this legacy, and to view the Black community and Black culture as the standard of human excellence relative to which other groups or cultures must be evaluated.

The work of early Black theologians like James Cone exemplifies this tendency. Early Black theologians took Black experience to be a principal norm and source for theology and ethics. Black experience was conceived by Black theologians as fundamentally and uniformly different from White experience; it was construed as irreducibly unique. At the same time, Black experience was considered superior to White experience, supremely emblematic of God's presence in the world, and reflective of God's special favor. White experience and White persons were viewed not only as inferior, but as downright demonic. Accordingly, what it meant to be Black and human became defined in terms of the drive to destroy the White oppressor, to be other than White.

It is important to understand that this sort of absolutist tendency emerged as a reaction to the intense pain and frustration that many Black religious thinkers felt in the late 1960s over the prolonged and virtually complete neglect – especially on the part of White theologians and ethicists – of the suffering of Black people in America. Black theology and ethics arose in tandem with the wider Black community's persistent attempts to gain self-understanding, self-determination, and social justice in America. Black theology and ethics emerged during a time when Black social protest was gathering strength, and when the advocates of Black freedom within the Black community, both religious and secular, were calling for revolution and armed resistance.

During the 1960s Black anger and frustration in American society had reached its boiling point. Within that volatile social setting, a number of Black poets, theologians, ethicists, artists, and commentators took the opportunity to speak for the first time from the vantage point of those who had suffered grave injustice due to race discrimination. Feeling ignored or dismissed by many of their fellow Americans, Black advocates spoke, wrote, and communicated their concerns animated by heated emotion, and this emotion undoubtedly affected their rhetoric. This same kind of angry, piercing rhetoric can still be heard today among the

Black underclass, whose alienation, nihilism, and despair permeate the lower strata of African-American society, especially the young and poor.

Whatever its causes and explanations, however, absolutized particularism is a problem for Black theology and ethics. Although few Black theologians and ethicists would speak today in the vitriolic words of the early Cone, it is important to notice that few of these scholars have managed fully to transcend the bipolar Black-White structure of that rhetoric, and few have offered a compelling critique of the questionable assumptions that are implicit in the use of that structure. Left to function as a largely unacknowledged undercurrent within the development of Black thought, the problem of absolutized particularism will likely undermine the future of Black theology and ethics. It will likely undermine the ability of Black theologians and ethicists to reflect in deeply liberating ways on the religious and moral dimensions of Black life. It will also undermine their ability to speak persuasively to persons outside the Black community who could potentially be of help in righting racial injustice, and who could benefit from engaging some of the insights that have been gained through Black American struggles for self-definition, self-affirmation, and social transformation.

In what follows, I want to show that the tendency toward absolutized particularism has been present since the inception of Black theology and ethics.[1] In later chapters, I will show that certain aspects of this problem have been addressed by a variety of Black thinkers; nevertheless, the problem remains, albeit in more subtle forms. I want to display this tendency within the context of a brief and focused history of Black theology and ethics.

The Struggle for Self-Affirmation

African-American life has been marked by the experience
of an ongoing struggle for responsible identity. W.E.B.
DuBois gives powerful expression to the dilemma that is
encountered on some level by most, if not all, African-
Americans who seek a mature sense of identity. He speaks
of the experience of "twoness," which is the experience
of being aware of oneself as a worthwhile Black human
being while, at the same time, also being aware of and
inescapably influenced by conflicting White interpretations
and evaluations of one's life.

> The history of the American Negro is the history of this
> strife – this longing to attain self-conscious manhood, to
> merge his double self into a better and truer self. In this
> merging he wishes neither of the older selves to be lost.
> He would not Africanize America, for America has too
> much to teach the world and Africa. He would not bleach
> his Negro soul in a flood of white Americanism, for he
> knows that Negro blood has a message for the world. He
> simply wishes to make it possible for a man to be both
> a Negro and an American, without being cursed and spit
> upon by his fellows, without having the doors of
> opportunity closed roughly in his face.[2]

I would posit that, until only recently, the experience of
virtually all African-Americans has been checkered by this
dilemma, and by feelings of displacement and insecurity
in the American social community. As Henry Young has
noted, as one of the oldest minority social groups in
America, Blacks have sought from "the inception of

Anglo conformity and the erection of the color line barrier"
to find full membership in the category of "human
experience."[3] The search for identity and full personhood,
the struggle to find a self-image that is truthful, admirable,
and defensible within a context where Black people are
maligned, lies at the heart of the many challenges that
African-Americans have faced from the inception of their
presence on this continent, and in this nation.

The place that the Christian religion has had in this search
for Black personhood has been formative and controversial.
Most African-Americans were exposed to the faith of the
Judeo-Christian tradition, and from the beginning of their
forced arrival to the continent used the stories, symbols,
theologies, and experiences associated with that tradition
to find hope in and beyond their servitude. Gayraud
Wilmore carefully documents the adjustments made to
Christian theology and symbolism by Blacks historically
as they sought a more meaningful existence within the
American context:

> What we may call "white Christianity" in Europe and
> North America has made a deep and lasting impression
> upon blacks everywhere, including Africa. But blacks
> have used Christianity not so much as it was delivered
> to them by racist white churches, but as its truth was
> authenticated to them in the experience of suffering
> and struggle, to reinforce an enculturated religious
> orientation and to produce an indigenous faith that
> emphasized dignity, freedom, and human welfare.[4]

Early Black Christianity was a faith that incorporated
certain traditional elements of an inherited faith, as well
as elements of a new faith that spoke to experiences of

cultural difference and social exclusion. Wilmore
comments further on the distinctive extension of Christian
religion by Blacks:

> It is true that the first independent Black churches, the
> African Baptist and African Methodist, patterned their
> orders of worship and creeds after the white churches
> from which they separated in the latter half of the
> eighteenth century. But it is also true, and even more
> significant, that these churches called themselves
> 'African' and developed, particularly in the South, out
> of that so-called 'invisible institute,' the slave church.
> From the beginning these churches developed what
> whites recognized as a "Negro style" of devotion and
> theology. Whatever those first gatherings of slaves for
> religious purposes outside the supervision of whites may
> have been like, it is inaccurate to think of the religious
> institutions that made their first appearance among
> blacks as "churches" in the sense of the European or
> American model.[5]

The emergence of Black Theology, which came into
existence with its greatest energy in the late 1960s, ought
not, then, to be perceived as a completely new and unusual
attempt on the part of African-Americans to interpret the
Christian faith with eyes focused on their liberation within
American society. In their ongoing historical struggles for
identity and self-determination, many African-Americans
have chosen all along to make sense of their lives in
light of this faith, expecting the gospel to speak to their
oppressive situation and reveal a way through and beyond
it.[6] Benjamin Mays provides a convincing argument that
the notion of God in Black poetry and writings from the

very beginning (as early as Jupiter Mammon in 1761)
reflects the persistent belief that the Christian God is no
respecter of persons, and is creator of all humankind.
Further, Mays details a clear trend within the spirituals
and Black writings through the 1930s expressing the
belief that God is on the side of the Negro, whose cause
is just. This trend existed notwithstanding the doubt
and frustration that characterized the younger and
post-War writers.[7]

Abundant evidence exists, then, to substantiate the claim
that many African-Americans throughout their history in
this country have believed that the Christian faith and its
ethic is the primary source of hope for the descendants of
African slaves seeking to experience liberated selfhood in
the midst of horrible oppression.[8] Evidence also exists to
show a deep ambivalence among many Blacks concerning
the legitimacy of a faith that was endorsed by White
slaveholders, some of whom justified brutal acts of injustice
on the basis of Christian dogma and practice,[9] but
virtually all historians of the African-American community
agree that Christianity and its religious practices lie at
the root of a distinctive African-American culture.
Christianity, largely in its Protestant forms, has been cited
as the key source of African-American religion in general,
and of the diverse traditions of Black Christian experience
in particular.[10] Cornel West argues that Black cultural life
developed through its ongoing connection to Black
Christian tradition and liturgy, and that many if not most
of the Black community's formative leadership base (i.e.,
its political leaders, orators, activists, journalists,
professionals, and scholars) has arisen from the church's
institutional experience and community life.[11] His

conclusion on this connection is clear: "The unique variant of American life that we call Afro-American culture germinated in the bosom of this Afro-Christianity, in the Afro-Christian church congregations."[12]

The Emergence of Black Theology and Ethics

The activism and reform inspired by the religious convictions of African-Americans came to a head in the late 1960s.[13] The Black theology and ethics that came into view during this period is best understood as a response to three cultural phenomena, namely, the civil rights movement of the 1950s and 60s, the beginnings of the Black Power movement, which was strongly influenced by Malcolm X's early philosophy of Black nationalism, and the mid-sixties writing of and reactions to Joseph Washington's controversial *Black Religion*. I want to introduce each of these in turn.[14]

Martin Luther King, Jr., clergyman and social activist, is clearly one of the most important figures in the history of Black theology and ethics. One of King's most famous theological and ethical declarations, the "Letter from Birmingham City Jail" (1963), argued vehemently that only in partnership with God and among all human beings could the evils of racism, militarism, and poverty be overcome. We shall analyze the thought of King in a later chapter. For now it is enough to note that King used a biblically-based Christian vision of a "Beloved Community" as the principal ground for a social movement that was designed specifically to promote political

enfranchisement for Blacks in America. King made plain
the connection between participating in an authentic
Christian faith and struggling together for equal human
rights. This was a connection that would captivate
other Black thinkers. As James Cone recalls,

> All those involved in the rise of Black Theology were
> also deeply involved in the civil rights movement, and
> participated in the protest demonstrations led by Martin
> Luther King, Jr. Unlike most contemporary theological
> movements in Europe and North America, therefore,
> Black Theology's origin was not in the seminary or the
> university. In fact, most of its early interpreters did not
> even hold advanced academic degrees. Black Theology
> came in to being in the context of Black people's
> struggle for racial justice, which was initiated in the
> black churches but was chiefly identified with such
> protest organizations as the Southern Christian Leadership
> Conference (SCLC), the National Conference of Black
> Churchmen (NCBC), the Interreligious Foundation for
> Community Organization (IFCO), and many Black
> caucuses in white churches.[15]

During the 1960s most liberal White Christian churches,
with few exceptions, remained silent on this connection
between the gospel and social justice; they felt ambivalent
about King as a spokesman for the practical outworkings
of a Christian vision in America.[16]

Just one year after King wrote his "Letter from Birmingham
City Jail," Malcolm X published his autobiography. A
growing Black population began to resonate with his
experience. More and more Black people came to believe

that King's calm, collected, and universalist language
of mass civil disobedience through nonviolent direct
action was not proving effective. Shortly after the March
on Washington in 1963, the sentiment in favor of an
integrationist vision began to wane, and it was replaced
to a significant extent by a nationalistic fervor that
was associated especially with the life and teachings of
Malcolm X, who became a key spokesman for the Nation
of Islam under Elijah Muhammad.[17] It may safely be said
that Black theology and ethics was influenced more by this
cynical and separatist strand of Black protest thought than
it was by the chords and cadences of King's thought.[18]
Malcolm X provided a strong impulse for the formation of
a Black Power vision, which competed with and eventually
triumphed over King's vision among Black intellectuals,
including those who considered themselves Christians.
Malcolm X's life experience, his eloquent articulation of
the lessons of that experience, and his stinging social
criticism made him an attractive leader, causing many
Blacks to join the Nation of Islam and many others, who
did not join the Nation, to try to knit his views into an
alternative, more revolutionary Christian program.[19]

Malcolm X was especially critical of White Christianity in
his earlier years. He believed that there was a religious as
well as a socio-political conspiracy to keep Blacks numb to
their true personhood. In a speech in Paris in 1964, he
maintained that, "Christianity was used in America on us,
on our people, not to take us to Heaven but to make us
good slaves, primarily by robbing us of our right to defend
ourselves in the name of Jesus."[20] Speaking of the tactical,
anger-suppressing role that Christianity played to keep
Blacks docile and tame, he urged:

> Brothers and sisters, the white man has brainwashed us
> black people to fasten our gaze upon a blond-haired,
> blue-eyed Jesus! We're worshiping a Jesus that doesn't
> even look like us! Now, just think of this. The blond-
> haired, blue-eyed white man has taught you and me to
> worship a white Jesus, and to shout and sing and pray to
> this God that's his God, the white man's God. The white
> man has taught us to shout and sing and pray until we
> die, to wait until death, for some dreamy heaven-in-the-
> hereafter, when we're dead, while this white man has his
> milk and honey in the streets paved with golden dollars
> right here on this earth![21]

This critical awareness of common distortions within
Christianity grew throughout the second half of the 1960s.
With the occurrence of the Watts riots in 1965, and a
growing militancy elsewhere around the nation, King's
dream of equality and justice for Black Americans, to
be realized through nonviolent direct action, gave way
to a nightmare of rage and cynicism, not only about
Black life, but also about the potential of Christianity
to make a liberative difference to Black life.

Black theology thus emerged out of the theological-
political connections that were made by King, and out
of the more critical Black Nationalist approach which
construed those connections differently. It also emerged
out of related political-philosophical ideas espoused
by Black Nationalist leaders like Bishop Henry McNeal
Turner[22] and the founder of the Universal Negro
Improvement Association, Marcus Garvey.[23] Along
with Malcolm, these leaders championed in one form
or another a notion of God as one who is Black, who

has the liberation of Blacks specifically in mind, and who
leads Blacks to discount and discard the values of White
society and religion. The arguments proposed for a Black
God were straightforward. Turner argued that "We have
as much right biblically and otherwise to believe that God
is a Negro . . . as you . . . white people have to believe that
God is a fine looking, symmetrical, and ornamented white
man."[24] Garvey likewise held that if Whites embraced a
notion of a White God, then Whites were free to worship
God as they desired; Negroes, however, believed in the
one everlasting God, who was the Black God of Ethiopia.[25]
These impulses to reveal a God that looked like and thus
affirmed the lives of Black people would receive further
articulation later in the twentieth century.

Another important goad that helped to generate energy
among Black thinkers to create a more comprehensive
appraisal of the meaning of the Christian gospel to the
Black revolutionary movement was Joseph Washington's
widely read and controversial *Black Religion* (1964).
This book offered a stinging, negative assessment of the
role and utility of Negro Christianity within the Black
community. In Washington's judgment, Negro folk
religion was a kind of religious amalgam, a syncretistic
emotionalism which "produced no Negroes who advance
'orthodoxy.'"[26] The Negro Christian church, in his view,
lacked its own credible theological underpinnings, made
no authentic contribution to the theological advancement
of Christianity, and ought therefore to be disbanded.
Washington urged Negro Christians to do the only
respectable thing that they could in light of the complete
inadequacy of their theological vision, which was to
accept their assimilation into the White Christian church.

Assimilation into the mainstream is the endeavor of the
Negro in every field except that of social relations and
the religious life. The responsibility of white Protestantism
is to create conditions wherein the Negro will realize
assimilation is in his best interest and that of the Church.
To do that without pain there is no social growth and
that the pain of new life and growth is preferable to the
pain of meaninglessness. Were congregations open
to assimilation of the Negro Christian into the Christian
community, it would not be a question of how many
Negroes would take this opportunity, but of the quality
and kind of Negro.[27]

Washington was convinced that Black churches contained
such a paucity of original theological thought that they
were at best inferior versions of their White counterparts,
if indeed they were churches at all. The lack of credible
theology among the Negro churches left them vulnerable
to the shifting winds of their own unreflective cultural
bigotries and socio-political agendas. Black congregations,
without the aid and instruction of the more refined and
theologically astute White churches, had no resources for
correcting their tendencies toward emotional extremism
and ideological exaggeration:

At least white Protestantism in its turn to cultural
religion does so under the judgment of a theology which
declares there is a tension between faith and culture and
calls attention to the conflict between spurious religious
concerns and the Christian faith. In this difference lies
the seeds of renewal, however far white Protestantism may
stray from its roots. In seeking economic and social
status under the guise of religious affiliation and class

congregations, the Negro is not only imitative but has no
theology which judges his response in the sphere of culture.
Negro congregations are free (or perhaps damned is
equally theological) to treat economic values and class
symbols as sanctions of religion.[28]

Washington's critique of Negro Christianity was
thoroughgoing. Not only did the Black church lack
a theology capable of securing it from ideological
and cultural error; it was a distortion of Christianity
in practice:

> The Negro has grounded his belief in Christianity in an
> ethical code, the principles of which are not founded in
> an enduring faith and [are] therefore devoid of content
> and the refreshment of a critical dimension. The Negro
> is forced to depend upon civil rights, religious feeling,
> sentiment, and color as substitutes for faith. It is the
> absence of historical loyalty to the Christian faith which
> expresses itself as religious sentiment. This feeling for
> religion is not inherent but nurtured, and to make virtue
> of necessity does not justify the title of Christian faith.[29]

The thesis that the Black Christian experience, although
unique and vibrant, was theologically empty and controlled
by political ideology, rather than faith, was one of the
central causes of the emergence of a more systematic Black
theology. Cone suggests that Black theology was partly
a rejoinder to Washington's dual claim that Black religion
was not even Christian and that the true Christian gospel
had nothing to do with the struggle for justice in American
society.[30]

Whether or not Washington's portrayal was correct or
legitimate, it was provocative. It was soundly denounced
in the Black community, and in fact it was repudiated by
Washington only a few years after he articulated it. With
an entirely different theological vision and sentiment
towards Negro Christianity, Washington argued in his
subsequent work, *The Politics of God*,[31] that Negro
churches should not assimilate, but should instead build
political muscle to work effectively for the fulfillment
of their self-chosen goals. The call for disbanding Negro
Christianity was rescinded, and the appeal for Black
Christians to assimilate into "legitimate" White Christian
churches was withdrawn. Instead, Washington made the
case for conceiving of the Black Christian community as
a suffering, servant people that should harness the requisite
political and social power to effect lasting social change
on behalf of the Negro.

Several explanations could be offered for this dramatic
turnaround in Washington's thought. Perhaps the most
important reason for Washington's change of mind was
the response of the Black community: his arguments had
been thoroughly spurned. Another likely explanation
was the evolving mood of the Black community, which
as I have mentioned was becoming more and more
cynical about the viability of an integrationist vision.
Even after King's march on Washington in August 1963,
many within the Black intellectual community began to
invest in the more nationalist philosophy of Black Power.
The outbreak of the riots provided clear signs of the
heightened frustration and despair of many urban poor
Blacks. During the eventful Mississippi "March Against

Fear," which was organized on behalf of James Meredith, who was shot during the first part of the march, Stokely Carmichael trumpeted the now well-known slogan of "Black Power." This slogan became an anthem that left an indelible mark on Black theology and ethics:

When Carmichael and other Black activists separated themselves from King's absolute commitment to nonviolence by proclaiming Black Power, White church people called upon their Black brothers and sisters in the gospel to denounce the Black Power slogan as un-Christian. To the surprise of White Christians, Black ministers refused to follow their advice. Instead they wrote a Black Power statement that was published in the *New York Times* on July 31, 1966. The appearance of this statement may be regarded as the beginning of the conscious development of a Black theology by Black ministers. It was in these two contexts, the civil rights movement and the Black Power movement, that Black theology emerged.[32]

Black Power, Black Christ

By 1966, then, it had become clear that Black theologians and ethicists wanted to articulate a theology that would provide, so to speak, the theological arm of the Black Power movement. There was, from the start, some ambivalence about using the phrase "Black Power." The ambivalence stemmed largely from King's concern that use of the term would cause White backlash and would link Black theology in the minds of both Blacks and Whites with the most violent elements of the Black freedom movement. In Cone's early apology on behalf of Black Power, he acknowledges that when it was first coined, the term was indeed ambiguous in its meaning. It was used during the civil rights movement by Stokeley Carmichael to designate "the only appropriate response to White racism."[33] It was used to refer to the "complete emancipation of Black people from White oppression by whatever means Black people deem necessary." It also referred to the power of Blacks to chart their own futures through a creative engagement with the historical structures that were designed for their humiliation and exclusion. Colloquially speaking, Cones suggests that Carmichael thought of Black Power broadly as meaning "T.C.B." – Black folk taking care of Black folks' business, not on the terms of the oppressor, but on those of the oppressed.[34]

Informed and inspired by the Black Power movement, Albert Cleage, a Black minister from Detroit, published in 1968 a book called *The Black Messiah*.[35] This book envisioned Jesus of Nazareth as a Black revolutionary leader whose explicit aim was to free the oppressed Black population from its White antagonists. Cleage opened his book with a clear outline of his thesis:

> For nearly 500 years the illusion that Jesus was white dominated the world only because white Europeans dominated the world. Now, with the emergence of the nationalist movements of the world's colored majority, the historic truth is finally beginning to emerge – that Jesus was the non-white leader of a non-white people struggling for national liberation against the rule of a white nation, Rome. The intermingling of the races in Africa and the Mediterranean area is an established fact. The Nation Israel was a mixture of Chaldeans, Egyptians, Midianites, Ethiopians, Kushites, Babylonians, and other

dark peoples, all of whom were already mixed with the
black people of Central Africa.[36]

Cleage argued that Black Christians needed to appreciate
that Messiah Jesus was Black, the Madonna Mary was
Black, and Israel was composed of Black people, the Black
Christian church and nation. This appropriation of these
symbols would provide Blacks with the tools for understanding their legacy and their destiny – the liberation of
the Black Nation by the Black Messiah. This was for
him an obvious historical fact.

Beyond this, Cleage urged Black religious leaders and
the members of their congregations to comprehend the
liberative implications of this fact. Christianity belonged
uniquely to Black people as their religion, and historically
Israel was a Black Nation. He urged Black Christians to:

> Put down this white Jesus who has been tearing you
> to pieces. Forget your white God. Remember that we are
> worshiping a Black Jesus who was a Black Messiah.
> Certainly God must be black if he created us in his own
> image. You can't build dignity in black people if they go
> down on their knees everyday, worshiping a white Jesus
> and a white God. We are going to communicate with
> black Churches. We are going to talk to them, reason
> with them, shame them if nothing else works saying,
> "Accept the historic fact. Christianity is our religion. The
> Black Church is the beginning of our Black Nation."[37]

In what could be claimed to be a daring theological
maneuver, Cleage began in his writing and sermonizing to
identify, without careful nuancing or qualification, Black

existential reality with the God revealed in Jesus Christ. He infused the concept of "Blackness" with a new critical import, using it to refer to something more than a color, a race, or a culture. He used it to refer to a transcendent reality that could give new life and power to those who participated in it. The implication was that racially and ethnically Black people could participate in this transcendent reality in a unique and superior way. Black people were set apart from others in their ability to represent and further the liberative work of the Black Messiah. Seeds of the enduring problem of absolutized particularism were thus planted and nourished with the broad rhetorical claims of Cleage.

Much of Cleage's language is associated with strong emotional invective, but it is important not to dismiss Cleage's words as angry rhetoric given in the heat of sermonic or social appeal. He sought to offer an argument concerning the nature of ultimate reality and the relationship between that reality and the lives of oppressed Black people. Cleage's claim that Blacks are, in their very Blackness, associated in a unique and superior way with the divine reality is an expression of a theological conviction. If the claims seem flamboyant and even appear to be beyond rational comprehension or defense, they are nevertheless not to be dismissed or ignored. On the contrary, only when these claims are taken seriously as theological claims can one address them on their own terms and begin the work of delineating precisely in what sense, if any, God could be said to be Black, and in what sense, if any, Black people could be said to stand in a special relationship with a Black Messiah.

On the heels of Cleage's explicit association of the Black
Power movement with the Black Christian church came
the *Black Manifesto*, written by James Forman. During a
Sunday service at the famous Riverside Church in New
York City, Forman interrupted the morning worship by
issuing a demand, on behalf of all African-Americans, for
reparations from White churches and synagogues in the
amount of 500 million dollars:

> This demand for $500,000,000 is not an idle resolution
> or empty words. Fifteen dollars for every black brother
> and sister in the United States is only a beginning of the
> reparations due us as people who have been exploited
> and degraded, brutalized, killed, and persecuted. Under-
> neath all of this exploitation, the racism of this country
> has produced a psychological effect upon us that we are
> beginning to shake off. We are no longer afraid to demand
> our full rights as a people in this decadent society.[38]

Forman's Marxist and revolutionary proposal in his *Black
Manifesto* had dramatic effect within the Black church,
again especially among its intellectuals. It gave voice to the
opposition that many Black Christians felt toward the
nonviolence and open-heartedness of King's vision. While
many, including James Cone respected King's integrity,
they felt that King's assumptions about universal humanity
and nonviolent direct action were naive. King did not take
seriously enough the recalcitrance in the hearts of White
oppressors and their unwillingness to acknowledge the
humanness of their Black counterparts. Many Black thinkers
who were moved by Forman's declaration called for the
articulation of a radical Black identity, which would assert
itself fundamentally over and against Whiteness. These
thinkers believed that Black life alone was emblematic of

God's liberative action in the world, and they saw historical Christianity as culpable in its acceptance of Black misery as theologically justified. Forman's assertion thus provided further impetus for Black religious thinking to unfold along the lines of absolutized particularism.

 ## James Cone

Despite the flurry of discussion in the Black community about the relationship between Christianity and the struggle for social justice, it was not until 1969 that someone attempted to develop a systematic or comprehensive Black theological vision. It was in that year that James Cone offered a full-blown theological interpretation of the meaning of Black Power for Black Christians. Seeking to refute the arguments of those who wanted to equate Black Power with the work of the biblical Anti-Christ, or those who suggested that Black Power was inconsistent with a Christian ethic of love and forgiveness, Cone argued that "Black Power, even in its most radical expression, is not the antithesis of Christianity, nor is it a heretical idea to be tolerated with painful forbearance. It is, rather, Christ's central message to twentieth-century America."[39]

Black Power, according to Cone, means "complete emancipation of Black people from white oppression by whatever means Black people deem necessary."[40] Black theology and Black Power correspond to each other in that the express intent of the Black Power movement is to engender within the Black oppressed an inward affirmation of the essential worth of Blackness, and Black theology's sole purpose is "to apply the freeing power of

the gospel to Black people under white oppression."[41]
Black Power and Black theology are both about the
struggle for dignity, liberty, and justice. Black Power is
thus, for Cone, a revelatory movement. God displays
God's deepest identification with the poor and the
oppressed through the struggles of those who have
been most injured, American Blacks:

> It would seem that Black Power and Christianity have this
> in common: the liberation of man! If the work of Christ
> is that of liberating men from alien loyalties, and if racism
> is, as George Kelsey says, an alien faith, then there must
> be some correlation between Black Power and Christianity.
> For the gospel proclaims that God is with us now, actively
> fighting the forces which would make man captive. And
> it is the task of theology and the Church to know where
> God is at work so that we can join him in this fight
> against evil. In America we know where the evil is. We
> know that men are shot and lynched. We know that
> men are crammed into ghettos. Black Power is the power
> to say No; it is the power of blacks to refuse to cooperate
> in their own dehumanization. If blacks can trust the
> message of Christ, if they can take him at his word, this
> power to say No to white power and domination is
> derived from him.[42]

Because Christ is the Liberator who fights against the
dehumanization of persons, and since Blacks above all
others in the American context are the objects of
systematic dehumanization, it follows that Christ is
himself involved in the Black Power movement, energizing
it and serving as its confirmation and justification.[43]

Cone's Christ is Black in the sense that he identifies with
Black people and their struggle. "The blackness of God
means that God has made the oppressed condition God's
own condition . . . [and] the liberation of the oppressed
is a part of the innermost nature of God. Liberation is not
an afterthought, but the essence of divine activity."[44] Cone
argues for a direct correlation between Christ and Black
Power. Since both are concerned with liberating human
beings from oppression, there must be some correlation
between them; they both shout an uncompromising "No!"
to Black dehumanization. Christ is Black, then, in the
sense of being of being anti-White. It is Christ's nature to
be against anything that is anti-Christ, and Whites are
anti-Christ in that they have instigated and profited from
the systematic dehumanization of Blacks. The idea of a
race-less Christ will not do, for Cone, because so many
Christians have become convinced that Christ has
"light skin, wavy brown hair, and sometimes – wonder
of wonders – blue eyes,"[45] and this image of Christ
must be negated. It can only be negated by being opposed
by the image of a Black Christ. Whether Whites want to
hear it or not, "*Christ is black, baby*, with all the features
which are so detestable to white society."[46]

With the writing of Cone's first major work, the ground
had been laid for the emergence of a distinct discipline of
Black theological and ethical discourse. A year later Cone
wrote a second book, *A Black Theology of Liberation*
(1970), which sought to make the concept of liberation
the "organizing center" of his theology. In this text, Cone
speaks of Blackness as a universal ontological symbol for
both oppression and liberation.[47] What comes through

with striking clarity here as well is the notion that God is not only unequivocally on the side of Blacks, but God is also unequivocally opposed to Whites. Speaking of the exhilarating experience of finally throwing off the chains of the White oppressor, Cone explains that "The black experience is catching the spirit of blackness and loving it. . . . The black experience is the feeling one has when attacking the enemy of black humanity by throwing a Molotov cocktail into a white-owned building and watching it go up in flames."[48] In short, Cone's God takes sides with Blacks in a holy war against Whites:

> Black theology cannot accept a view of God which does not represent God as being for oppressed blacks and thus against white oppressors. Living in a world of white oppressors, blacks have no time for a neutral God. The brutalities are too great and the pain too severe, and this means we must know where God is and what God is doing in the revolution. There is no use for a God who loves white oppressors the same as oppressed blacks. We have had too much of white love, the love that tells blacks to turn the other cheek and go the second mile. What we need is the divine love as expressed in black power, which is the power of blacks to destroy their oppressors, here and now, by any means at their disposal. Unless God is participating in this holy activity, we must reject God's love.[49]

Cone suggests that "blacks are those who say they are black, regardless of skin color," suggesting that God is not opposed to people who happen to have white skin color, but to White people who are part of the system of White racism. Cone gives no indication, however, of how it would be possible for a person with white skin to "become black with God by joining God in the work of liberation."[50] He leaves the impression that God, quite simply, hates all people with white skin. It is at this point that the problem of absolutized particularism appears in its starkest form.

The writing of Cone's first two works marks the beginning of the Black theological project formally, and would spawn considerable intramural critique and dialogue regarding Black theology's validity and viability. Some of Cone's commentators supported his vision of Blackness as ultimate ontological symbol, and others for various reasons called Cone's thesis into question.[51] As we will see in the next chapter, J. Deotis Roberts in his *Liberation and Reconciliation* (1971) supported Cone's general intention of constructing a theology of liberation, but argued that Cone had ignored reconciliation as a central component of the gospel's understanding of liberation in general, and of Black-White relations in particular. Major Jones advocated a similar position in his *Black Awareness: A Theology of Hope* (1971), where he argued that Cone's strident position against Whites could claim no basis in a distinctively Christian theology and ethic.

Ironically, Cone's approach and method also came under attack for being too Eurocentric in its substance and methodology. One of the key critics of this early period who criticized Cone for being overly dependent on White theological sources was his brother, Cecil Cone. His book, *Identity Crisis in Black Theology* (1975), marks a high point in the early period of Black theology, and a culmination of its initial intramural critical dialogues. Cecil Cone argued for a Black theology that would become increasingly more aware of the distinctively

African origins of Black religion. He suggested that the theology of his brother, James Cone, failed to engage the Black religious traditions on their own terms. James Cone's theology interpreted Black religion through the jaundiced lenses of White philosophical theology, which obscured rather than clarified the distinctive nature of Black religion.

Cecil Cone was critical, not only of his brother's use of White theological sources, but also of his over-reliance on the Black Power motif, which tended to reduce Black religion "to a social, economic, and political movement."[52] Cecil Cone urged his brother to make a choice: "[James] must make up his mind concerning his confession commitment: Is it to the Black religious experience of to the Black Power motif of liberation with a side-long glance at the Black religious experience? As long as it is the latter, so long will he suffer an essential inconsistency."[53] In sum, Cecil Cone argued that what was needed was a Black theological vision that would, on the one hand, transcend the uncritical acceptance of White theological categories as illuminative of Black experience and would, on the other hand, avoid reducing the Black theological vision to the Black power vision of Black radicals.[54]

Cecil Cone's critique of Black theology was championed by Gayraud Wilmore in his *Black Religion and Black Radicalism* (1972), which argued for the construction of a Black theology that seeks distinctly African and other uniquely Black sources for understanding Black religiosity. Analyzing the growth of Black religion from its early period in American slavery to its association with the radicalized dimensions of the Black Power movement,

Wilmore argued that undergirding the largely conservative, evangelically-oriented thought of Black Christians there is a distinctive Black religious experience that is deeply rooted in a distant African past. There is also a connection to religious experiences that gave hope and direction to the slaves. Wilmore argued, like Cecil Cone, for an investment in the study of the African and African-American religious history in order that it might be possible to draft a theology capable of binding Black people together both inside and outside their churches, "in the solidarity of a new faith in God and humanity."[55] It is to these and other response that we shall turn, after a further investigation into the theology and ethics of James Cone.

 ## Conclusion

This brief overview of the classic formulation of Black theology and ethics reveals the emergence of its central problematic. Although Black theology and ethics have gone in many different directions since these initial expressions, the tensions that arose during this formative period have never been resolved. The tendency to absolutize Black experience was displayed from the very beginning, largely as a result of the close connection of this discourse to the Black Power motif of the Black consciousness movement of the late 1960s. Claims regarding the ontological priority, exclusivity, and superiority of Blackness and Black people have received some intramural critique, but not as much as they deserve. The absolutized particularism that came to the fore with thinkers like Cleage and gained ground with Cone has given rise to various kinds of theological and ethical projects that simply overlook or deny the categorically chauvinistic and potentially destructive implications of this approach, which makes the approach too easy to dismiss, in my judgment. It leaves buried or invisible what is right and genuinely liberative about the project of constructing a particularistic Black theology and ethic.

Cone claims that Black theology is a discourse that "must speak with a passion consistent with the depths of the wounds of the oppressed."[56] But again, it would be wrong to dismiss his theology as mere rhetoric, and thus leave its claims unexamined and uncritiqued. It is important to probe deeply, for example, into the question of how Blackness could function universally as an ontological symbol of both oppression and liberation. It is important to probe the tendency to define Blackness in a way that implies uniformity within the Black community; it is important to question the way that Blackness, Blacks, and the Black Christ are defined over and against Whiteness, Whites, and the Christ of White Christianity; it is crucial to reflect critically on the relationship between violence and liberation. Black theology and ethics needs, to wrestle with the question of how it can speak cogently and critically to a world whose populations are growing more complex, diverse, and divided. In the next chapter, we will take a closer look at Cone's work, focusing on his vision of humankind and the good of human beings in an effort to further isolate the tendency towards absolutized particularism in his thought and the implications it has for his theological project, as well for Black theology in general.

CHAPTER 2
Black and White: James Cone's Theological Anthropology

As we have seen, there is a predilection within Black theology and ethics to absolutize the experience of Black life in America. The failure fully to recognize and correct this inclination has resulted in a troubling opaqueness within many of Black theology's arguments and proposals. One often wonders about whom theologians are talking when they refer to "Blacks." The assumption seems to be that Black people constitute a monolithic, unified group – a group of people who are more alike (especially in their not being White) than they are unalike. The category of "Black life" or "Black experience" does point to something very important that most, if not all, Black people in America share, which is the experience of racial discrimination and the painful struggle to attain self-definition and a sense of dignity within a racist society. Many people thus have an interest in retaining the category of Blackness because it signifies and calls attention to a similar set of experiences undergone by people who have labored under the same, systemic oppression because of the color of their skin or other of their physical features. Capturing these similarities is crucial to the work of exposing the reality of racism; it may also be crucial to the bonding that is necessary for effective resistance.

Yet the category of Black experience is problematic in that it obscures or leaves invisible noteworthy differences among and between persons of African descent in the U.S. It lumps together the experiences of people of different classes, genders, cultures, philosophies, and lifestyles. In addition, the category is problematic because of the tenor that it took on originally, within the context of the Black Power movement, which was a tenor of over-againstness. Early Black theologians and ethicists sought to define Black experience as non-White or anti-White. What is more, early Black theologians and ethicists sought to define that which is non-White or anti-White as superior to White, as being linked in a unique way to ultimate reality and the plan of God for the salvation of humanity. This over-againstness, associated as it was with the assumption of ontological superiority, is not and has never been regarded by ordinary African-American Christians as a constructive program for attaining authentic self-regard or social transformation. As I will show in chapter three, it tethers the attainment of full Black personhood to a rejection of Whites and White values, which threatens to keep Black people in an emotionally reactive mode, rather than a mode of deliberate self-determination. In short, Black theology and ethics, by virtue of its historical association with the race politics and polarizing rhetoric of the Black Power movement, has failed to address the most pressing existential questions of Black American Christians.

The tendency within Black theology and ethics to oversimplify and in certain respects romanticize Black experience, and the failure fully to transcend the racial polarization of Black Power, has also confounded the intention and the effort to articulate cogent and compelling interpretations of the Christian gospel to persons who are oppressed, but who do not readily identify with the historical African-American community and the experiences of oppression that are to some extent peculiar to that community. Much Black theology has failed to appreciate, and to signify adequately with its rhetoric, the notion that oppressed persons around the world share in certain experiences of being neglected, abused, and exploited by members of dominant groups, yet these experiences are undergone and reflected upon by persons in terms that are to a significant degree historically and culturally particular, i.e., not reducible to the rather specific terms of Black Power-defined Black American experience.

If Black theology and ethics are to reach rank and file Black Christians who continue to struggle for self-definition, and if they are at the same time to speak the liberating Word of God in a way that is likely to be heard and acted upon by other oppressed people – and, one would hope, by oppressors who are also in need of liberation – then Black theology and ethics will have to find a workable answer to a question that is becoming more and more important: How can one articulate the gospel of liberation persuasively to people who are wrestling (or need to be wrestling) with the problems and promises of a particular community that has been defined and confined as "Black"; and how can one simultaneously draft theological and

ethical formulations that resonate with the experiences
of other human beings who are not – and do not wish to
be – defined with reference to the perennial, historical
struggle between Blacks and Whites in America?

Much is at stake in the construction of a Black theology
and ethic that seeks to integrate attention to both Black
particularity (the definition of which is still under
construction) and the moral connections that are implicit
in universal humanness. How do we, in a post-revolutionary
context of thoroughgoing heterogeneity, continue to
make sense, theologically and ethically, of a discourse of
Blackness, particularly a discourse that was originally
formed polemically, as a distinctly anti-White rhetoric
within a particular political wing of the Black community?
Can the current search among African-Americans for
self-definition and dignity transcend the earlier project's
penchant to define itself through the negation of
Whiteness? Can Black theologians and ethicists further
the cause of Black liberation, not in competition but
in coordination with the efforts of other people to expose
and transform the attitudes and social structures that
keep all human beings from achieving their full potential?

James Cone has offered a theological anthropology that
provides a partial response to these questions. He has
sought to define what it is to be fully human as a Black
person, in a situation of oppression. The impact of Cone's
response on the tradition of Black theology and ethics
can hardly be overestimated. In my view, his contribution
is in many respects valuable. There are, however, several
problems with his theological anthropology that relate to
the problem of absolutized particularism. In this chapter,
I elucidate Cone's view of authentic human existence,

specifically as it exposes this problem. My focus is primarily on Cone's early thought. While Cone is an evolving thinker who continues to write on questions of theological anthropology, his early view, developed in the 1970s and 80s, continues to exert a considerable influence in theology and ethics, and the features of this view that I regard as problematic have remained unedited, uncorrected. They need to be critiqued.[1]

This chapter is organized in three sections. In the first section I sketch Cone's concept of the human being, paying particular attention to his use of the contrasting notions of "Blackness" and "Whiteness" as anthropological categories. I examine also the roles that freedom, sin, and the future play in his conception of human existence. In the second section, I highlight some of the positive contributions that Cone's view makes to our understanding of human existence. Finally, I conclude by discussing some of the critical problems with Cone's anthropology, which weaken both its theological validity and ethical appeal.[2] Black theology and ethics are still in need of a theological anthropology that is capable of generating and sustaining active, rather than predominantly reactive, efforts toward Black self-definition, self-affirmation, and self-determination.

 ## Cone's Conception of the Human Being

It is helpful to begin a discussion of Cone's theological anthropology with reference to his views regarding the personal limits that must be acknowledged by anyone who seeks to say something true and meaningful to others about the nature of human being and human flourishing. Cone argues that a thinker and her thinking are ineluctably rooted in a given socio-cultural situation that shapes all elements of her interpretive and evaluative enterprise. All theological and ethical reflection is tied to the reflector's personal background and experience. Cone expounds on his own rootedness in a poor Black southern experience; he acknowledges this experience as formative of his consciousness, and thus of his theological and ethical project.[3] Carlyle Fielding Stewart III, in analyzing Cone's work, explains:

> . . . the black theologian is not a detached observer who subsumes his subjective interpretations to dispassionate objective analysis; nor for that matter is he an armchair theologian given to quixotic ruminations on the nature of oppression, but is one who like Ezekiel, "Sits where they sit . . . ," because the categories of interpretation must arise out of the thought forms of the black experience itself. The raw data of Black Theology is gleaned not only from the experience of racism and oppression of the black déclassé en masse, but also from the experience of oppression encountered by the theologian himself. His personal experience of oppression along with the extant truths of the gospel of liberation authenticates and corroborates the truth claims of his theology, which differentiate his claims from those articulated from outside the black experience.[4]

This vision of the personal dimension of theological discourse carries critical import for Cone's understanding of how theology and ethics are to be done. Cone disallows all talk about God and persons that is not grounded in first-hand experience of suffering due to the evil of oppression.[5]

What is more, Cone discredits theological and ethical reflection that does not focus sharply on the problem of oppression as its subject matter. Given this focus, ". . . our definition of the human being must be limited to what it means to be liberated from human oppression."[6] Any esoteric conceptions of human being that do not attend to the human *qua* oppressed, suffering, and longing for freedom are useless and perhaps even corrupt. According to Cone, "The inability of American theology to define human nature in the light of the Oppressed One and of particular oppressed peoples stems from its identity with the structures of white power."[7]

Finally, Cone extends his point about the personal qualifications that are necessary for reflecting theologically and ethically on the human to a broader epistemological point about the source of all genuine knowledge regarding the human. It is only the poor and wounded, only those who have "encountered both the depravity of human behavior from oppressors and the healing powers revealed in the Oppressed One who know what human personhood is."[8] It is therefore to them, and to the lessons of their lives, that theologians and ethicists must turn.

In reflecting upon the human, then, Cone tries to construct a view that will emerge out of and reflect the concrete reality of people who live under oppressive social conditions. It is Black reality, in particular, that he knows and feels qualified to address.

> Because Black theology begins with the Black condition as the fundamental datum of human experience, we cannot gloss over the significance and the concreteness of human oppression in the world in which Blacks are condemned to live. In its concern for concreteness, Black theology resembles existentialism, with its conviction that

> "existence precedes essence" (to use Sartre's phrase).
> This means that the concrete human being must be the
> point of departure of any phenomenological analysis
> of human existence. . . . [T]here is no essence or universal
> humanity independent of persons in the concreteness
> of their involvement in the world. All persons define their
> own essence by participating in the world, making
> decisions that involve themselves and others.[9]

Cone, then, is dismissive of any theological discourse that
attempts to define the human apart from the engagement
of suffering human beings who seek an end to their
suffering. A discourse that seeks in the abstract to offer
universally valid interpretations of human reality becomes
a kind of specialized, guild-based language game that
tends to be oriented toward philosophical speculation
for its own sake, and this sort of speculation makes
no positive difference to the plight of the poor and
downtrodden. Because it makes no positive difference,
it is in effect supportive of the social status quo.[10]

Ingredient in Cone's method is the assumption that there
is a fundamental, identifiable difference between Blacks
and Whites, and it is only in the crucible of distinctively
Black experience and culture, which is set up by Cone
as the complete opposite of White experience and culture,
that theology and ethics can truthfully and responsibly
be done.[11] What, more specifically, does Cone mean by
Blackness, and what is the relationship between Blackness
and authentic humanness?

It is apparent that for Cone Blackness has at least
something to do with skin color, and with the experiences
that a particular group of people in America have had

because of the way that a dominant social group, Whites of European descent, have sought to construct the meaning of their skin color. Reflecting on the history of Black theology, for example, Cone says that, "Black theology . . . was not created in a vacuum and neither was it simply the intellectual enterprise of Black professional theologians. Like our sermons and songs, Black theology was born in the context of the Black community as Black people were attempting to make sense out of their struggle for freedom."[12] Being Black seems to have something to do with physical blackness and the shared ethos of physically Black people.[13]

Yet Blackness is not a matter of color alone. It is not merely an issue of pigmentation, phenotypical characteristics, race, or social customs. For Cone, Blackness refers more fundamentally to a way of being human in relation to other humans; it refers to a set of desires, attitudes, and allegiances that place one in solidarity with the oppressed.

> Being Black in America has very little to do with skin color. To be Black means that your heart, your soul, your mind, and your body are where the dispossessed are. We all know that a racist structure will reject and threaten a Black man in Whiet skin as quickly as a Black man in Black skin. It accepts and rewards Whites in Black skins nearly as well as Whites in White skins. Therefore, being reconciled to God does not mean that on's skin is physically Black. It essentially depends on the color of your heart, soul and mind.[14]

To be Black is, above all, to love and fight for those who know through personal experience the evil of suffering due to oppression and who long for release from this suffering.

Cone uses the term Blackness in a narrow sense, to refer to
the experiences of evil and the good within people who are
descendants of African slaves in America; he also uses it in
a very broad sense to refer to people – of any color – who
experience both the evil of oppression and the good of
striving toward freedom. A problem in his work, which
makes interpreting it a challenge, is that he equivocates
in his use of the term Blackness. He shifts back and forth
between different senses of the term apparently with
little awareness of the trouble that this shifting causes in
understanding his meaning.[15] It could be that this slippage
is intentional, but is difficult to see the clear advantage
of it. It is difficult to see the benefit of having non-African-
American readers and hearers, including non-white-
skinned people, wonder whether or not they really are
or can be included in the category of Black.

Blackness seems primarily to function as a symbol in
Cone's work. It is a symbol that stands for suffering,
struggle, and resistance in the face of social, political, and
economic evil. Whiteness is the antithetical correlate
symbol that Cone uses to represent greed, injustice, and
brutality.[16] Whiteness is also a symbol for sin, which
is "the desire of whites to play God in the realm of human
affairs."[17] As this quotation hints at, however, there is
considerable slippage in Cone's use of the category of
Whiteness, just as there is in his use of Blackness. Whiteness is a symbol that represents a hateful state of being
(in a person of any color) and an orientation toward
unjust domination; it also refers to everything of Northern
European origin; it is also descriptive of skin color.
Evidently, for Cone, most if not all people with white
skin participate in Northern European cultural values

and support structures of White racism, which render them in the fullest, symbolic sense, White.

Cone sometimes seems to identify Blackness with humanness, but I think that what he intends to do, more precisely, is to identify Blackness with the possibility of full humanness. He intends to identify people of African-American heritage, as well as others who are Black in the general sense of being on the side of the oppressed, with the possibility of full humanity. First, Cone argues that in America today God in Christ aligns Godself with the cause of a particular Black people, namely, members of the African-American community who continue to engage in the centuries-old struggle against White racism within the North American context. As far as Cone is personally concerned, God's chosen ones are those of African ancestry whose identity has been formed by painful (and sometimes also hopeful) memories of struggle, from the days of slave ships, to emancipation, to Jim Crow, to the civil rights movement, and beyond.[18] If pressed, Cone would likely acknowledge that the risen Christ is at work wherever people say "No!" to oppression; but his particular interest and expertise lie in reflecting on the way that Christ is revealed in the historical African-American community.[19]

Second, Cone argues that it is those of any race or color who make the struggle for liberation their own struggle who have the possibility of being fully and authentically human. It is those, and only those, who are engaged in active resistance of White culture and values who are realizing their humanity. For Cone, "To be (fully) human is to be involved, participating in societal structures for human liberation."[20] This conception of full humanity is rooted in a faith in the God who has revealed the meaning of humanhood in Christ.

> The definition of Jesus as black is crucial for christology if we truly believe in his continued presence today. Taking our clue from the historical Jesus who is pictured in the New Testament as the Oppressed One, what else, except blackness, could adequately tell us the meaning of his presence today? Any statement about Jesus today that fails to consider blackness as the *decisive factor* about his person is a denial of the New Testament message. The life, death, and resurrection of Jesus reveal that he is the man for others, disclosing to them what is necessary for their liberation from oppression. If this is true, then Jesus Christ must be black so that blacks can know that their liberation is his liberation.[21]

Cone draws a tight connection between his ultimate reality as a Black person, and Ultimate Reality as revealed in Christ: "The fact that I am Black is my ultimate reality."[22] The meaning of Cone's life resides in the recognition and the realization of his potential as a Black human being, that is, as a member of a particular African-American community as well as the larger community of the poor and dispossessed. His struggle for Black humanity is also God's struggle, and God's liberative work is done in and through the world of Black people like him.

Cone's conception of the human being is that she is the sort of being who is called to take sides, to struggle in solidarity with the abused against all that is White. To proceed, the human being is called to struggle as one who is free, but exercises her freedom within a fallen world.

A human being is essentially free, and in order to actualize her humanity, she must exercise her freedom. The question of what the exercise of freedom amounts to, and what form it ought ideally to take, is a question that cannot appropriately be asked or answered apart from participation in particular struggles for freedom within particular contexts of oppression. The question of freedom is "not a matter of rational thought but of human confrontation. It is not solved by academic discussion but by risky human encounter."[23] Using Paul Tillich's language, Cone asserts that freedom is the power to stand out from nonbeing, particularly in the form of White oppression, and to *be*.[24] For Cone, it is the power to be both Black and human, which is to struggle with courage, with others and for others, against the constant threat of nothingness.

> Cone relates human freedom to the *imago dei*, as spoken of in scripture and tradition. The image of God, for Cone, refers to the way in which God intends human beings to live in the world. The image of God is thus more than rationality, more than what so-called neo-orthodox theologians call divine-human encounter. In a world in which persons are oppressed, the image is human nature in rebellion against the structures of oppression. It is humanity involved in the liberation struggle against the forces of inhumanity.[25]

For Cone, the image of God is revealed within humans in the way that we choose to become oppressed with the oppressed, to make their cause, which is their full humanity, our own cause. "*No one is free until all are free.*"[26]

The choice to identify with victimized people in their quest for self-determination is a weighty matter. Our own

authenticity hinges on the choice. In Cone's view, to fail
to join a particular community of oppressed persons in the
war against oppression is to forego the possibility of being
fully human. To be allied with the oppressed is the true
meaning of Christian conversion.[27] To undergo the kind
of conversion that Cone has in mind involves suffering. To
take sides with the victims of oppression[28] is inevitably to
suffer economic, social, and political hardship, and in some
cases even to die, as the violent deaths of Jesus of Nazareth,
Martin King, Jr., and Malcolm X demonstrate.[29] Anguish,
forlornness, and temptations to despair await those who
change their communities for justice's sake. Such is the price
to be paid, according to Cone, for true human existence.

Part of the reason why freedom entails suffering is
because we live in a sinful world, which resists the good
of liberation. Sin is partly

> . . . the attempt to be God, to take his place by ordering
> the societal structures according to one's political interests.
> Sin is not primarily a religious impurity, but rather social,
> political, and the economic oppression of the poor. It is
> the denial of the humanity of the neighbor through
> unjust political and economic arrangements.[30]

Elsewhere, Cone defines sin as a state of separation
from the source of being, from the essence of the life of
a community. It refers to the state of denying others or
ourselves full participation in God's liberating work in
Jesus Christ.[31]

Consistent with his epistemology, Cone maintains that one
can know what sin is, just as one can know what freedom
is, only when one experiences the depths of oppression at
the hands of the powerful, and has at least an inkling of

the possibility of overcoming it. Without that inkling, one cannot recognize the sin of the oppressor for what it is. While free Blacks can know the sin of their oppressors, Cone argues that Whites cannot know their own sin as sin until they step out of it and stop committing brutality against Blacks. And they are in no position whatsoever to make valid judgments on the nature of sin in the Black community.[32] Only Blacks can understand their own sin. In Cone's judgment, even though Blacks are favored by God, they can still get caught up in sin, which is to say that they can still fall into a state of estrangement from the source of their being.[33] For Cone, the sin of many Black people is the desire to be White; it is "the refusal to be what we are," which is free beings who are called to destroy "the filthy manifestations of whiteness" in American society.[34]

This definition of sin has implications, according to Cone, for how we see the relationship between the ends sought and the means employed to attain Black freedom and self-realization. Violence, which had been summarily rejected in the nonviolent direct action of Martin Luther King, Jr. was kept open as an option within the Black nationalist perspective. It was perceived as necessary for self-defense in an extremely violent culture that seeks to destroy Blackness. The only question, for Cone, is whether the violence perpetrated is proportionate to the good of the ends sought, and the people who are in a position to answer that question are the victims of injustice, who alone know just how bad, how deadly their situation is, and how necessary violent action is to survival.[35]

There is no neutral ground, for Blacks. They are already suffering systemic, structural violence, as well as personal violation; they must either allow that violence to continue to occur, or respond in a way that will likely exhibit – and in turn elicit – violence.

> Concretely, ours is a situation in which the only option we have is that of deciding whose violence we will support – the oppressors or the oppressed, whites or blacks. Either we side with Blacks and other unwanted minorities as they try to redefine the meaning of their existence in a dehumanized society, or we take a stand with the American government whose interests have been expressed in police clubs and night sticks, tear gas, and machine guns. There is no possibility of neutrality – the moral luxury of being on neither side. Neither the government nor black people will allow that![36]

Cone argues that peaceful reliance on the ideals of American democracy is not enough for Black people: "The country was founded for whites and everything that has happened in it has emerged from the white perspective. The Constitution is white, the Emancipation Proclamation is white, the government is white, business is white, the unions are white. What we need is the destruction of whiteness, which is the source of human misery in the world."[37] What Blacks need is the destruction of Whiteness "by any means necessary."[38]

The emphasis on Black self-realization "by any means necessary" is sometimes bounded by comments within Cone's thinking on the necessity of working for justice and peace on behalf of all persons, regardless of background or station. At certain times, Cone has elucidated a vision of the ideal human future is profoundly egalitarian – non-sexist, and non-racist.[39] He has envisioned a new social order that is non-classist, at least in the sense that the necessities of life (food, shelter, work, and play) are accessible to everyone in society. This vision of the human future seems to derive from and builds upon an emphasis on unity within Black history and culture, and it includes at least a tacit recognition of and commitment to the "integrationist tradition" as developed by Martin Luther King, Jr.[40]

It is difficult, however, to understand how these sparse and undeveloped references to an egalitarian future square with Cone's absolutizing of Black particularity. Due to the many vitriolic statements about demonic Whiteness, which have essentially gone uncritiqued by Cone, we are left with, at the very least, an unclear picture of precisely what the human future ought to be, and how such a state will incorporate the plethora of human cultures and groups who have historically abused and mistreated each other. It appears that the White role in a just future would be to deny itself, to identify with the sufferings of the Black oppressed by converting (at least symbolically speaking) to Blackness, and to join the Black community in its efforts towards self-affirmation and self-determination. Cone's failure to attend with precision to the nature of the White role in Black liberation, however, makes speculation on these matters tenuous.

 ## Positive Aspects of Cone's Theological Anthropology

This account of James Cone's anthropology reveals the highly provocative nature of his theological imagination. Despite its overly polemical tone, Cone's conception of the human contributes important insights. First, Cone's emphasis on the historical rootedness of human inquiry accentuates the limitations placed on any community or theologian purporting to do completely objective theology. Every theological statement is produced in a social environment that affects its style and content. Whether the subject is anthropology, soteriology, eschatology, or any other feature of theology or ethics, people simply cannot reflect in a manner that is wholly unconstrained by the contingencies of their historical and cultural situations. Each theological and ethical proposal must thus be offered with a great degree of modesty, since none can claim to have been written in a value-free, neutral setting.[41]

Cone's treatment suggests that there cannot be (and perhaps never has been) a single "Christian anthropology," but only "Christian anthropologies."[42] I agree with Cone that all too often the social context of a theologian's thought, if given at all, is given as mere background material, as if his or her thoughts were not intrinsically related to the particular social situation that conditions and frames the theologian's experiences and interpretations of reality. By emphasizing the legacy of thought and history that sets the stage for and animates his own discussion (i.e., poor African-American life and culture), Cone does what he thinks other theologians ought also to do, which is to limit their presumptions regarding the universalizability of their theological and ethical constructions.

A second contribution of Cone's anthropology concerns the way that he includes reflection on African-American culture, experience, and history within the project of theological anthropological research. Although he seems to me to use the category of Blackness primarily as a symbol for all people, of whatever race or hue, who engage in acts of resistance against oppressive people in positions of power, he uses the term also to call to mind members of a particular human community and their particular history of struggle.

> Until recently, theological anthropology has been dominated by Euro-American figures, many of whom appear to have no interest in people who have been crushed by the cumulative effect of generations of economic and social injustice. Few Euro-American theologians have demonstrated a concern in their theologizing for what it would be for crushed people, in particular, to become fully human, while struggling against their debilitation, yet without the expectation that much will change in their external situation during their lifetime.[43] Most theological anthropological studies are, frankly, of no direct relevance to African-Americans who are on the edge of despair and even death within a society that has historically structured itself both for their diminishment and destruction. Cone is to be commended, I think, for emphasizing the momentous practical import of all theological work. In a comment on EATWOT's vision of theology (Ecumenical Association of Third World Theologians), which he helped to formulate, Cone states:

> Therefore, the initial motivation that compels us to do theology is not our desire to place books in university and seminary libraries for professors and their graduate students. On the contrary, our reason for making theology arises from our experience in the ghettoes, villages,

and churches of the poor in our countries. We do not believe that it is necessary for them to remain poor. Something must be done about their misery.[44]

Cone writes theology strategically, that is, with the liberation of Blacks in mind, and I share his judgment that Black people are worth this sort of theological and ethical attention.

A third contribution of Cone's anthropology is the way that it highlights the importance of freedom and liberation – not simply spiritual liberation, but social, political, and economic justice – to the realization of authentic human existence. Liberation has always been the central theme of Cone's theological writing, and his persistent concentration on this concept constantly reminds us not to allow our discussions of human being to devolve into abstract theoretical discussions about metaphysical or ontological cores, structures, or essences. His definition of freedom as the power to actualize one's humanity precisely by siding with the oppressed, by suffering and by struggling for justice alongside them, and on their behalf, is an excellent corrective. To be fully human has nothing really to do with satisfying individual interests or attaining personal happiness. It has to do with binding oneself to others and to the project of liberation, even though on the face of it this binding of ourselves to the pained and powerless appears to involve the loss of freedom.

We may wish that Cone had developed his view of human being and freedom in more depth and with more philosophical precision. It seems to me that Cone offers an analysis that deliberately avoids metaphysical speculations that do not appear to have any direct and immediate relevance to the lives of the poor and oppressed. His analysis displays the promise of an approach to ethics that begins with the experiences and the ideas of persons who perceive reality from below, from the position of poverty and powerlessness, without recourse to (or much interest in) sophisticated theories of the human soul or the human composition. What the oppressed are most in need of is not a highly refined, systematically developed account of the nature of human being, but a vision of a way of being in relation to each other that generates hope for something better and the courage to seek it.[45]

Deficiencies of Cone's Theological Anthropology

These insights – the value of developing different conceptions of humanhood that are rooted in and pitched to different historical communities, the value of turning to African-American experience as a resource for understanding the human condition, and the value of a conception of freedom that is linked to the work of solidarity – are all important contributions made by Cone. There are, however, several problems with his theological anthropology, which need to be addressed.[46] He has recognized certain limitations in his early approach, yet he has not repudiated the limiting features that are of most concern to me and, I think, to the future of Black ethics and theology.

The main concern that I have with Cone's work is that he uses Blackness in two different senses without clarifying when he is using the term in which sense, and without explaining possible intentions behind this equivocation. This is a problem because, to the extent that a reader focuses on Blackness as a symbol for the oppressed, he or she readily loses sight of particular oppressed people and their stories. The reader can thereby fail to appreciate that experiences of suffering and of hope are to some extent specific to people's unique personal, cultural and historical situations. One can hear repeatedly about the poor and the oppressed in Cone without ever attaching names and faces to these people, which leaves the reader ironically in a world of abstraction that elicits little genuine care.

I would argue for an approach that attends much more explicitly and in more detail to the lives of individual African-Americans, in their unity as well as their diversity. I would begin an analysis of human being and freedom, for example, with the story of Suella Orange, a neighbor of mine who died recently in an urban ghetto community where I live and work. Suella (whose friends affectionately called "Tee") was an elderly African-American poor urban dweller whose entire life had been marked by exclusion and oppression on the basis of race. Tee had grown up at a time when it was hard to be Black in the South. A commoner who had worked for nearly nothing in the cotton fields, Tee migrated from the South after World War II (like millions of other African-Americans) in the hope of finding greater stability for herself and her daughter, who was physically deformed and suffered from cerebral palsy. Abandoned as a young woman by her husband and forced to work odd jobs because of poor education, Tee also suffered from a host of physical ailments (e.g., she had only a few teeth, could not afford dentures, was acutely diabetic) and environmental challenges. Always on the verge of being completely destitute, and never having enough to eat, Tee lived in a tiny, unkempt house in a neighborhood riddled with crime and violence. By any standard one can imagine, Tee's daily existence was filled with suffering and despair.

In the midst of this turmoil and despair, however, Tee demonstrated a resilience in her moral agency, a discernible power to affirm her own human dignity as one specially created by God. Tee was the most grateful person I had ever met, without a tinge of bitterness, even in the face of terrible stories of White rejection, abuse, and censure. She freely expressed her gratitude for all she had (which was virtually nothing), and for her daughter, who needed Tee's around-the-clock-care just to remain alive. Furthermore, Tee singlehandedly raised her niece's children, and was of constant encouragement to all of us who knew, loved, and served her. In a house where the plumbing and heating never seemed to work, and in a community where young street gangsters terrorize the neighborhood, Tee was this petite, African-American woman of clarion voice and the most incredible dignity. Her life was model of grace, cheer, humor, and warmth that was inspiring and challenging. Tee attributed this strength and courage to her faith in God, her reliance on God's justice and guidance, and the hope and promise of God's providential care in her life and those who she loved.

I would suggest that starting an analysis with Tee's experience as an urban poor African-American woman who had experienced firsthand and for her whole life long a terrible kind of racial animus would make a significant difference to the way that Black theology and ethics has been done by scholars like Cone. His reflection and rhetoric are really about the poor in general, which has its place, but if his analysis of human being and freedom is not tied explicitly to particular people's stories, like the story of Tee, then he falls into unhelpful abstractions. Cone's discussion begins on the right track, but he needs to follow through even further with his own best insights, bringing to life the actual struggles of particular Blacks who through their faith in God have come to affirm their own dignity in the face of terrible suffering largely due to prolonged racial exclusion and injustice.

A second concern I have is that Cone does not make clear the connection between attending to particular poor and oppressed people's lives and saying something about human beings or about poor and oppressed people in general. On the one hand, he indicates that all legitimate talk about authentic human being is radically restricted by the socio-historical reality that spawns it. He seems to deny the possibility that someone in particular could speak truly and universally about the meaning of human existence. At the same time, however, he makes many general and apparently universal statements about human freedom, liberation, and oppression. The challenge for Black theology and ethics is to be unabashedly interested in the lives of diverse African-Americans who share a certain heritage and, at the same time, to show how reflecting on these people's lives can provide invaluable insight into what it means to be human and to have dignity within situations of devastating poverty and violence.

Because of the way that Blackness can be read in particular or in general, Cone's theological anthropology raises yet another difficult issue. He associates Blackness with full humanness. He associates it with the full humanness made manifest in Jesus Christ. Blackness thus becomes a symbol for human perfection and even divination. Insofar as a reader stays on the level of the symbolic, in reading Cone, he will read Blackness as the term for goodness, without associating Blackness with black-skinned people. But it is highly unlikely that readers will not associate Blackness also with members of the African-American community. Here is where the problem of absolutized particularism becomes clearest. The experiences of African-Americans, indeed, all African-Americans are implicitly construed as uniquely representative of the divine life in the world. No internal check is evident that would inhibit the idolization of African-American life. Cone admits that Black people sin, but he suggests that their worst sin is succumbing to the temptation toward Whiteness, which makes the sin of Whiteness the ultimate sin for which Whites are ultimately responsible. Black theologians who follow Cone's method and speak in the same terms are opened up to ideological blindness and theological imbalance.

What is more, I think it is a mistake for Cone to construct the meaning of Blackness, whether in general or in par-ticular, over and against Whiteness. This argument will be developed more fully in the next chapter, but let me suggest here that constructing Black humanity over against White inhumanity creates a kind of logical correlation between the two, so that the meaning of Blackness becomes logically dependent on the perceived reality of Whiteness. In effect, Cone creates a necessity for there to be White oppressors to resist, in order for Blacks to become fully human and fully alive. Within Cone's conception, Blacks do not appear to derive their identity from an intrinsic worth bestowed upon them by God, who is the ground of their human being. Rather, they appear to attain their identity by opposing White definitions of Black reality, which keeps Blacks in a kind of servitude to White definitions and interpretations of Black reality.

In a similar vein, Cone's conception of Blackness, and its antithesis, Whiteness, are treated as conceptions that are not subject to the examination or criticism of Whites. This is an implication of Cone's view concerning the finitude of theologies and their vulnerabilities to ideological distortion. It is also a point that Cone makes explicitly. Regarding the meaning for sin for Black people, for example, he says that, "only blacks can talk about their sin. Oppressors are not only rendered incapable of knowing their own condition, they cannot speak about or for the oppressed. This means that whites are not permitted to speak about what blacks have done to contribute to their condition. . . . For whites, to do so is not merely insensitivity, it is blasphemy!"[47] It is difficult to know how other theologians who are not members of the African-American community can enter the conversation that Cone has started. If White theologians are excluded *a priori* from criticizing Black theology because they are White (that is, due to the oppressive heritage of which they are a part), then there can be no rational dialogue between White and Black theologians concerning the arguments and evidences that underpin Black theology's view of human existence.[48]

> Similarly, Cone's emphasis on emancipatory praxis is in some respects admirable, but it tends to obscure the need for theoretical justification of one's theological and ethical proposals. Too often Cone suggests that the practice of rational argumentation is an enterprise peculiar to Whites and not to be expected of Blacks.
>
> . . . Black faith assertions [with their focus on the living presence of Jesus] were never intended to be answers for the intellectual problems arising out of the European experience. They are Black reflections on life and were

> intended as testimonies for the oppressed so that they
> would not give up in despair. They are not rational
> arguments. . . . The truth of the Black faith claim is found
> in whether the people receive that extra strength to
> fight until freedom comes. Its truth is found in whether
> the people who are victims of White philosophy and
> theology are led to struggle to realize the freedom they
> talk about. . . . Pure theory is for those who have the
> leisure for reflection but not for the victims of the land.
> The truth, therefore, of our theological analysis ought
> to be decided by the historical function of our assertions
> in the community we claim to represent.[49]

In his determination to keep reflection on the human
condition relevant to the community of the oppressed and,
perhaps more specifically, the oppressed members of the
African-American community, Cone has disallowed White
philosophy any access (through debate and discussion) to
Black theological and ethical truth claims. Accordingly, his
views are likely to have no appeal outside of his particular
community, and his analysis becomes parochial and
ineffectual. Cone's view appears to have relevance and
appeal only to a certain faction within his community,
and only because it serves the pragmatic aims of (Cone's
view of) liberation.[50] If Cone's claims concerning the
nature of human existence lie beyond the scope of White
philosophical, theological, or ethical consideration and
refutation, then Black theology becomes accountable
only to the Black world, and thus can speak only to the
Black world.

This rejection of White intellectual involvement in Black
theology and ethics implies likewise the rejection of White
involvement in Black communal and social practices,

including liberative practices, and it thus erodes the
possibility of reconciliation among Blacks and Whites.
While Cone presents Whiteness as symbolic of the
oppressor, he also uses the term to refer to the institutions
and practices that are associated in any way with the
intellectual, social, cultural, and historical movements
of mainstream America. His assessment leaves no hope
for those who are rooted, to any significant extent, in this
culture. All things associated with Whiteness are culpable
and useless: White rationality, White truth, White moral
judgments, White philosophical and theological analysis,
and the White Church. While Cone's later writings argue
for a more egalitarian conception of society that makes
room for people with Euro-American backgrounds, one
is hard-pressed to find resources within his anthropology
for seeking a reconciliation between Black and White people,
which could make a difference for human liberation
locally and globally.[51] The antipathy towards Whiteness
can become so ideologically charged that violence
against those associated with White culture seem not
only necessary, but attractive.[52]

To this whole line of reasoning I ask: without the
possibility of criticism from without, how can the Black
community safeguard itself from error, blindness, injustice,
or moral ineptitude? How does a Black theologian protect
herself from imbalance or demagoguery? How can the
Black community resist unreflective, myopic or distorted
visions concerning its own liberation efforts, or the results
of fallacious concepts within its view of human existence?

It must be noted that Cone himself has been willing to
modify many of his views in light of criticisms leveled at
his early theological writings. He has recognized, for

example, his superficial social and economic analysis, and his blindness to the problem of sexism.[53] Along the same lines, Cone ought to modify his theoretical approach to allow explicitly for an open and critical dialogue with others about problems that arise in attempting to understand the human and the good of humanity. These problems may show up in particular terms within particular communities. That is, the problem of understanding and realizing human well-being may appear, for some, in terms that make the most sense to poor, elderly, urban African-American women. But these problems of self-understanding and self-realization are not unique to African-Americans or to any sub-group of African-Americans. They are problems that all humans share, in some form, to some extent.[54]

 ## Conclusion

James Cone's view of human being is both provocative and informative. His understanding of the standpoint of the theologian is instructive for those who would seek to speak a liberating Word, but without paying attention to the particular problems faced by those who may be in the greatest need for such a Word. His theological anthropology, motivated primarily by his commitment to Black liberation, accentuates (albeit mostly in principle) the validity of African-American experience as a starting point for theological reflection.

However, Cone's view of human existence, as it currently stands, is unsatisfactory. By using Blackness as the symbol for oppression, liberation, and the possibility of authentic human existence, even as he refers to Blacks also as a particular people with a particular history of racial discrimination in America, his thinking gives rise to a tendency to absolutize the experiences of a particular people, to construe people's response to the experiences of African-Americans as emblematic of their relation to the divine, and thus to invest Black experience with a kind of exclusive moral value. This construction limits the appeal of the Black theological project within the African-American community, and hinders its overall appeal to other communities who seek a way of articulating the meaning of their own situation in terms that will also link them in solidarity with other suffering and resisting human beings.

Cone's theological anthropology illustrates clearly the persistent proclivity within Black theology and ethics to make ontological Blackness the foundation for the possibility of full humanity. It illustrates the tendency for Black theology and ethics to single out Blackness as a *sui generis* reality, and to define it over and against Whiteness, in a way that keeps Black identities tethered to the conceptual framework and rhetoric of the Black Power movement. Cone's work has been subjected to a variety of critiques, within the ongoing Black theology movement. Other Black theologians and ethicists have critiqued certain features of what I am calling the problem of absolutized particularism. Yet my argument is that they have not finally transcended the stifling hold of the basic, polarizing Black-White framework that has set the terms of internal Black theological and ethical debate since the publication of Cone's early writings.

CHAPTER 3
Self-Critique of Absolutized Particularism within Black Theology and Ethics

Black theology and ethics, as a developing discourse and literature, has from its inception been a forum that encourages vigorous debate among its participants. At no time has there been within Black theology a lockstep conformity among its commentators concerning the central meanings of Black religion, theology, or ethics.[1] As one would expect, Black theologians and ethicists have not allowed Cone's theology to go without critical response. For our purposes, it is important to note that some critics have responded to Cone in a way that touches on the problem of absolutized particularism.

There have been several different kinds of critiques of Cone's construction of Blackness and its polar opposite, Whiteness. Some critics have sought to take the offensive edge off of Cone's polarizing terms; some have sought to shift the focus within the Black-White polarity, giving further specificity to the meaning of Blackness; others have sought to extend Cone's terms, to show that there are polarities within the Black community itself that need to be addressed, even as Black people address the problems between Blacks and Whites.

In my judgment, none of these critiques cuts deeply enough. The critiques have been carried out, to a significant extent, within the terms originally set by Cone. None of them move beyond an overly-simple, unrealistic Black-White dichotomy, into the post-revolutionary context of striking diversity, pluralism, and syncretism. None has succeeded in articulating an ethic that is deliberately particularistic, without being dichotomous. And none has pushed far enough in the direction of articulating an ethic that promises to make important contributions to the self-understandings and liberation of people other than African-Americans.

Specifically, in this chapter, I present three different responses to Cone's approach within the community of Black scholars. First, I present two similar critiques that followed swiftly on the heels of Cone's early and provocative works, and which provided a point of departure for additional vital dialogues. J. Deotis Roberts and Major Jones, among a few other Black scholars, responded to Cone's claims primarily by emphasizing that reconciliation between Blacks and Whites, rather than a sharpening of the division, was integral to the cause of Black liberation. Second, I present the central tenets of the Black theologians and ethicists who responded to Cone by making a sharper turn toward particularity, by concentrating their attention on the specifically African roots of Black religion, and also on the symbols, folklore, and testimonial data of the slaves. Third, I examine briefly some of the central components of womanist theology – a form of Black theology and ethics that extends a critical

perspective beyond the problem of racism to the problem
of sexism (and other related forms of oppression) within
the Black community and also outside this community.
Womanists[2] have responded to Cone partly by exposing
his tendency to treat Black male experience as if it were
normative of all Black experience. They have responded
also by treating the diversity of Black women's experiences
of oppression and liberation not merely as footnotes on
the page of Black male theological and ethical discourse,
but as part of the defining body of this discourse.

After each of these three sections, I evaluate the adequacy
of the critical response to Cone within Black theology and
ethics. I show that while these critiques have pushed the
Black theological and ethical project far beyond its original
formulation, a need exists to step self-consciously out of
the constraining and distorting framework that is still
implicitly present in so much of this reflection, which is
the framework of the 1960s Black Power conceptions of
Blackness, Whiteness, and the problem of race in America.
In my mind, there is an urgent need within Black theology
and ethics to articulate clearly the essential connectedness
of all human beings and the fundamental dignity of all
humans, in all of their uniqueness and diversity. Accordingly,
there is a need to acknowledge the impossibility of constructing a liberating vision of self and community that
implies in any way the denial of the dignity of others.
Beyond this there is a need to acknowledge, despite endemic
problems of race relations in this country, that the
situation for many African-Americans (especially in the
arena of civil rights) has improved dramatically over
the last several decades. Black theology must expand its
frame of reference not merely to oppose forces that
continue to undermine the Black struggle for freedom,

but also to propose a constructive vision of God's working and of human flourishing that is convincing for a wide variety of people within our increasingly complex, heterogeneous, and international cultural context.

To foreshadow the argument that I will develop further in later chapters, whole populations of human beings, ranging in the millions, even billions, have no historical connection to or remote cultural memory of the Black and White racial controversies of the 1960s as construed in terms of the language of Black Power. One of the highest priorities of Black theology and ethics must be to make new connections between African-American struggles for courageous self-affirmation and similar struggles among other human beings around the world, in ways that pay attention to differences in culture, gender, and class, but refuse to allow such differences to undermine the ethical assumption of equal human dignity. If Black theology fails to stand firm on the ethical ground of equal human dignity, so that all differences appear through the lens of that dignity, Black theology will fail the millions of people who currently live in situations of poverty, abuse, militarism, and suffering, and would benefit greatly from hearing a liberating Word.

Early Critiques of Cone's Black Theology and the Need for Reconciliation

From the beginning, Black theologians identified certain dimensions of the absolutizing tendency of the new discourse represented by James Cone. J. Deotis Roberts and Major Jones were two of the first commentators to recognize potential problems with Cone's formulation. These authors sought to soften Cone's angry rhetoric and to point out that any viable and Christian answer to the problem of racism in America would have to include the goal of reconciliation between Blacks and Whites.

Roberts outlined a Black theology that refused to construe Whites as ontologically inferior to Blacks and as enemies. Roberts' theology recognized Whites as human beings who had a God-given dignity equal to the dignity of Blacks. He insisted that the work of Black liberation had to include the work of reconciliation. Indeed, he identified the core of the Christian gospel with the message of liberation *and* reconciliation:

> We are aware of the gospel of freedom, to which Christist
> as Liberator has called us. But as Christians, black and
> white, we surely know that separation, however rewarding
> to set the record straight, cannot be an ultimate Christian
> goal. Separation must give way to reconciliation. The gospel
> is a reconciling as well as a liberating gospel, and Christ
> is at once Liberator and Reconciler. At the same time that
> black Christians are set free, they are called together
> with all other Christians to a ministry of reconciliation.[3]

For Roberts, the life of faith requires that Blacks make reconciling movements toward Whites, and Whites make reciprocal movements toward Blacks, out of a mutual commitment to Christian love. Whites need to learn to accept all human beings as equal to them, equal before God, and Blacks need to pursue true self-understanding, self-respect, and personal fulfillment as beloved children of God.[4] A lack of self-acceptance and a failure to acknowledge the God-given humanness of the other breeds a hatred that is self-corrosive and self-defeating for both Whites and Blacks.

While James Cone could envision a human future where Whites, due to their complicity in the oppression of Blacks, were only marginally involved in the construction of a new, just society, Roberts finds such thinking untenable.[5] He affirms the value of paying particular attention to the needs of Black people, in the employment of a Black theology, but he argues that these needs ultimately include the need of overcoming hatred, offering forgiveness, and incorporating Whites into their liberating future.

> My understanding of the Christian faith leads me to speak of both liberation and reconciliation as proper goals for the Christian church in general and of the black church in particular. I understand the church to have a center but not a circumference – and exclusiveness to be a means to universalism and not its own end. Therefore, the black church, in setting black people free, may make freedom possible for white people as well. Whites are victimized as the sponsors of hate and prejudice which keeps racism alive. Therefore, they cannot know for themselves the freedom of Christians, for they are shackled by a self-imposed bondage. The cry for deliverance, for authentic freedom for existence, on the part of black people, may be salvific for all regardless of the nature or cause of oppression.[6]

Roberts sees Black theology's purpose as the empowerment of Black people, the affirmation of Black personhood, but also of the possibility that justice and peace could one day characterize relationships between Black and White Christians.

Roberts's vision of reconciliation was echoed by his contemporary, Major Jones. Jones's *Christian Ethics for Black Theology* approached the issue of reconciliation through the ethical theme of Black power understood as the ground of authentic Black selfhood. He argued that

> the quest for black liberation will end with the self-empowerment of the now powerless black people so that they may have the power to participate in all decisions affecting their welfare and fulfillment. The black man must achieve a counter power to offset the current power of the collective white society. He must of necessity empower himself; this power will never be given to him.[7]

Black theology, for Jones, had given new meaning to the concept of Blackness. It had placed Black people for the first time in touch with a deep and beloved core within themselves. This was a core which, once found, could provide Black people with all the resources they needed to attain genuine self-affirmation.[8]

The new sense of self-love and self-assertion coming to be within Black self-consciousness was a sign of a kind of revolution – a revolutionary recovery of hope. The hope rooted in the realization of Black humanity was thought to be liberative for all who encountered it, including Whites:

> It seems totally impossible to dismiss the deeper ethical obligations which the black Christian has for the ex-master, oppressor, the white man. There can be no true liberation as long as it excludes the oppressor; he is the key to liberation, however it may be conceived. It is from him that one must be liberated. He has to be considered.

> However, the black Christian can never dismiss the fact
> that the white oppressor is also God's child in need of
> a redemption of a different kind. . . . Christian love would
> demand no less than that the ex-slave, oppressed, black
> man must maintain a spirit of love which will dominate
> his attitude and his response toward both insult and
> injury from the oppressor. Revenge will, and must be
> left to God. . . . [A]pplied Christian love would bring
> the oppressor and the oppressed into a totally new
> relationship wherein there is a new dimension of
> mutual understanding, not of indifference, but of
> active, positive goodwill.[9]

Like Roberts, Jones was convinced Black theology would
be dramatically weakened if it failed to inform Black people
of the meaning of God's will for all people. If Black
theology's message were for Blacks alone, it would fail
to acknowledge the obvious scriptural testimony that
God sent God's son to save all who were caught up in the
trap of sin. The truly revolutionary character of hope in
God is reflected in the assumption that God seeks the
well-being of all human beings, both Black and White.[10]

These commentators made an important move by
insisting, in effect, that the liberation of Black people
could not be effected apart from the liberation of
White people. Surely they were right that Black people
will not be liberated from the effects of White racism
as long as they are dominated by their own hatred of
Whites, just as they will not be liberated from racism
as long as Whites continue to hate Blacks. The only way
to move forward in the work of liberation is to seek
reconciliation, to extend an olive branch, to initiate
a conversation in good faith.

The problem with these early pieces, however, is that they concentrate on Black-White relations in a way that implies that all Blacks are basically the same, all Whites are basically the same, and the differences between Blacks as a group and Whites as a group are pretty plain. Reconciliation amounts to respecting each other's dignity, despite each other's differences, where the shape of each other's differences is taken for granted as obvious. These early works reflect a kind of race analysis that is no longer tenable. While it still makes sense to talk about race relations, and specifically about relationships between Blacks and Whites, it is no longer possible to do so apart from a concomitant recognition of the fact that members of both groups are very diverse, and thus relationships between members of each group are equally diverse. Beyond this, there is no longer a stark line of demarcation between these two groups, or between these and other groups, in a country that is increasingly multiracial and multiethnic. The problem, then, is not with the insistence upon reconciliation per se, but with the fact that this goal was conceived by Roberts and Jones in overly simplistic terms. Even though these authors move beyond absolutized particularism by denying its claim that Blackness alone is normative for authentic humanness, they remain trapped within its dualistic conceptual structure.

For instance, Roberts reflects upon all of the classic theological themes (e.g., humanity, sin, forgiveness, God) in terms of the racial problems confronting Blacks and Whites.[11] The focus is first on Black life and potential, and then on how Blacks and Whites relate. Within such a framework, which focuses narrowly and exclusively on the historically-bound problem of race relations in America, one is destined to lose sight of the larger, more global human context of the issues at stake. One of the fruits of absolutized particularism is the tendency to reference only a narrow band of human concern. As egregious and unjust as the tragic legacy of racism in America is, it is not the only example of oppression and injustice in the history of human affairs. To address these momentous human issues of liberation and reconciliation only in terms of Black experience is to miss opportunities to note their significant ramifications outside of the Black-White American historical conflict.

Constructive Black Theologies and the "Hermeneutics of Return"

Whereas this first line of critique that emerged during the initial debates over Cone's theology argued, in effect, that his theology was not universalistic enough in that it was not sufficiently concerned with reconciliation between the races, a second line of critique argued that it was not particularistic enough in that it was not sufficiently grounded in the details of Black life. In its early form, this critical approach concentrated on the way that Cone had relied (ironically) on European, White philosophical and theological sources to explicate Black experience and culture. Cecil Cone and Gayraud Wilmore were especially vigorous in their critique of Cone's early work, which appeared to be too dependent upon the Protestant theological visions of Barth and Tillich. It was argued that in order for Black experience to be exegeted in a way that yields an authentic understanding of oppression and liberation for Black people, Black theological and ethical inquiry must be grounded in and informed by conceptual frameworks that capture the exigencies of Black experiences.[12] According to Cecil

Cone and Wilmore, a theology and ethic that is "Black"
must be rooted in an internal-critical analysis of the folklore,
symbolism, and cultural products of Black culture and
Black history.[13]

Theologians and ethicists are usually trained to speak in
generic and universal terms of "humankind" or "the human
condition" or the "needs of humanity." This tendency
toward abstraction makes most traditional theological and
ethical systems appear sterile and superfluous to many
Black thinkers. Rather than seeing such language as aiding
in the work of understanding what it means to be both
Black and human, this language is perceived as a sleight-
of-hand pulled by mainline theologians who have no
intention of addressing Black problems directly. Every effort
at dealing with "human life," rather than "Black life" is
thus rejected by thinkers like Cecil Cone and Wilmore as
either naive or turncoat. It is not enough, from this point
of view, to modify the theological and ethical constructs
of Whites as needed in order to treat the reality of Black
suffering. Rather, the language of Black theology must be
for Blacks, written by Blacks, informed by Blacks. It must
speak knowingly about the pain and agony of Blacks as
descendants of African slaves.[14]

In an effort to answer critiques regarding the over-reliance
of Black theologians on European and Euro-American
theoretical constructs and, at the same time, in order to
lay new methodological ground for its own reflections,
in a way that is likely to appeal to a broad and diverse
Black audience, other Black theologians have recently
focused their attention on distinctively Black narratives,
historical accounts, experiences, and religious symbols.
Commentators such as Dwight Hopkins, Riggins Earl, Jr.,

Theodore Walker, Jr., Cain Hope Felder, and James H. Evans, Jr. have sought to move Black theology beyond its absolutized particularistic beginnings, in effect, by uncovering and retrieving the African and early African-American roots of a view of God and the good life that is happily and proudly particularistic, yet has no explicit pretensions of being normative for the rest of humanity.[15]

In a sense this hermeneutics of return[16] within Black theology can be seen as an attempt to transcend the impulse of early Black theology to reduce itself to an angry reaction to the problem of White racism. This hermeneutic seeks to place Black discussions of the holy and of morality within a framework that is, for people whose identities are rooted in a historical African past, authentically self-defining and self-determining. This more proactive, rather than simply reactive, impetus reflects some of the changes that have occurred in America since the beginnings of the Civil Rights movement in the early 1950s. While one may dispute the nature and extent of the gains that Blacks have achieved over the last five decades, few commentators will deny that the present represents for at least some Blacks a great opportunity for social participation, especially in terms of social mobility, economic security, and society acceptance. The hermeneutics of return seeks to address this new situation by tapping rich, ancient resources that are likely to enhance the lives of Black people, many of whom feel a growing freedom of self-discovery and self-development.

Dwight Hopkins, as much as any other thinker, has stood at the center of this new movement within Black theology. His position is represented in *Shoes that Fit Our Feet: Sources for a Constructive Black Theology* (1993) and *Cut Loose Your Stammering Tongue* (1991). Hopkins holds that enslaved Africans were profoundly religious people who "felt the powerful living presence of the Divine in the midst of their daily burdens."[17] Once exposed to the Christian message, most Africans tried to find a way to articulate their spiritual vitality in terms of a workable amalgam of traditional West African religion and the Christian view of radical religious transformation. Slave religion created an independent theology of liberation that can serve, in Hopkins' view, as a kind of proto-Black theology for contemporary Black religious studies.

The hermeneutics of return thus requires that Black theologians find sources that can provide a legitimate basis for the construction of a new Black theology:

> What important sources of faith in the African-American community can foster the construction of a contemporary black theology of liberation? Simply put, what is the connection between black theology and black sources? A black theology of liberation today is woven together from at least the following political and cultural strands found in the fabric of black North American life: the African American church, black women, African American cultural folklore, major black political representatives, and an analysis and vision coming out of the African American legacy of struggle. Furthermore, an authentic account of the God of freedom, whom black people have worshiped and continue to worship in its sources, dictates that a contemporary black theology of liberation must start from the perspective of achieving justice for the "least of these" – God's poor.[18]

Black theologians seek sources that will allow them to construct a theology that answers to the new situation

within which most Black Christians now find themselves.
As Victor Anderson puts it, Black sources are sought,
which will ensure

> . . . the legitimacy of a black theology in a
> postrevolutionary context. The theological gaze here
> returns to African traditional religions and slave narratives,
> autobiography, and folklore in order to assure the vitality
> of the black church (church theologies) and the cultural
> solidarities that transcend the individualism that drives
> our market culture and morality, and rob the black
> community of moral vitality. The hermeneutics of return
> is a decisive element of African-American fundamental
> theology. As a function of fundamental theology,
> hermeneutics is therefore prolegomenon to African
> American constructive theology.[19]

The hermeneutics of return is not simply a modification of
the methods and formulas used by early Black theologians.
It is an attempt to move the discourse in a new direction –
toward the recovery of authentic African-American roots.
Its language does not mirror the revolutionary rhetoric of
the previous phase of Black theology, which was often tinged
with genuine anger at Whites and a disdain for anything
that was perceived as European or North Atlantic in origin.
Correspondingly, the hermeneutics of return appears to
be more modest in its claims regarding the ontological
superiority of Blacks and Black culture relative to Whites.

The hermeneutics of return thus represents a significant
retreat from the problem of absolutized particularism, as
manifest in the writings of James Cone. Nevertheless, this
new movement has not yet transcended the problem. First,
there remains, even in this new movement, which seeks to

highlight and celebrate Black particularity, a tendency
to overgeneralize and romanticize Black experiences,
particularly the religious experiences of African slaves in
America. The claim is made, for example, that a clear
correlation was made in the minds of many slaves between
the notion of an African High God and the Christian
theological vision of God and Jesus Christ, and that the
slaves generated from this correlation a unique and
independent theology of liberation. The claim is also
made that the original, hybrid theology of liberation
constructed by the slaves is meaningful for Blacks today.
Anderson rightly suggests that such a correlation is not
easily discovered in the writings concerning the religious
experience of the slaves, and that sometimes the correlations
made by those who engage in this hermeneutic of return
seem forced.[20] Even if the correlation is present, it is not
apparent what this implies about the applicability of the
slave vision to the situation of Black American Christians
today, or to the situations of others who struggle with
legacies of oppression.

A second and more important problem associated with the
hermeneutics of return is that it is still too wedded to the
old attempt to articulate the meaning of Black experience
negatively, over against the problem of White oppression.
This approach to Black theology focuses on the slaves'
experiences of struggle, crisis, resistance, and survival, and
these experiences are naturally constructed vis-a-vis the
specter of the brutal slave owner. It is important to attend
to these features of slave life, and such attention may
prove helpful for some African-Americans who are still
tragically preoccupied with the basic struggle to survive in
situations of unspeakable poverty and violence, and need
models of people who refused to give up. Many African-

Americans struggle today to survive in environments
where it makes sense to focus on White people as the
main source of their problems, for they still live in rational
fear of being murdered by racist Whites simply because
they are Black. Yet it is problematic, I think, to encourage
African-Americans as a group to construe the realization
of their full humanity negatively, in terms of an ongoing
struggle against the generalized "other" of White
oppression. This is so for several reasons.

When Black struggles for self-affirmation and self-
determination are effectively reduced to struggles against
abstract, outside evils, as they tend to be today, Blacks
are undermined in their efforts to understand and
acknowledge the ways that certain evils, which originated
in the agencies of wicked White people have, over time,
had a profound effect on many Black people. Many of the
evils of racist society have been internalized by Blacks
and have thus taken root within the characters of Black
people.[21] These evils must be addressed, and they cannot
be addressed simply by seeking to understand more fully
the evil of slavery and post-slavery oppression, and the
goodness of Black resistance. Nor can these evils be
addressed by implicitly blaming Whites for the evil in
Black life (even though Whites are blameworthy for many
evils). These evils must be addressed with a new sense of
responsibility and hope that is grounded, positively, in acts
of courageous self-affirmation that are guided by a clear
vision of personal and communal well-being.

When the goal of self-determination is construed
mainly in terms of overcoming egregious racial bigotry,
discrimination, and injustice, there is a tendency to

fasten the potential of Blacks to the active undermining
of Whites, who are construed as a relatively uniform class
of historical oppressors. In this way, Black self-affirmation
remains ironically tethered to the will of Whites, for Blacks
become prone to conceive and plan their reactions always
in relation to the action of Whites. There is a tendency, as
one focuses one's eyes on the evil of White oppression, to
be governed by the dictates of anger, resentment, and hatred
toward Whites, which cannot possibly be liberating, in the
long run, for Black people. At a certain point, destructive
human emotions begin to enslave people and stifle their
ability to experience joy in being human.

When the struggle for self-determination is set up as a
struggle against White oppression, it appears that Blacks
have no goal, no constructive vision of Black life beyond
the ending of White supremacy, hegemony, and oppression.
It appears, accordingly, that the Black imagination is held
in bondage to White oppression, for White oppression is
still setting the terms for what counts as the liberation of
Black life. Black identity remains conceptually dependent
upon the figure, the foil, of White resistance. Victor
Anderson expresses in similar terms the dilemma in which
much Black theology continues to be caught:

> The difficulty arises here: (a) Blackness is a signification
> of ontology and corresponds to black experience. (b) Black
> experience is defined as the experience of suffering and
> rebellion against whiteness. Yet (c) both black suffering
> and rebellion are ontologically created and provoked
> by whiteness as a necessary condition of blackness.
> (d) Whiteness appears to be the ground of black experi-
> ence, and hence of black theology and its new black

> being. Therefore, while black theology justifies itself as
> radically oppositional to whiteness, it nevertheless
> requires whiteness, white racism, and white theology for
> the self-disclosure of its new black being and its legitimacy.
> In this way, black theology effectively renders whiteness
> identifiable with what is of ultimate concern.[22]

The dilemma here is not humorous; this circularity places the Black theological project (and any other particularistic theological or ethical project) in jeopardy unless it can find a way to ground its critical reflection on the meaning and value of Black humanity in something beyond the experience of the White oppression that precipitated the discourse in its original form and force.

From a different angle, one can discern another kind of problem with the tendency to construe Black self-affirmation primarily in terms of the negation of Whiteness. The act of affirming both one's particularity and one's humanity in the midst of protracted suffering is an act that is mirrored in the lives of millions of people other than Black Americans, who seek to survive as unique people, with rich personal and cultural histories, under inhumane conditions. Other people have sought – and are presently seeking – to affirm their dignity and freedom in ways that are analogous to the efforts of African-Americans. There must be a way for Black theology to honor the experiences that Black people have had of specifically White racism, while at the same time breaking free of the discourse of Black-White polarity, so that Blacks can make connections with other people who are trying to understand and affirm themselves as valuable human beings within contexts that seem to have been deliberately designed for their destruction and humiliation.

Can the Black theological and ethical project provide Blacks with ways of pursuing what it is to be Black and human that incorporate reflection on the history and experiences of racism in America, yet also transcend the categories originally set up by the Black Power movement? Is there a theological or ethical vision that can give Black Americans a larger, more sublime, nobler purpose than simply survival or resistance, even as it asserts the need for resisting all efforts to thwart human beings in their attempts to live full human lives? If so, what is the shape of this vision, and what is its theological ground? The hermeneutics of return must continue to seek answers to these questions as it searches for new sources for a constructive Black theology.

Womanist Theology and the Critique of Absolutized Particularism

Perhaps the most important internal critique that bears on the problem of absolutized particularism comes from Black women theologians and ethicists who have sought to expand the discussion of the Black theological project from issues of race alone, to issues of race, class, and gender. Womanist theology, a theology that is written in the North American context, represents what is often referred to as the third trajectory within the literature of Black theology and ethics, which complements the first trajectory of Black theology's initial formulation and extension, and the second trajectory of the hermeneutics of return.[23] Womanist scholars such as Katie Cannon, Cheryl Townsend Gilkes, and Jacquelyn Grant, have given rise to a dynamic discourse, one original purpose of

which was to address the proclivity within Black
theological and ethical discourse to absolutize Black
male experience, i.e., to take Black male experience
as representative of all Black experience.

The classic formulation of Black theology highlighted the
issue of race and, to some extent, class without offering
an interpretation of how race, class, and gender oppression
are inter-structured so as to form complex webs of
dehumanization and exploitation. The basic premise of
womanism builds upon the thought of W.E.B. DuBois,
which was considered earlier. DuBois characterized the
awareness of being both Negro and American as a
"double consciousness," which produces within Blacks
a chronic sense of confusion, an ongoing and painful
ambivalence regarding who they are, where their loyalties
lie, and whether or not they belong within the context
in which they find themselves.[24] Womanist scholars add
a third element to DuBois's double consciousness by
suggesting that Black women must endure experiences
within American society that engender a triple consciousness, which produces ambivalences that are more
complex than DuBois and other Black male thinkers
have realized. Many Black women struggle in American
society, according to womanists, not only because they
are Black and poor, but also because they are women.
And their struggle as women takes place within the Black
community and the Black church, and specifically in
relation to Black men, as much as within the broader
American society.

Black women's experience did not, in fact, receive
attention in the classic formulation of Black theology.[25]
Some of the reasons for this are plain. First, Black

theology developed largely in the conceptual and social context of Black Power. The Black Power movement (spurred on through the strategic resistance of student groups like the Student Noviolent Coordinating Committee, i.e., SNCC, and the Congress of Racial Equality, i.e., CORE) was not itself egalitarian: Black male and Black female roles were distinguished, and Black male roles were valued more highly than those of Black females.[26] With a few notable exceptions, such as Angela Davis, Black women were ignored within the leadership of the Black Power movement.[27]

Second, although Black women make up the vast majority of all the participants in the Black church and play prominent roles within it, the Black church has often been a vehicle for the overlooking and misrepresentation of Black women.[28] C. Eric Lincoln and Lawrence H. Mamiya argue persuasively that even though Black women formed "the backbone" of both the civil rights movement and the Black church they were largely marginalized, relegated to positions of taking orders, rather than promoted to posts of authority.[29]

Womanists are thus rightly critical of Black theology for leaving invisible the problems that they faced within the freedom movement and still face within many churches – as women who want to be the full partners of Black men within various Black communities, but are commonly relegated to a second-class status relative to Black men. But this was not the only major problem faced by Black women. As they struggled for the acknowledgment of their full humanity by Black men, many Black women also struggled alongside White women in the women's move-ment for basic human and civil rights that they had been denied partly because they were women. Yet this relationship, too, was strained, for White women did not appear to have much interest in or understanding for the ways that sexism took on different dimensions and dynamics among women of color. In short, Black women were in a unique situation: they struggled with White women against patriarchy, which pitted them against Black men; at the same time, they struggled with Black men against racism, which pitted them against White women.

Womanists have focused most of their attention on marking out a distinct place for themselves relative to a predominantly White women's movement. In *White Women's Christ and Black Women's Jesus* (1989), Jacquelyn Grant tries to differentiate womanist theology from its "feminist" theological counterpart by suggesting that feminist theology is essentially "White theology," and "racist theology."[30] Feminist theology is White and racist because those doing it are White in terms of their race, they rely exclusively on "White" sources, and they cannot help but be bound in their analyses by racist assumptions, given their social status.

> In a racist society, the oppressor assumes the power of definition and control while the oppressed is objectified and perceived as a thing. As such, White women have defined the movement and presumed to do so not only for themselves but also for non-White Women. They have misnamed themselves by calling themselves feminists when in fact they are White feminists, and by appealing to women's experience when in fact they appeal almost exclusively to their own experience. To misname themselves as "feminists" who appeal to "women's experience"

is to do what oppressors always do; it is to define the
rules and then solicit others to play the game. It is to
presume a commonality with oppressed women that
oppressed women themselves do not share. If White
women's analysis were adequate, they would be more
precise in naming their own movement and would not
presume to name or define the experiences of others.[31]

In womanist thought, the devaluation of "Black
womanhood," within the Black community and Black
church and also within feminism and the White
religious academy, diminishes Black women's *humanity*.[32]
Delineating for themselves what it means to be Black
women is thus critical for womanists.

Womanists have derived much of their inspiration from
the definition of womanism that was first proposed by
author and social critic Alice Walker.[33] Delores Williams
has spoken to the characteristics of a womanist in her
interpretation of Walker's definition:

Walker identifies a womanist as Black or of other color.
Cone has shown well enough how Black people's color
has been the basis upon which many white Americans
have judged Black people to be subhuman. Walker lifts
up Black women involved in the single-parenting act of
passing on advice to the female child. The relationship
between mother and child in a single parent household
is not valued as the proper circumstance out of which
"normal" and psychologically healthy children can come.
These kinds of relationships and family life are devalued.
Needless to say, American culture does not value the
advice that women give. Walker, in her description of a

womanist, challenges stereotypical ideas devaluing Black
women. She describes a Womanist as "Responsible . . .
in charge . . . serious." This challenges the stigma of
"childlike," "girlish," and "frivolous," which patriarchal
and demonarchal social attitudes assign to Black women.
According to Walker, a womanist loves men and women
sexually or nonsexually. This challenges those who
devalue the humanity of lesbian women. A womanist
defines universality in terms of an array of skin colors.
This gives intrinsic value to *all* skin color: "brown, pink
and yellow" as well as "white, beige and black." Walker
describes Black women's love in terms of dance, the moon,
the spirit, love, food, roundness, struggle, the folks, and
love of themselves as women. This affirms the cultural
elements through which Black women express their
humanity. To devalue any of this understanding of a
womanist is to devalue Black women's womanhood, to
devalue their humanity, to be guilty of sin – the sin that
denies that Black women's humanity is in the image of
God as is all humanity.[34]

What is clear from this extended interpretation of Walker's
definition of womanist is that Black women like Williams
are thoroughly invested in the project of redefining their
identities and affirming their value as Black women.
Womanist theology and ethics is a fresh attempt at
reassessing the life possibilities and promises of Black
women as perceived through their own lenses and
articulated in their own voices.

In seeking to further their own self-understanding, most
womanists are disinclined to turn to the traditional sources
of the predominantly White academy. Katie Cannon

speaks of the dilemma posed by refusing to "join the
canonical boys":

> To prove that she is sufficiently intelligent, the
> Black woman as Christian ethicist must discount the
> particularities of her lived experiences and instead focus
> on the validity of generalizable external analytical data.
> The dilemma she faces in joining the canonical boys is
> that of succumbing to the temptation of mastering only
> the historically specified perspective of the Euro-American
> masculine preserve. In order to be a respected scholar in
> the discipline, the Black woman is placed under a double
> injunction. She has to face a critical jury, primarily White
> and male, that makes claims for gender-neutral and value
> free inquiry as a model for knowledge. The Black female
> scholar will have little opportunity to expand her creative
> energy in the direction of liberation ethics if she con-
> centrates on searching for universal truths unhampered
> by so-called incidental matters such as race, sex, and
> class differences. In other words, there is an unspoken
> informal code within the guild that the Black woman
> academician must engage in this type of abstract moral
> discourse or else she runs the risk of being misunderstood,
> misinterpreted, and frequently devalued as a second-class
> scholar specializing in Jim Crow subject matter.[35]

Most womanists have responded to this dilemma by
turning away from traditional resources and methods,
despite the risks. They have turned their attention to Black
women themselves as resources for understanding the
weighty questions of life, God, and community. Womanists
research the writings of African-American women writers
such as Zora Neale Hurston, Harriet Tubman, Sojourner

Truth, Mary Prince, Toni Morrison, Mattie Jackson, Alice Walker, and others.[36] Black women's narratives, spiritual autobiographies, essays, poetry, and preaching help Black women to identifying the values that provided their "foremothers" with the most direction, meaning, and courage in their struggles toward self-determination.

By engaging in its own hermeneutic of return, but including women's lives within its broadening scope, womanist theology provides a powerful challenge to both traditional Black theology (and the traditional Black church) and the predominantly White feminist movement. The challenge is to do theology, and to engage in political struggle, in way that reflects some awareness of the distinctiveness of Black women's lives, particularly their moral lives. As false and misleading assumptions about Black women are uncovered and disputed, it will become possible to perceive Black women more truthfully, and thus to engage in theology and ethics in a way that is more truthful.

Womanist theology, perhaps more than any other trajectory within Black theological and ethical discourse, reveals in at least some of its conversations a growing inclination to move beyond the old, pejorative constructions of early Black theology. Although the intention is not thematized in so many words, there seems to be a growing openness among womanists to the possibility that Black women's experiences could speak, in a broadly humanistic vein, to women, and even to men, outside the Black community. In their attention to Black women's past and present experiences, womanists focus primarily on the concerns of those who have experienced the triple threat

of oppression – racism, classism, and sexism. Yet, with
a method and disposition quite different from early
Black theology, womanist reflections have the possibility
of promoting the liberation, not only of Black women,
but of others who experience unjust treatment in
analogous ways.[37]

Has the womanist critique and trajectory, then, settled
the question of absolutized particularism? While it is clear
that the womanist strand of Black theological discourse
is more receptive, egalitarian, and dialogical than the
classic formulation of Black theology, it does not, in my
judgment, adequately transcend the problem. Womanist
theology and ethics continues to express in its language
and analyses a strong reliance on survival and resistance
motifs. As with classic Black theology and ethics, and
with the narrower hermeneutics of return trajectory, this
reliance belies a subtle, enduring over-dependence on
the foil of White oppression. By focusing on survival and
resistance, Black women seem to surrender too much
of the power of self-definition to the obstacles that they
struggle to overcome.

My point is not that a liberation theology or ethic is
somehow less than credible merely because it emphasizes
resisting oppression or surviving in an unjust, evil context.
Indeed, in some situations this may be the only kind of
response possible. Still, as a mature discipline, Black theology
must eventually transcend this as its sole or even primary
emphasis. A more tenable and persuasive ethic, I think,
would present Black women not only as survivors and
resistors of evil, but also as unfathomably dignified and
powerful contributors to the good of the whole human

community. A more persuasive theology would make plain how God is present to Black women, and to others, as the power to make these contributions to the common human good.

Perhaps the greatest challenge facing womanists is to insure that their ongoing debates about what it means to be Black and female do not divide them unnecessarily among themselves – or relative to other people who have concerns that are similar to theirs. In an important roundtable discussion among womanist thinkers on the subject of Christian theology and ethics, Cheryl Sanders contributed an essay that has produced much discussion on the nature of the womanist project as a whole.[38] Sanders asks the question, "Does the term womanist [as defined by Walker] provide an appropriate frame of reference for the ethical and theological statements now being generated by Black women?"[39] She argues on several different grounds that it may not. She argues, first, that black womanhood is not likely to be promoted with reference to a self-conception that celebrates lesbian loving. For Sanders, Black women's well-being is integrally bound up with the well-being of the (traditional) Black family, which is conceived, in turn, as an integral part of the Black church. Sanders argues, second, that Walker's definition is too "secular"; it fails to connect the meaning of Black womanhood with the experience of the (traditional) Black Christian God. Sanders argues, third, that reliance on Walker's definition seems to require that one uphold all aspects of the definition if one is to be admitted into the ranks of "womanist," and this is something that Sanders is unwilling to do.[40]

Sanders' comments received vigorous response, especially
from Black lesbian Christians. What emerged from the
discussion is the realization that Black women may have
fewer particulars in common than they tend to imagine,
and it is not a simple matter to develop a definition of
Black womanhood that is inclusive of, and therefore
affirmative of, all Black women. This is an important
realization because it signals the need to think critically
about what it is, in the end, that binds all Black women
together. Even if Black women agree that all have an
interest in promoting the well-being of Black women and
their families, there is evidently much disagreement
regarding what this means, not to mention how it can
best be brought about.

Womanists, like other Black theologians and ethicists, need
to find a way to affirm themselves as a diverse group, on the
basis of a clear and indisputable commonality. They need
also to uncover a commonality that binds them, not only to
each other, but also to other women, and to other human
beings who are in situations that may be, in important
respects, analogous to theirs. It is crucial, I think, that Black
women look beyond their relationships to each other and
consider the larger, global context of their reflections: For
instance, why should a discouraged, poor Guatemalan
mother of twelve, who struggles each day to feed her family,
but wants to do more than simply survive, find "womanist"
thought intriguing and liberating? Why should she read it?
Is there a connection between her experience as a poor rural
woman laboring in the fields to make ends meet and a poor
single woman in the Watts ghetto of Los Angeles? The
challenge for womanist thought is to make plain what this
connection is, or at least to initiate conversations aimed
in that direction.

Conclusion

Various aspects of the problem of absolutized particularism have been addressed by authors of the Black theological tradition since Cone. What is evident from the discussion above is that the problem needs further attention. J. Deotis Roberts, Major Jones, and others took an important step forward by urging Blacks to let go of the hatred for all things White, which found expression in the sharp rhetoric of early Black theology. Nevertheless, these authors spoke of forgiveness and reconciliation between Blacks and Whites, within a dualistic Black-White conceptual framework, which was understandable for the time, but is too limiting for today.

The hermeneutics of return extends the critique against absolutized particularism by trying to step outside the Black-White polemic and focusing on investigations of Black particularity. The impulse appears to be a constructive one, but since the particular experiences to which these authors attend are the experiences of slaves, and many of the slaves were preoccupied with surviving in wretched circumstances, the effort to elucidate slave experiences keeps Black theological and ethical reflection in a reactive mode, overly-dependent on the terms set by the historical struggle of Blacks against Whites in a racist society, and unable to connect its reflections on God and the moral life to people who do not conceive of themselves in these historical terms.

Finally, the most significant response to the absolutized particularism of Black theology and ethics is contained in womanist thought. Womanists have made evident how Black theology's original formulations of Blackness unthinkingly reflected Black men's experiences to the neglect of Black women. Womanists have clarified the importance of engaging in a kind of theological and ethical reflection that attends to the triple threat of racism, classism, and sexism, which affects so many Black women. Moreover, many of the most recent womanist writings are more open in that they do not employ a rhetoric that immediately discourages anyone other than Black women from engaging it. Still, womanists face the challenge of pursuing their self-definitions and affirmations without focusing too narrowly on Black American women's lives, particularly as dominated by the motifs of struggle and resistance. They face the challenge of theorizing in a new and creative way how to connect what they are learning about themselves and their foremothers to what other women – and men – around the world need to hear.

In the following chapter I offer a proposal based upon the thought of Martin Luther King, Jr. which suggests a way to do Black theology and ethics while, at the same time, moving decisively beyond absolutized particularism. In King's writings, we will see how a Black theological and ethical project can affirm a ground of liberation greater than Black experience itself, such that the problem of idolizing Blackness is alleviated; it can affirm the equal dignity and sacredness of all human beings, so that the problem of making Black experience appear utterly unique and even normative for others is avoided; and it can recognize a fundamental interconnectedness among all human beings, and for that matter, all of life, so that Black theology and ethics is compelled to at least try to speak a liberating Word that will to reach people other than Blacks.

CHAPTER 4
Coming Full Circle: Martin Luther King, Jr. and a Black Ethic of Dignity

In the last chapter we examined some contributions that various thinkers within the Black theological tradition have made in their efforts to account for the meaning and value of Black life in America, while moving beyond the original, overly-simple, Black Power framework that focused on the historical struggle between Blacks and Whites. In spite of the efforts of these creative scholars, I believe that the Black theological tradition has not yet been able to find an adequate answer to the problem of absolutized particularism. It has not yet found the right strategy for constructing a compelling particularistic ethic.

One of the things that makes a theological and ethical vision compelling is its ability to explicate the universal significance of particular human concerns. A successful proposal articulates with clarity the specific form in which its theological and moral concerns arise, and it offers answers that are suitable to that form, yet at the same time, it makes clear the relevance of its answers for other people, who may seek new ways of understanding their own, distinctive situations. Can a critical engagement with Black experience carry significance for all human beings who seek to engage in a full and free participation in their society and community, yet, for whatever reason, have been denied that freedom? What are the possible connections between the life of a poor, Black woman in an American ghetto and the life of a young boy, orphaned through the violence in Kosovo? Can a critical engagement with Black experience carry significance, as well, for humans who are presently doing the work of oppressing and victimizing others? What are the possible connections between Black gang members in the streets of Los Angeles and KKK members who want more than anything to belong to a group that seems to bestow power?

The classic formulation of Black theology and ethics, with its appeal to ontological Blackness as ultimate reality is not workable. What is needed is a theology and an ethic that can incorporate the original intention to understand the way that God is at work in Black American individuals and communities, yet can also communicate God's liberative reality in ways that are likely to reach a wide variety of human beings who share, on some basic level, the same human condition. Particularistic Black thought, if it can manage to conjoin the effort to deepen Black self-understanding with a deliberate attempt to reconnect with the hopes and longings of the broader human family, can overcome its inclinations towards isolationism and exclusivism. A reconsideration of the work of Martin Luther King, Jr. can provide an excellent foundation for this endeavor.

Retrieving King

Martin Luther King, Jr., is arguably the most important
preacher, theologian, and social activist produced by
20th century America. This judgment is shared by James
Cone: "If theology is a disciplined endeavor to interpret
the meaning of the gospel for the present time, and if the
gospel is God's liberation of the poor from bondage, then
I would claim that no one has articulated the Christian
message of freedom more effectively, prophetically, and
creatively in America than Martin Luther King, Jr."[1] King's
life and thought have been the subject of intense study.[2]
His influence on the Black theological project has been
well-documented, and his writings continue to exert a
strong influence on the academy, the church, and the study
of religion in America. It is not my intention to provide
a thorough analysis of his theological and ethical work.

I do propose, however, to discuss three elements in
King's theological and ethical vision which, if properly
understood and retrieved within the context of the
dynamic, multi-racial, global society of the new millennium,
could offer the Black theological project a way to reframe
a liberating message for humanity, while continuing to
concentrate upon the full explication of the religious and
ethical significance of Black culture, the Black church, the
Black family, and the struggle for full Black participation
within the American socio-political and economic situation.
I hope to highlight these themes in the life and thought of
King so as to point in a preliminary way toward a more
deliberate and explicit transcendence of the problem of
absolutized particularism. The first theme to be treated is

that of God as the creator and providential underpinning of all that is, who guarantees that ultimately good will triumph over evil. The second theme is that of the equal, unfathomable dignity of every human being, who is created in the image of God. The third theme is that of the interconnectedness and interdependence of human beings, who do best as humans when they seek to live according to an ideal of a beloved community.

Although King's writings do not make explicit the full implications of his thinking for the project of Black theology and ethics, I will argue that his vision of the transcendent moral God, the equal dignity of God's human creatures, and the interconnectedness of all life, which is ideally to be embodied in the beloved community, suggests the possibility of a Black ethic that can come full circle – beginning with a sincere attempt to relate the divine to the exigencies of Black lives and culture and ending with a proposal of how those lives fit into the larger world story of which we are a part.

 ## Relevant Influences on King's Life and Thought

Before examining these three conceptual strands in King's thought, it is appropriate to consider briefly the various influences that shaped King's view of God, humankind, and the beloved community. His views did not, obviously, arise in a vacuum. It is quite commonplace for thinkers, in assessing the sources that influenced King, to focus on the multiplicity and variety of the sources that King, ever the eclectic social activist, preacher, and theologian, employed.[3] We shall consider briefly some of the most prominent sources.[4]

One source that had a significant impact on King's vision of social justice, freedom, and equality was the Black integrationist tradition, which issued from the thought of Frederick Douglas, was later refined by W.E.B. Dubois over against Booker T. Washington, and is still advocated in visions such as that of the NAACP and the National Urban League, which have their own vigorous and articulate contemporary advocates. This tradition rejects separatism among the races and seeks to bring about a society where, in King's words, the content of one's character takes precedence over the hue of one's color (and more than this, the reality of one's God-given dignity ultimately takes precedence over the content of one's character). King reveals the influence of this tradition most poignantly in his "I Have a Dream" address in Washington in 1963. This tradition was influenced by the optimism of Protestant liberalism, and drew much of its philosophical power from the documents of the American democratic tradition, especially the Constitution and the Declaration of Independence.

King was influenced also by reading authors of the White Protestant liberal tradition himself, although scholars disagree about the extent and significance of that influence. James Cone notes that the liberal theological tradition, represented especially by Walter Rauschenbusch, George Davis, and Harold DeWolf, helped King to "[apply] the critical spirit of rational reflection to theology and the Bible and [insist] on the reasonableness of the Christian faith."[5] Cone notes that, within an essay entitled

"Pilgrimage to Nonviolence," King mentions liberal
Protestant theology's impact on his optimism about human
nature, his accent on beloved community, his conviction
that love is the gospel's central meaning, his understanding
of Jesus' unique God-consciousness, and his views
concerning the value of human personality, the necessity
of ethical activity as a corollary of the Christian faith,
and God's imminent presence in the world.[6]

King was also influenced by the Protestant theologian Paul
Tillich. He wrote his dissertation on the doctrine of God
in the thought of Paul Tillich and Henry Nelson Wieman.
While King rejected both of their conceptions of God as
impersonal,[7] he nevertheless borrowed from Tillich's
theology insofar as it helped him to articulate a vision of
Black liberation. King resonated with Tillich's theological
method of correlating the mode of the Christian message
with the existential concerns and questions of those who
would hear the message.[8] In addition, King was influenced
by Tillich's notion of the courage to be.[9] In the last chapter
of this thesis, I show how King alludes to Tillichs' conception of courage as essential self-affirmation, in the effort
to articulate the courage needed by Blacks and by others
to withstand threats to their lives and their personhood.

Mohandas K. Gandhi and Henry David Thoreau both
influenced King's understanding of nonviolent direct
action, and the justification of its application to the
American social justice scene. As Cone notes, a visit
to India, reflection on Gandhi's philosophy, and much
discussion led King to speak about "the inevitability
of black suffering through nonviolence before the goal of
an integrated, beloved community" could be achieved.[10]

White it is clear that King was fed by the insights of Gandhi, it is also clear that he integrated these insights into his own powerful vision for the Black community:

> We will match your capacity to inflict suffering with our capacity to endure suffering. We will meet your physical force with soul force. We will not hate you, but we cannot in all good conscience obey your unjust laws. Do to us what you will and we will still love you. Bomb our homes and threaten our children; send your hooded perpetrators of violence into our communities and drag us out on some wayside road, beating us and leaving us half dead, and we will still love you. But we will soon wear you down by our capacity to suffer. And in winning our freedom we will so appeal to your heart and conscience that we will win you in the process.[11]

Cone rightly notes that this kind of theology was more appealing to liberal Whites than to oppressed Blacks, and King was warned by many Black scholars that such a position was illegitimate for Black people because it inflicted upon them too much psychological damage.[12]

The influence of Thoreau's concept of civil disobedience is evident in King's call for the open disobedience of unjust laws, particularly his call for Black people and their supporters to disobey the segregation laws of the South and to participate in sit-ins, the freedom rides, and the Birmingham demonstrations. King agreed with Thoreau, who said that "it is not desirable to cultivate a respect for the law, so much as for the right. The only obligation which I have the right to assume is to do at anytime what I think right."[13]

Although these various traditions and sources (i.e., the secular Black integrationist tradition, the White Liberal Protestant vision, and the thoughts and writings of Gandhi and Thoreau), contributed to the overall vision of the beloved community, which was advocated by King, they cannot be compared, in my judgment, to the influence that the Black Church and its vision of the God of the needy had upon King's life and work. King's vision of social justice and peace was grounded primarily in the Black church's faith in, and experience of, the God of the prophets, and the Christian God and Father of Jesus Christ.

In speaking of the influence that the Black church and the Black religious tradition had upon his life, King asserted:

> I am many things to many people; Civil Rights leader, agitator, trouble-maker and orator, but in the quiet resources of my heart, I am fundamentally a clergyman, a Baptist-preacher. This is my being and my heritage for I am also the son of a Baptist preacher, the grandson of a Baptist preacher, and the great-grandson of a Baptist preacher. The Church is my life and I have given my life to the Church.[14]

King was a product of the Black church. He had been quarried out of the Black Christian experience in its struggle for justice and peace on the North American continent.

Richard Lischer is correct when he suggests that conventional inquiries into the roots of King's thought and action tend to portray King as a theological thinker who was shaped primarily by his seminary and graduate education.[15] Conventional inquiries focus on tracing the relation of King's thought to the thinking of Rauschenbusch, Hegel, Marx, Tillich, and a host of other thinkers whose work King likely read during his academic and public service careers. What Lischer finds faulty in such accounts is that they over-intellectualize or over-academicize the process by which King's mind and heart were formed. They do not capture the lived religiosity of the man, who was steeped in the symbols, metaphors, narratives, and rituals of the Black church, and in its theology of a God who loves the poor and needy. As Lischer writes, the outlines and homilies that constitute the lion's share of King's addresses had been

> absorbed from sources deep within the African-American tradition. The arguments he used are as venerable as Richard Allen's defense of the integrity of all human beings, Daniel Coker's teachings on redemptive suffering, David Walker's indictment of Christian hypocrites, and even Nat Turner's terrible prophecy of deliverance. The Bible and the Black church taught him that you reap what you sow. The sources of his opposition to oppression and violence were as ancient as the Hebrew prophets, who insisted that the poor deserve justice, and the Sermon on the Mount, which forbids hate and counsels peace. These were his convictions.[16]

This brief introduction to some of the more notable influences on King's thought provides a backdrop for a discussion of King's notion of God.

God as the Ground of Life and the Guarantor of Human Liberation

Even the most cursory reading and interpretation of King's articles, books, sermons, speeches, and interviews reveals a deeply theological dimension to his thinking about human freedom. Rather than separating the theology of his Black church experience from his public advocacy for equal human rights, King kept his theology center stage in his social justice work. King based his understanding of the righteousness of the struggle against racism, militarism, and poverty on his faith in the personal God of the Christian scriptures, a deity whose mandate was plain regarding our sacrifice on behalf of the poor and needy:

> The Christian ought always to be challenged by any protest against unfair treatment of the poor, for Christianity is itself such a protest, nowhere expressed more eloquently that in Jesus' words: "The Spirit of the Lord is upon me, because he hath anointed me to preach the gospel to the poor; he hath sent me to heal the brokenhearted, to preach deliverance to the captives, and recovering of sight to the blind, to set at liberty them that are bruised, to preach the acceptable year of the Lord.[17]

From the very beginning of his social justice efforts until his last public address prior to his assassination in Memphis – during the successful Montgomery bus boycott (1955-56), his defeat in Albany (1961), his demonstrations and imprisonment, in Birmingham (1963), his memorable "I Have A Dream" speech and march on Washington in 1963, his march for voting rights in Selma (1965), his marches in Chicago (1966), his dialogue with Black

Power advocates in Meredith Mississippi in 1966, and his preparation for the Poor Peoples March and his stand against Vietnam in 1967 – at every stage of his outward encounter with recalcitrant social structures of evil, King invoked his confidence in God to engage and overthrow any and every force of evil that sought to degrade and destroy human life.

In *The Measure of a Man* King discusses what he deems to be the three dimensions of a complete human life.[18] The first dimension involves the full acceptance of one's own integrity and inner powers, and the determination to use them as fully as we have opportunity. The second dimension involves the breaking out of individualism into an authentic altruism toward all human beings. The third and most important dimension is the affirmation of God as the ultimate ground of all life and the center of human liberation and well-being. Speaking of persons who appear to master the first two dimensions but ignore the third, King suggests:

> They develop their inner powers; they love humanity; but they stop right here. They end up with the feeling that . . . humanity is the end of all things and that humanity is God. Philosophically or theologically, many of them would call themselves humanists. They seek to live life without a sky. They find themselves bogged down on the horizontal plane without being integrated on the vertical plane. But if we are to live the complete life we must reach up and discover God.[19]

No human being can be fulfilled by loving only himself, which is the length of a person's life, or even by loving his neighbor as himself, which is its breadth or width. That which underlies and gives purpose to life's joys and struggles and integrates every dimension of life is the cultivation of a love for God. This love, properly sought, understood, and realized, is the most significant dimension of a life that is fully human and fully alive. This love, says King, represents the "height of life. And when you do this, you live the complete life."[20]

King is speaking of Black life here, but under the banner of human life. His analysis is not exclusive to any particular group. For any human being to come to authentic self-love and authentic care for others demands this initial acknowledgment, this admission that in and of oneself one cannot be complete. Human life is derived life; the power to survive and thrive is not self-generated. Only as a man or woman seeks and discovers God as the ultimate power of life can he or she possible find the strength to become an integrated personality, a fully aware person who does not succumb to the kind of self-idolatry that is characteristic, in King's judgment, of humanism. Only through the power of God can a human being, regardless of his or her culture, clan, nationality, or social categorization, find the hope needed to sustain a meaningful human life:

> So I say to you, seek God and discover him and make him a power in your life. Without him all of our efforts turn to ashes and our sunrises into darkest nights. Without him, life is a meaningless drama with the decisive scenes missing. But with him we are able to rise from the fatigue of despair to the buoyancy of hope. With him we are able to rise from the midnight of desperation to the daybreak of joy. Saint Augustine was right – we were made for God and we will be restless until we find rest in him.[21]

All human beings, in King's view, in all of their
distinctiveness and their diversity, derive their elemental
human worth, their strength to go on, and their strength
specifically to do what is right from a source beyond
themselves and each other. The power to engage in acts
of self-sacrifice on behalf of those least cherished and
most vulnerable does not well up from within humankind
unaided. The vision and passion necessary to sustain
the "Freedom Movement," as the civil rights struggle was
called in the late 1950s, was not simply the product of
the finite imaginations of Black people and their White
supporters. It was, for King, the gift of a just God.

The success of the movement was, more specifically,
the product of a cosmos that was and is oriented by the
benevolent will of God toward the restoration of justice
for the hopeless and the helpless. In King's first national
address in May of 1957, he stated that the victory won
in Montgomery only months earlier and the new cry for
freedom throughout the world was in line with the
providential work of God. The struggle for freedom,
which was unfolding in Asia and Africa, as well as
America, revealed something about the nature of the
universe:

> It tells us something about the core and heartbeat of the
> cosmos. It reminds us that the universe is on the side of
> justice. It says to those who struggle for justice, "You do
> not struggle alone, but God struggles with you." This
> belief that God is on the side of truth and justice comes
> down to us from the long tradition of our Christian faith.
> There is something at the very center of our faith which
> reminds us that Good Friday may occupy the throne for
> a day, but ultimately it must give way to the triumphant

beat of the drums of Easter. Evil may so shape events
that Caesar will occupy a palace and Christ a cross, but
one day that same Christ will rise up and split history
into A.D. and B.C., so that even the life of Caesar must
be dated by His name. There is something in this universe
which justifies William Cullen Bryant in saying, "Truth
crushed to earth will rise again."[22]

Similarly, ten years after this address, in a Christmas
sermon delivered in Ebenezer Baptist Church at Atlanta
on Christmas Eve of 1967, King reiterated his belief that
God has invested the universe with its own fundamental
morality which cannot be overwhelmed, however
pernicious or injurious the evil may be that appears,
at least on the surface, to have extinguished the
hope of justice and compassion:

> If there is to be peace on earth and goodwill toward
> men, we must finally believe in the ultimate morality of
> the universe, and believe that all reality hinges on moral
> foundations. Something must remind us of this as we
> once again stand in the Christmas season and think of
> the Easter season simultaneously, for the two somehow
> go together. Christ came to show us the way. Men love
> darkness rather than the light, and they crucified Christ,
> and there on Good Friday on the Cross it was still dark,
> but then Easter came, and Easter is an eternal reminder
> of the fact that the truth crushed to the earth will rise
> again. . . . And so this is our faith, as we continue to hope
> for peace on earth and goodwill toward men: let us
> know that in the process we have cosmic companionship.[23]

What is thus plain is that King's idea regarding the nature
of human good and the prospects of human well-being,

was not rooted in a faith in human beings themselves. It was rooted, instead, in a faith in God's "cosmic companionship," which bends and inclines the universe towards justice and love, and ensures that lies, hatred, and malice cannot and will not ultimately triumph. King concedes that this is a proposition that is difficult to defend on purely rational grounds, in light of what appears to be the considerable success of evil in the world, but he nevertheless embraces it as a central tenet of his Christian faith.[24]

The conviction that God alone is the ground and guarantor of human liberation allows those who struggle on behalf of the poor and abused to keep clear on the fact that certain people and groups can indeed be the bearers and the instruments of God's providential concern in the world. Yet these persons and groups are not themselves God. They do not have God at their disposal. Their status as loci for the revelation of God's will for humanity does not place them in a special category where they are immune from common human failures and the need for broad human consideration and criticism. In other words, the fact that God reveals Godself partly in the liberative work of Black people like King does not mean that God is Black, if in asserting that God is Black one has the slightest inclination to imagine that Black is God. What is so striking about King is that he took on enormous responsibility in his leadership role in the civil rights movement, yet he always and unambiguously pointed away from himself and to God as the ground of his action and the cause of any success that was realized in the movement.

In reminiscing about her initial days with Martin King, as they readied themselves for the long struggle in Montgomery, Coretta Scott King speaks of an ongoing dialogue among leaders of the movement about why Montgomery, of all places, would be where African-Americans would unite peacefully for the cause of freedom. In the course of their exchange they found one final explanation.

> Though some of the impetus came from the Supreme Court decisions, and some was due to the particularly unjust actions of the city bus company, these were not enough to explain it. Other blacks had suffered equal or greater injustices in other places and had meekly accepted them. I suggested that it was due to his own leadership and to his devoted coworkers, but Martin said, "No." There was no rational explanation that would suffice. Therefore we must accept something else. The birth of the Movement could not be explained "without a divine dimension." My husband devoutly believed that there is "a creative force that works to pull down mountains of evil and level hilltops of injustice." As we have seen, he regarded himself as an instrument of this force, and he said, "God still works through history, His wonders to perform." He believed that "God had decided to use Montgomery as the proving ground for the struggle and the triumph of freedom and justice in America."[25]

Martin King makes this point himself in *Stride Toward Freedom*.[26]

With reference to the above quotation, notice first that in the mind of King, no rational, human explanation exists for why the Montgomery struggle met with the success that it did, at the time that it did. The attempt to read human

history as a roadmap that shows and predicts the cause
and effect relationship between God's action and the
success of human action in the world is futile. Regarding
the Montgomery bus boycott, for instance, King says
that many of the elements that one would have looked
for in the movement were noticeably absent; instead
of a preexistent unity, for example, there was division,
indifference, and complacency. Nor can the idea of
"new leadership" be sufficient to explain the success
since, in King's mind, the story of Montgomery would
have unfolded in much the same way that it did even
if the leaders of the protests had never been born.
Whatever one wishes to call this providential force,
King suggests, whether it be the principle of concretion
of Alfred N. Whitehead, the process of integration of
Henry N. Wieman, the Being-itself of Paul Tillich, or the
personal Lord and Savior of the Black church, "some
extra-human force labors to create a harmony out of the
discords of the universe."[27] God's work in history on
behalf of the broken and the despised cannot be tracked,
and no prophetic gaze can detect the timing, place, or
event that will finally trigger such intervention from God.
Yet, the intervention is certain to happen, according to
God's will.

Second, King believes that the goal of liberation does
not depend on the charisma of a given movement's
participants. Who could have envisioned that one of the
greatest movements of the twentieth century would
take place among Negroes who were denied equal access
to public accommodations, or that the entire civil rights
movement would be triggered through the fatigue of a
gentle "colored woman" who refused to give up her seat
on the bus to a White male passenger, on a typical day in

the segregated town of Montgomery, Alabama? Again,
King refuses to ground the movement's energy or progress
in his own leadership or in that of his coworkers. God, in
King's view, works according to God's own will to secure
the goal of cosmic justice; King is merely an instrument
and a willing agent of that work.

James P. Hannigan makes this point when he argues that
"this God who was the Father of humankind was quite
real and personal to King. If one does not grasp just how
alive and how central this God was in King's mind and
heart, it is likely that he will never comprehend King's
message of militant nonviolence. The fact of the matter
is that King believed – he entrusted himself to and staked
his life upon the God in whom he believed."[28] In King's
vision, no human moral agency, Black or otherwise, could
ever become the foundation of the struggle for right in
the universe. No human being, Black or otherwise, could
ascribe to his or her particularity or group membership
a special place, position, or power, except as one finite
vehicle among many for the embodiment of God's
providential care. In King's estimation God is the only
one who could guarantee the success of the helpless.
God was the final arbiter in the affairs of humankind.

At least one other insight can be drawn from the dialogue
described by Mrs. King. Having faith that God is ultimately
in charge of the freedom struggle and will one day bring
this and other similar struggles to completion does not mean
that humans can sit back and let God do the work of
liberation; King does not even consider this as a possibility
for thought. Nor does it mean that it will be relatively easy
to engage in the day to day work of liberation. Instead,
allegiance to the struggle demands human suffering and

sacrifice. From the very beginning of King's public career, there were numerous threats made on his life and his family, and the themes of death and the need to be free from the temptation to turn away from the terrifying face of evil were ever present in his speeches, relationships, and conversations. Melbourne Cummings and Lyndrey Niles have documented this ongoing inner struggle.[29] The authors quote one of King's sermons early in the movement, in 1956, during the boycott, where King admits that their stance on behalf of human dignity and equal rights could mean that some will have to suffer serious loss:

> Sometimes it might mean going to jail. If such is the case you must honorably grace the jail with your presence. It might even mean physical death. But if physical death is the price that some must pay to free their children from a permanent life of psychological death, then nothing could be more Christian.[30]

King's view of God was neither sentimental nor naive. Evil exists in the world. The more one seeks to stand against the onslaught of evil, the greater the risk to one's person in this life, and the greater the temptation to abandon the cause, for risk of loss, abuse, and even death.

At the same time, however, as one gradually comes to understand God as the ground of all life and hope, a fundamental shift occurs where the resources of God are mysteriously substituted for one's own resources. In his sermon, "Our God is Able," King relates a powerful personal experience that may account, to some extent, for King's conviction on this matter.[31] Contrasting his pre- and post-Montgomery days, he says that the former were days of fulfillment; the burdens of his high school,

college, seminary, and graduate school days were minor
and of little consequence. The latter, which began when he
agreed to be the leader of the Montgomery Improvement
Association, were difficult from the beginning, and were
often characterized by trials, threats, and confrontations.
Immediately, King began to receive threatening telephone
calls and letters in his home, and although he discounted
the initial threats as "the work of a few hotheads," he soon
discovered that many of the threats were in earnest. King
said that he "felt myself faltering and growing in fear."[32]

After an extraordinarily strenuous day, after the beginning
of the Montgomery bus boycott, on the evening of January
27, 1956, King received a call. The caller said, "Listen,
nigger, we've taken all we want from you. Before next week
you'll be sorry you ever came to Montgomery." King hung
up the phone, and could not sleep afterwards. His fears,
all of them, began to bear down on him at once, and he
reached "the saturation point." While many such threats
had come to King before, this particular threat stayed with
him. He was tortured over it, was not able to go to sleep,
went to the kitchen to heat some coffee, and began to
search for answers. King recites the incident:

> In this state of exhaustion, when my courage had almost
> gone, I determined to take my problem to God. My head
> in my hands, I bowed over the kitchen table and prayed
> aloud. The words I spoke to God that midnight are still
> vivid in my memory. "I am here taking a stand for what
> I believe is right. But now I am afraid. The people are
> looking to me for leadership, and if I stand before them
> without strength and courage, they too will falter. I am
> at the end of my powers. I have nothing left. I've come
> to the point where I can't face it alone." At that moment

I experienced the presence of the Divine as I had never
before experienced him. It seemed as though I could hear
the quiet assurance of an inner voice, saying, "Stand up
for righteousness, stand up for truth. God will be at your
side forever." Almost at once my fears began to pass
from me. My uncertainty disappeared. I was ready to face
anything. The outer situation remained the same, but
God had given me inner calm.[33]

In a different account of the same incident, King drew
upon the theology and the philosophy that he had just
studied in the universities, trying to arrive at a rational
explanation for the existence, power, and nature of evil,
but the answers didn't come. In agony, King turned to
the God of his Black faith:

Something said to me, you can't call on daddy now; he's
in Atlanta, and 175 miles away. . . . You've got to call on
that something, on that person that your daddy used to
tell you about, that power that can make a way out of no
way. And I discovered then that religion had to become
real to me and I had to know God for myself. And I bowed
down over that cup of coffee. I never will forget it. Oh
yes, I prayed a prayer. And I prayed out loud that night.
I said, "Lord, I'm down here trying to do what's right. I
think I'm right. I think the cause that we represent is right.
But Lord, I must confess that I'm weak now, I'm faltering,
I'm losing my courage, and I can't let people see me like
this because if they see me weak and losing my courage
they will begin to get weak.[34]

In recalling this event again in his book, *Stride Toward
Freedom*, King mentions hearing the inner voice, which
said, "Martin Luther, stand up for righteousness. Stand up

for justice. Stand up for truth. And lo, I will be with you, even until the end of the world."[35]

What is striking in these renderings of one of the most agonizing events in King's life, which was so formative for his leadership in the freedom movement,[36] is that his nearly paralyzing agony was answered by a powerful conviction that God will indeed provide the readiness and the resources to do what is necessary to endure, and if need be, to suffer and die on behalf of the truth. This conviction was renewed again and again in King's life, whenever he most needed that renewal. During an imprisonment in the Birmingham jail, to provide one more example, King heard from his lawyer and friend Clarence Jones that the actor Harry Belafonte was going to raise money for the imprisoned demonstrators. King reflects:

> I found it hard to say what I felt. Jones's message had brought me more than relief from the immediate concern about money; more than gratitude for the loyalty of friends far away; more than confirmation that the life of the movement could not be snuffed out. What silenced me was a profound sense of awe. I was aware of a feeling that had been present all along below the surface of consciousness, pressed down under the weight of concern for the movement: I had never been truly in solitary confinement; God's companionship does not stop at the door of a jail cell. I don't know whether the sun was shining at that moment. But I know that once again I could see the light.[37]

As James Cone argues, whether we speak about the Montgomery boycott, the demonstrations in Birmingham, or the Selma march, whether we address his dialogue with Black Power or his views concerning the Vietnam War, we must take note of King's way of returning consistently to the personal God of his Black church tradition as the ultimate ground of strength and hope.[38]

The Dignity and Worth of the Human Personality

King's notion of God seems to eliminate any hint of the possibility of an absolutized particularism because of the way that God infinitely transcends any and all manifestations of God in particular human beings, groups, or movements. Similarly, the tendency toward absolutized particularism is undermined by King's theological anthropology, which would never allow an entire group of people, even White racists, to be characterized as a manifestation of the Anti-Christ and thus reduced to something less than human.

To begin with, King asserts that every human being[39] is a creation of God, a beloved child of God, who is made in the image of God. Every human being is therefore crowned with glory and honor.[40] Despite the fact that a human person is chemically, in King's estimation, worth only around ninety-eight cents, the artistic genius of a Michelangelo, the poetic genius of a Shakespeare, or the spiritual genius of Jesus of Nazareth cannot possibly be explained in light of that sum – nor can the spirit of an "ordinary" person like Rosa Parks or "Tee," whom I introduced in chapter two:

Deeply rooted in our religious heritage is the conviction that every man is an heir to a legacy of dignity and worth. Our Judeo-Christian tradition refers to this inherent dignity of man in the Biblical term "the image of God." The "image of God" is universally shared in equal portions by all men. There is no graded scale of essential worth. Every human being has etched in his personality the indelible stamp of the Creator. Every man must be respected because God loves him. The worth of an individual does not lie in the measure of his intellect, his racial origin or his social position. Human worth lies in relatedness to God. An individual has value because he has value to God. Whenever this is recognized, "Whiteness" and "Blackness" pass away as determinants in a relationship and "son" and "brother" are substituted. Immanuel Kant said that "all men must be treated as ends and never [simply] as means." The immorality of segregation is that it treats men as means rather than ends, and thereby reduces them to things rather than persons.[41]

The conviction that "there is no divine right of one race which differs from the divine right of another"[42] is upheld by sources other than the Christian tradition, including the Declaration of Independence, but the ultimate warrant for this belief is theological. "'All men...are created equal. They are endowed by their Creator with certain inalienable rights, among these are life, liberty, and the pursuit of happiness.' Never has a socio-political document proclaimed more profoundly and eloquently the sacredness of human personality."[43]

The sacredness of the human personality is, for King, both a gift and a task. As a gift, this sacredness is bestowed freely, generously, and equally to all. It is neither earned nor can it be negotiated. This dignity cannot be blotted out (e.g., within oppressors) by the corruption of human character or community, nor can it be destroyed (e.g., within the oppressed) through wicked programs of dehumanization, victimization, and abuse. The actions of others and one's own actions can be so corrupt that they could hinder one's ability to see – and to be duly moved by – the image of God in every person, but the image is nonetheless there for those who have eyes to see. Quite simply, as long as a person lives, she or he lives as a being whose essential nature reflects the goodness and glory of God.[44]

As task, human dignity must be acknowledged and publicly upheld. Every person, regardless of how much her dignity has been violated, must try to resist the temptation to regard herself as less than profoundly and irreducibly valuable. Every person, regardless of how much she has been wronged by other people and regardless of the prospect that those people will change their ways, must also resist the temptation to dehumanize her oppressors. She must resist this, not on cultural or social grounds, but by virtue of a theological conviction that the image of God is stamped upon all, without exception. All are due respect, and all ought to be accorded the freedom that is appropriate to that image, especially the freedom to realize one's full human potential.

King was aware, of course, that not everyone shared his conviction on this matter. He observed that there was another strand of thinking within the American psyche, which reflected the belief that the Negro is not stamped, in the same way as White people are, with the image of God. It is, ironically, human freedom, which is an element of the image of God in humans, that allows some humans to close their eyes to the reality of equal human dignity.

> Human beings are free to choose if they will affirm the truth or follow lies, misrepresentations designed for the well-being of their own in-group. Human beings are free beings made in the image of God, and are not led by instinct; they can choose between alternatives, and so can choose to reject the truth and embrace the lie, to choose the good or the evil, the low or the high.[45]

King knew that many Whites chose to deny the truth of the sacredness of human personality. He also knew that many Black people had become convinced, by the lies of White racists, of the sub-human value of Black people. Garth Baker-Fletcher quotes King in an address to the New York State Civil War Centennial Commission where he speaks about the "imposition of inferiority" as the "slave chains" that continue to fetter the minds of Blacks:

> The imposition of inferiority externally and internally are the slave chains of today. What the Emancipation Proclamation proscribed in a legal and formal sense has never been eliminated in human terms. By burning in the consciousness of white Americans a conviction that Negroes are by nature subnormal, much of the myth was absorbed by the Negro himself, stultifying his energy, his ambition, and self-respect. The Proclamation of Inferiority has contended with the Proclamation of Emancipation, negating its liberating force.[46]

The liberation of the Black soul would have to involve, more than anything else, the coming to a secure conviction of one's own essential, God-given dignity.[47]

Speaking of the greatest victory won during the civil rights movement, King points to "something internal. The real victory was what this period did to the psyche of the Black man. The greatness of this period was that we armed ourselves with dignity and self-respect. The greatness of this period was that we straightened our backs up. And a man can't ride your back unless its bent."[48] King made the same assessment during an interview with Merv Griffin in July of 1967. When asked what the civil rights movement had done for the Negro individually King responded:

> Well, I think the greatest thing that it has done is that it has given the Negro a new sense of dignity, and a new sense of somebodyness. And this is the greatest victory we have won. Turning away from the external changes that have come about, I think that the greatest thing that has taken place is the internal change in the psyche of the Negro. And the Negro has a sense of pride that he's desperately needed all along. And, uh, he is able to stand up, and, uh, feel that he is a man.[49]

King realized that unless Blacks who had been classified as sub-human rejected the culturally and religiously sanctioned lies about their humanness, they would continue to live in the shadow of these lies. Believing them, they would likely fall into the trap of acting in ways that appeared to confirm the lies.

King knew that it was no simple matter to overcome the ambivalence that characterized Black identity. The question that each person must confront is, "Who am I?"[50] To grapple with that question, in the midst of the White American rejection of the Negro, is what constitutes "the Negro's greatest dilemma."

The Negro is the child of two cultures – Africa and
America. The problem is that in the search for wholeness
all too many Negroes seek to embrace only one side of
their nature. Some, seeking to reject their heritage, are
ashamed of their color, ashamed of black art and music,
and determine what is beautiful and good by the
standards of white society. They end up frustrated and
without cultural roots. Others seek to reject everything
American and to identify totally with Africa, even to the
point of wearing African clothes. But this approach also
leads to frustration because the American Negro is not an
African. The old Hegelian synthesis still offers the best
answer to many of life's dilemmas. The American Negro is
neither totally African nor totally Western. He is Afro-
American, a true hybrid, a combination of two cultures.[51]

For King, this idea of the two-ness of the consciousness
of Black people in America, a concept that was articulated
so well by DuBois', was a signal insight. One the one
hand, King is quick to embrace the full meaning of having
African roots:

Who are we? We are the descendants of slaves. We are
the descendants of slaves, the offspring of noble men
and women who were kidnapped from their native land
and chained in ships like beasts. We are the heirs of a
great and exploited continent known as Africa. We are
the heirs of a past of rope, fire, and murder. I for one
am not shamed of this past. My shame is for those who
became so inhuman that they could inflict this torture
on us.[52]

This full acceptance of Black people as descendants of
African people was essential in King's understanding of the

African pole of the African-American identity. For any
Negro to be ashamed of her African past and its painful
matriculation to American slavery – as gnawed, frayed,
and bloodied as that past was – was to deny something
fundamental about one's heritage and oneself. King did
not view integration as the forgetting of the African past
or the dissociation of Negroes from their collective
memories of the slavery period. To the contrary, he urged
that Blacks integrate their African and African-American
heritage into a proud and dignified identity.[53]

On the other hand, King affirmed with no shame his
roots in American history and culture, as shaped as it is
by the White majority, and he encouraged other Blacks
to do the same. As difficult and terrifying as it may be for
some to accept, America is the home of Black Americans.
The destiny of Blacks is tied up with the destiny of America,
and although King acknowledged the psychological appeal
of becoming more identified with Africa, he urged the Negro
to "face the fact that America is now his home, a home
that he helped to build through 'blood, sweat, and tears.'"[54]
The only hope for Blacks lay, not in creating a separate
Black nation within this nation, but in binding together
with people of conscience from the too often apathetic
White majority to create a new, liberating environment
where all could enjoy security and justice.

The destinies of Blacks and Whites in America are
bound together: the fact that many White Americans
abandoned their country's vision of the sacredness
of human personality, and chose to exploit Blacks for
economic gain reveals that there is a fissure within
the soul of the nation, which must be healed if the nation
is to survive. The depersonalization of any segment of

the population by any other segment leads people to malign, abuse, even destroy others without recognizing the evil of their actions. Bigotry and discrimination are signs of a fundamental failure to acknowledge the truth regarding the nature of persons. Regardless of the reasons given to justify inequities or injustices, the person who inflicts abuse on other persons commits sacrilege. She profanes and desecrates a human being, someone who bears God's own image.

To deny the image of God in another – to discount our shared God-relatedness and our mutual sacredness as God's – is to "thingify" the other.[55] A person, people group, or nation that "thingifies" others quickly becomes brutal. Since certain others are not regarded as persons – not experienced as having the dignity of persons – these "things" can readily be used and exploited, denied basic human goods, tortured, and killed, with little consequence for human conscience. King's genius lies in his recognition and his dogged, costly insistence that this is a universal human truth. Whether thingification takes place on the part of the majority or the minority – on the part of the oppressor or the oppressed – it always and everywhere constitutes a violation, not only of the other's essential human dignity, but also of one's own. This belief drove a wedge between King and the Black Power movement that needs to be kept clearly in view as Black theologians and ethicists seek to articulate the meaning of Black liberation.

As we saw in the first chapter, Black theology was originally conceived as the religious arm of the Black Power movement.[56] King himself recognized many of the positive contributions that the Black Power movement

was making to the cause of Black freedom and equality.
He agreed that the problem of transforming the ghetto was
a problem of power that required a confrontation between
those committed to change and those advocating the status
quo.[57] He agreed with the need to call African-Americans
to a "new sense of manhood, to a deep feeling of racial pride
and to an audacious appreciation of [their] heritage."[58]
King thought that Black Power was right to seek to arouse
within Negroes a majestic sense of their own value, and
the elimination of shame in being Black. The goals of Black
Power, in its broadest and most positive meaning for
King, resonated to some extent with the goals of the civil
rights movement, which included the personal, social,
legal, economic, and political empowerment of Blacks.[59]

Despite these similarities between the civil rights and
Black Power movements, however, King rejected Black
Power as being inconsistent with the essential affirmation
of the dignity and worth of all human beings as made
in the image of God, and as a failed strategy for social
change. King perceived Black Power, fundamentally,
as a nihilistic philosophy born of the suspicion that the
Black cause cannot, in the end, succeed. No vital
revolutionary movement of love and justice can succeed
that is built on hate and disillusionment: "revolution,
though born of despair, cannot long be sustained by
despair."[60] The ultimate contradiction within the Black
Power movement was, on the one hand, its claim to
be the most revolutionary wing of the social revolution
taking place in America at that time and, on the other
hand, its failure to keep alive the flames of hope. King
stated plainly the reason why Blacks should reject the
way of Black Power: "The Negro cannot entrust his destiny

to a philosophy nourished solely on despair."[61] The
bottom line is that, "today's despair is a poor chisel to
carve out tomorrow's justice."[62]

There were other reasons why King rejected the Black
Power movement as a viable strategy for the Black
freedom struggle. He thought its advocacy of separatism
(the garnering of Black resources only for Black purposes)
was unrealistic, and he perceived their understanding
of the nature of power as naive. They seemed to assume
that Blacks would not be as abusive and negligent in
the use of power as their White counterparts had been.
Most importantly, however, King rejected Black Power's
advocacy of retaliatory violence as a strategy for Black
empowerment.[63] To adopt violence as a strategy, in King's
mind, was impractical and self-destructive; it would be
a suicidal act of despair, quickly quelled and thoroughly
defeated. Adopting violence was also unimaginative
and unregenerative: Rioting in the ghettos was not a
revolutionary act; it was simply reactionary.[64] Violent
response was also immoral.[65] To turn to violence was
to concede the high ground of good moral conscience.[66]
Violence destroys the moral character of those who
employ it; it lays the foundation for future bitterness
and chaos that our children will inherit from us.[67]

This does not mean that we ought to be passive in the
face of injustices that discount our fundamental human
dignity. Writing his "Letter from the Birmingham City
Jail," King saw himself as standing in the middle between
two identity extremes in the Black community. On the
one side stood those who were complacent, who as a
result of oppression had lost their ability to resist and to
dream and had thus accommodated themselves to

injustice. On the other side stood the Black nationalist
groups, represented by the Nation of Islam, who had
repudiated Christianity and concluded that Whites were
devils, the embodiment of evil in the world today. King
reflects: "I have tried to stand between these two forces,
saying that we need emulate neither the 'do-nothingism'
of the complacent, nor the hatred and despair of the Black
nationalist. For there is the more excellent way of love
and nonviolent protest."[68]

While violence engenders bitterness in an ever growing
vicious circle,[69] direct nonviolent resistance enhances
the self-regard of the protestor.[70] It affirms and respects
those who oppose us, while at the same time bringing
pressure to bear on them to face themselves and their
attitudes honestly, to acknowledge that they have a terribly
distorted view of their fellow human beings.[71] It sends
the message: "I am not avoiding penalties for breaking the
law – I am willing to endure all your punishment because
your society will not be able to endure the stigma of
violently and publicly oppressing its minority to preserve
injustice.[72] By advocating nonviolent protest, King
effectively reversed the assumed moral roles of the
oppressor and the oppressed. The authorities were
exposed as unjust, and going to jail no longer appeared
as a disgrace; it was transfigured into a badge of honor.

Nonviolent resistance allows the resistor to use her
suffering in a strategic way, to win the human regard
and perhaps even the friendship of the oppressor. The
resistor uses her suffering to tutor, instruct, and shame the
oppressor into the realization of shared sacredness. This
is not a matter of humiliating the oppressor; rather, it is a
matter of awakening human recognition and compassion.

To quote again King's use of Gandhi, "We will match your capacity to inflict suffering with our capacity to endure suffering. . . . [and] we will soon wear you down by our capacity to suffer. And in winning our freedom, we will so appeal to your heart and conscience that we will win you in the process."[73]

In sum, the struggle for justice must never be accompanied by hatred. Hatred destroys one's sense of values – one's tendency to be duly awe-struck in the presence of human beings. It eliminates the possibility of mutually respectful human regard.[74] Achieving dignified Black personhood requires letting go of the temptation to anti-Whiteness,[75] retaliation[76] and humiliation.[77] Bitterness is the true enemy. Only forgiveness, which removes all barriers for future relationship, creates the atmosphere necessary for a "fresh start and a new beginning." We must love or perish.[78]

 ## The Interconnectedness of All Things and the Beloved Community

The last of the three thematic strands in the theological and ethical vision of King flows from the first two and completes them. God is the ground of all life. God has created every human being in God's own image, with unfathomably deep dignity, and God calls human beings into modes of action and relationship that uphold and reflect this dignity. God calls humans into ways of being that reflect, not only the dignity of individuals, but also the dignity of the human race as a whole. All human beings are interconnected, in several related senses, and humans are called to acknowledge, value, and exhibit that interconnectedness in all that they do.

As we have already seen, King believes that all human beings are connected, metaphysically and morally, in the sense that they have their being in relation to the same Creator, who creates them with the same essential dignity. When one human being looks properly into the eyes of another, she sees, in a sense, a reflection of her own infinite depth. She sees a "thouness" in the other, which drives home the realization that every human being, and all human beings taken together, provide a kind of access to the infinite being and love of God.[79]

King believes that human beings are connected in other ways, as well. They are connected empirically, as forces within an enormous system of cause and effect relations. Every action that we commit has an impact on other human beings and, perhaps in some small way, on *every* other human being. And every act that others commit has, for good or for ill, some effect on us and those who matter most to us. In *Where Do We Go from Here*, King focuses on some of the practical and moral implications of this connectedness.

> All men are interdependent. Every nation is an heir of a vast treasury of ideas and labor to which both the living and the dead of all nations have contributed. Whether we realize it or not, each of us lives eternally "in the red." We are everlasting debtors to known and unknown men and women. When we arise in the morning, we go into the bathroom where we reach for a sponge which is provided for us by a Pacific Islander. We reach for soap that is created for us by a European. Then at the table we drink coffee which is provided for us by a South American, or tea by a Chinese or cocoa by a West African. Before we leave for our jobs we are already beholden to more than half the world.[80]

Just as we benefit from each other's productive actions, so we also suffer from each other's destructive actions. In his "Letter from the Birmingham City Jail," King reflects soberly about his responsibilities as a citizen of the entire U.S.:

> I am cognizant of the interrelatedness of all communities and states. I cannot sit idly by in Atlanta and not be concerned about what happens in Birmingham. Injustice anywhere is a threat to justice everywhere. We are caught in an inescapable network of mutuality, tied to a single garment of destiny. Whatever affects one directly, affects all indirectly. Never again can we afford to live with the narrow, provincial "outside agitator" idea: Anyone who lives inside the United States can never be considered an outsider anywhere within its bounds.[81]

Beyond this, King also reflected upon his responsibilities as a citizen of the world. As Cone notes, King "was as concerned about the life chances of brown children in Vietnam as he was about black children in America's cities. King's vision was truly international, embracing all humanity."[82]

Human beings have a God-given human dignity, whether they or other humans recognize it or not. But human beings are nevertheless dependent on others to treat them with respect and fairness if they are to survive and actualize their full humanity in the frame of their historical lives. In *Strength to Love*, King acknowledges this human vulnerability and the responsibility that humans have because of it: "I can never be what I ought to be until you are what you ought to be, and you can

never be what you ought to be until I am what I ought
to be. This is the interrelated structure of reality."[83]
Particularly in the current era of global communications
and global economic markets, this shared vulnerability
and responsibility cannot be denied. King appeals to
a story (about a story) to make his point:

> Some years ago a famous novelist died. Among his papers
> was found a list of suggested plots for future stories, the
> most prominently underscored being this one: "A widely
> separated family inherits a house in which they have to
> live together." This is the great new problem of mankind.
> We have inherited a large house, a great "world house"
> in which we have to live together – Black and White,
> Easterner and Westerner, Gentile and Jew, Catholic and
> Protestant, Moslem and Hindu – a family unduly separated
> in ideas, culture, and interest, who because we can never
> again live apart, must learn somehow to live with each
> other in peace.[84]

Unless all of us learn to live peaceably in this "world
house," all of us will suffer the stultification of our gifts
and capacities.

An implication of the metaphysical, moral, and empirical
connectedness of human beings is that no self can be fully
human and fully alive without the care and contribution
of other selves. And no self can become fully itself without
caring for and contributing to the well-being of other
selves. Individualism as a life choice is self-destructive; no
person, according to King, can shut himself or herself off
from others in this world and still pretend to be living
well, as God intended:

> The universe is so structured that things go awry if men
> are not diligent in their cultivation of the other regarding
> dimension. "I" cannot reach fulfillment without "thou."
> The self cannot be self without other selves. Self-concern
> without other-concern is like a tributary that has no
> outward flow to the ocean. Stagnant, still, and stale, it
> lacks both life and freshness. Nothing would be more
> disastrous and out of harmony with our self-interest than
> for the developed nations to travel a dead-end road of
> inordinate selfishness.[85]

King thinks that this individualized self-interest is a
problem, not only for persons, but also for nations and
racial groups, which can become preoccupied with their
economic position and their social status to the point of
losing all perspective on their membership in the larger
family of humanity.[86]

What King affirms is intriguing, in my judgment. All
human beings are involved in a single unfolding process –
one that involves and effects us all, for good and also for
ill, whether or not we are consciously aware of it. Our
willingness to concern ourselves with matters beyond our
own parochial interests is key to our active and responsible
participation in this process. It is key to our actualization
as relational moral agents. In King's view, humans need to
conceive and follow a longing "for genuine inter-group
and interpersonal living"[87] if they are to live decent human
lives. They *need* to become responsible to each other. In
order to display the full glory of their God-given dignity,
and in order to know the joy of this display, humans *need*
to become obedient to the "unenforceable obligations" of
the beloved community, where men and women live in
mutual self-interest, but also in mutual empathy, cognizant
of their interdependence and invested with the willingness

to suffer and sacrifice until every person, group, and nation enjoys full and free participation in the community.

As I interpret him, King is maintaining that the beloved community can be realized only when persons become aware of their essential, moral, and empirical interconnectedness with each other, and they begin to shift their loyalties accordingly, grasping that other selves are in some significant sense part of them and that the well-being of other selves is thus integral to their own well-being. This expansive quality of the self, is, in my mind, a critical point in King's overall ethical vision. As the self expands through empathy and loyalty-shifting to include the well-being of the other within its own well-being, the self takes a personal interest – realizes that it has a strong personal stake – in the concerns, burdens, problems, needs, and aspirations of the other. The other simply cannot be dismissed.

Remarkably, King holds that his welcoming of the other into the self's sphere of concern can and ought to happen on all levels, from the level of the personal self all the way up to and including the level of the national self (e.g., America). We realize the ideal of a beloved community inasmuch as we affirm and defend our mutual vulnerability and responsibility as brothers and sisters of a single, extended family, citizens of a single, global community.

> Now let me suggest first that if we are to have peace on earth, our loyalties must become ecumenical rather than sectional. Our loyalties must transcend our race, our tribe, our class, and our nation; and this means we develop a world perspective. No individual can live alone; no nation can live alone; and as long as we try,

> the more we are going to have war in this world. Now
> the judgment of God is upon us, and we must either
> learn to live together as brothers or we are all going to
> perish together as fools. Yes, as nations and individuals,
> we are interdependent.[88]

One of the signs that one has included another within
the sphere of one's most intimate self-concern is that
one becomes able and inclined, in compassion, to feel
the misery of others as partly one's own.[89] On his visit
to India, King spoke of many "depressing moments"
that he endured there, which could not be avoided as
he beheld with his own eyes millions of people going
to bed hungry, sleeping on sidewalks at night. Realizing
that in our country we spend millions to store excess
food, King exclaimed, "I know where we can store that
food free of charge – in the wrinkled stomachs of the
millions of God's children in Asia, Africa, Latin America,
and even in our own nation, who go to bed hungry at
night."[90] King was convinced that any person or group
can – and every person or group ought to – choose to
transcend their narrow perimeter of care or expand that
perimeter to include all human beings, at least in the
sense of finding it impossible to treat the suffering of any
human being as if it were of no account.

 ## Conclusion

King's ideas about God, humanity, and the beloved
community have important ramifications for Black
theology and ethics, particularly in their tendency toward
absolutized particularism. King's vision of what it means

to be Black and human posits an unambiguously transcendent ground of Black dignity, which is the same ground of the same dignity that resides in every other human being. King suggests that Black people who have been unjustly discriminated against, demeaned, and tortured must resist their dehumanization, and they can resist it best, not by appealing to some special (and essentially separate) status of ontological Blackness, but rather by disclosing the common ground of human value in which all human beings of all races participate. Rather than arguing that Blackness is in some sense a unique and superior locus of God's self-revelation, King argues that Black people do best to focus our attention first and foremost on the reality of shared humanness which reveals that, before God and in the eyes of all who love God, all human beings are essentially equal in value.

Because King shifts the focus of moral attention to this common ground of value, he can articulate an ethic that is more than an ethic of resistance. He can articulate an ethic that discloses, seeks to promote, and celebrates the goodness of God's creation and the dignity of the Creator, which is reflected in a potent way in the faces of our fellow human beings. He can articulate an ethic that turns the imagination and the heart to a pondering of the way that the destinies of human beings are linked together in a single cosmic process that has a loving God as its ultimate ordering principle. For King, human beings are called to reflect God's image in their relationships with each other; they are called to embody God's good intention for creation. In order to do this, they must resist the temptation to contract their circle of concern to include only their own family, group, nation, or race. More than this, they must

deliberately expand the circle of their concern, shifting
their loyalties to the "world house" of humanity.
According to his vision, it is unacceptable for Black
people, in particular, to restrict their concern to
Blacks, or even to "the oppressed," while relegating
Whites to some separate category of the less-than-human.

Within King's vision, the notion of Blackness as an
ontological symbol of oppression or freedom is absent.
At no time does King suggest that Blacks in any form
can or should want to claim any special regard or treatment
by God, on account of their unique relationship to God
or their unique history of suffering or resistance. In King's
view, claiming such a special status is simply inconsistent
with who he believed the God of scripture, tradition, and
his own experience to be. A God who is partial to the
plight of Blacks – who is by implication (as well as by
assertion) less concerned about the life chances of Whites
or is desirous of the destruction of all that is White –
cannot be identified with the God and Father of Jesus
Christ, in King's estimation. The God about whom
King spoke in thousands of sermons and hundreds of
interviews and articles, was the ground of all life, even
White people's lives, and the guarantor of human
liberation, even for the nastiest slave holder or oppressor.
Black people do not need to believe that they are
individually or as a group in some way special or better
than others; they need to affirm their basic human
dignity in a way that connects them, rather than alienates
them, from their fellow human beings.

The fiery polemic of Black versus White is thus
extinguished in such a theology and ethic. The essential
struggle is not, and must never be, against persons

(which is implied by the use of the ambiguous category of Whiteness), but rather against injustice. Because persons are ends in themselves, they are not reducible to the unjust actions that they commit or even to the injustice that rules in their hearts. The evil that must be fought is essentially the failure, on the part of persons and institutions, to acknowledge and reflect the irreducible and indestructible value of the human spirit.

Can such a theology, however, in the final analysis, claim to be Black? Yes, it can. The affirmation of essential equality does not in any way take away from the appreciation of the rich variety of ways that human beings seek, through diverse social and cultural media, to reflect the unfathomable dignity that they know and affirm to be theirs. On the contrary, the acknowledgment of equal human dignity establishes the true ground of the appreciation of cultural and ethnic diversity. King's perspective provides a valid ground for the kind of work that is being done under the rubric of the hermeneutics of return, including the work being done by womanists. This acknowledgment of equality and its sacred ground actually encourages people to look to the details of cultural difference in order to get a fuller, more compelling picture of that which, in the final analysis, transcends all finite human representations. It is important, then, that there be a Black theology and ethic that focuses specifically on the concerns of the Black community. It is important that there be a theology and ethic that pays attention to the ways that God is at work in the particularities of Black life, in all of its internal diversity. But there is no reason to suppose, in paying this attention, that Black culture will turn out to be in some sense ultimate or normative for others.

Perhaps the most important element of King's ethical and theological vision is how it prepares us as moral agents to live with integrity, to affirm the truth (the work of theology), and to live out its implications (the work of ethics). King does not allow in his thinking a separation between one's conception of God and humankind and the outworking of one's convictions in the formation of one's character and actions. To believe rightly in human dignity is to resist injustice and to embody justice in one's human relationships. King's ethic of dignity thus requires much from those who seek to follow it. Most importantly, perhaps, it requires the courage to affirm the truth about each person's dignity under God, and to work tirelessly to uphold that dignity in all of our engagements with the persons, structures, policies, programs, and laws that constitute our relational webs. In the next chapter we will explore in a preliminary way the meaning and role of courage that might be developed for a new Black theology and ethics.

CHAPTER FIVE
Making It Plain: The Use of Traditional Sources and the Future of Black Theology and Ethics

Richard Lischer, in his work detailing the homiletical style and substance of King's sermons, has noted an intriguing phenomenon that occurs "in all of the audiotapes of King's sermons in black congregations."[1] A phrase is heard, coming from the congregation, in the form of a single voice or a chorus of voices, shouting in affirmation: "Make it plain." Lischer reflects on the use of this phrase:

> When King begins to uncover the problems of contemporary society in light of the Word of God, the voice gives its encouraging interpretive advice: "Make it plain." "Tell our story. Make the connection." In some Pentecostal and Holiness churches a reader "lines" the Scripture and the preacher interprets with commentary. Sometimes the deacons and deaconesses create an elaborate antiphonal effect in answering their preacher. In churches where the preacher chants the sermon, the congregation sometimes anticipates the preacher by humming a tune just before he or she begins. King's congregation helped him make it plain

by completing his sentences for him, especially his
recitations of Scripture, by echoing his words, and by
resounding with encouragement and joy.[2]

Coretta Scott King reflects on this traditional Black
church plea, "make it plain," in her book, *My Life with
Martin Luther King, Jr.*[3] When she and her husband took
a trip abroad in 1964 so that Dr. King could receive the
prestigious Nobel Prize for Peace, Dr. King was invited to
speak in the great 17th century Anglican church, St. Paul's
Cathedral, in London. The contrast between the listening
styles of the King's home congregation and those of the
great crowd that was gathered at St. Paul's was striking:
the Anglican crowd sat silent and motionless during King's
passionate appeal for a complete human life. King's father
sat in the audience, and after the sermon he was teased by
the members of the King party. While King was preaching,
"[Daddy King] was muttering under his breath a favorite
phrase which he would have shouted out in [their] own
Baptist church. 'Make it plain, son, make it plain.'"[4]

Black theology and ethics is a discourse dedicated to
"making it plain" in the sense of making clear and vivid
the connection between ordinary Black life and the
symbols and stories of the Judeo-Christian tradition.
Black theology and ethics has sought to "tell the story"
of the Black community in historical outline – from
captivity in Africa, through enslavement in America,
through emancipation and segregation, through the
civil rights and Black Power movements, and into the
post-civil rights and post-revolutionary environment
of the 21st century – in a way that connects the "Black
story" with the story of God's love for humanity.[5]

In the past, Black theology and ethics has sought to
"make it plain" by focusing on (a seemingly singular)
Black experience in a way that absolutizes that experience
and thus comes close to idolizing it. In recent years, Black
theology and ethics has attended admirably to the rich
details of Black history and culture, but without appearing
to care about the connection between Black experiences
and the experiences of other human beings. Black theology
and ethics, even in its womanist forms, continues to be
written in a way that fails to make evident why anyone
other than Black people would want to read this literature
and study it.

With King, by contrast, what we see is an attempt to
"make it plain" that involves clarifying the meaning of
Black experience partly by clarifying the human dimension
of that experience. King articulates the meaning of being
Black in the same breath that he articulates the meaning
of being human. Because he takes this integrative and
universalistic approach, his work has the potential of
illuminating what is distinct and wonderful about Black
life in America at the same time that it invites a broad
audience (beyond the Black community and even beyond
the borders of America) to ponder the difference that
understanding Black life might make to them. King's
approach, suitably adjusted for the 21st century, is in
effect an invitation for all human beings who are concerned
about human well-being and global justice to share the
details of their own experiences in ways that are likely to
contribute to our common human understanding and
welfare.

Given King's interest in "making plain" what is human
and dignified about Black life, in a way that promises to

unite, rather than divide human beings, it is not
surprising that he turned to a wide range of sources
for support, including sources that were authorized
by White philosophers and theologians. It must be noted,
however, that King and other Black thinkers who used
these sources received criticism for doing so. Advocates
of the study of Black religion asserted that using White
sources to do Black theology is illegitimate, for it involves
letting the oppressor set the terms of the debate – the
terms of Black self-understanding and self-affirmation.
According to these advocates, Black theology must
rely on Black sources alone, it must understand these
sources on their own terms, and it must resist the
temptation to legitimize itself with references to traditional
"White" philosophical and theological systems. This
argument was persuasive to many Black thinkers, who
shifted their work away form the study of traditional
theology and toward the study of the religious dimensions
of indigenous African and African-American communities.

This focus on Black sources alone was never, however,
complete. How could it be? The majority of African-
Americans are Christians, and one cannot understand
what it means to be Black and Christian without engaging
at least some of the classics of the Christian tradition. In
fact, Black theologians and ethicists have always employed
key concepts that mainstream White thinkers have used
to elucidate the relation between God and humanity, and
they have done so with great ingenuity and acuity. The
claim that legitimate Black religious studies must steer
clear of the sources of the broader Christian tradition is
misguided. If King's assertions regarding the sacredness of
human personality have any truth to them, there is reason
to believe that each of us will learn something important

from the theological and ethical reflections of others who share our concern for illuminating the meaning and value of human life. Each of us is likely to learn something that allows us to be distinctively who we are while also functioning as integral parts of the extended human family.

In this chapter, we will revisit briefly the debate over the use of "White" sources in Black theology. Then we will consider some of the suggestive ways that one such source, namely, a text of Paul Tillich, has been put to use by James Cone, Katie Cannon, and Martin Luther King, Jr. Specifically, we will consider how these thinkers use Tillich's concept of the courage-to-be in order to articulate part of the meaning of God and goodness in Black life.[6] It is not within the scope of this thesis to give a complete analysis of the relationship between these three thinkers' ideas and Tillich's conception of courage. I intend only to call attention to some of the allusions to Tillich's concept within the work of Cone, Cannon, and King. I will also reflect on the significance of these allusions.

Cone, Cannon, and King refer to Tillich's conception of courage, but they do so without seeking to situate Tillich's conception within the framework of his theological system. Such an effort should not be expected. Selective, popular appropriations of certain Tillichian concepts must be understood contextually; they are employed because of their presumed ability to "make plain" how one can garner the hope and the strength to go on in an excruciating situation. King, in particular, never appropriated *any* thinker's entire system; rather, he selectively incorporated specific dimensions of other people's thought, which he expected to have liberative import for his listeners. Still, there is no reason to think

that a thorough analysis of Tillich's conception of
courage, within the framework of his system, would
not be a valuable endeavor for a Black theologian.
I do not provide such an analysis myself, but I provide
some reasons for expecting it to be profitable.

The suggestion that traditional western sources be reread
with new questions and with an openness to the possibility
that certain of those sources will provide some insight into
what it means to be Black and human is a call for a more
inclusive "hermeneutic of return" than the one discussed
in chapter three. Rather than asking only for a return
to the African roots of Black religion, to the slave-religion
roots of the Black church, or to the experiences and
literary works of courageous Black Christian women,
I want to advocate as well a return to certain traditional
theological texts. More specifically, I want to recommend
a hermeneutic that recognizes that any text or source that
speaks truthfully to the human condition can, by virtue
of this fact, speak well to many Black people, at least in
some way and to some degree. At the same time, I want
to recommend a hermeneutic that acknowledges the ways
that reflecting on the particularities of Black experience
can give readers new eyes to see what is good and right in
traditional texts.

The relationship between the particular struggles and
insights of the Black community and the theological and
ethical construals of the Western theological traditions
are best understood as dynamic and reciprocal. As I have
argued, no oppressed group should absolutize its own
experience, particularly in a way that denies the validity
of all external critique. Conversely, no traditional construal
of God or the human good should be adopted slavishly,

without openness to the possibility that certain of its
features may need to be critiqued or augmented with
reference to the growing self-understandings of various
oppressed people. King offers a way to approach the
project of reciprocal re-reading by laying, as it were,
a theological and ethical foundation for such readings.
By approaching texts with King's ethical affirmations
in hand, we are free to consider a wide variety of texts
for their potential to illuminate what it means to live
a dignified human life, even in the most dehumanizing
of environments.

The main argument of the thesis regarding the need to
overcome the problem of absolutized particularism, and
the contribution that a rediscovery of King could make
to that effort, has already been made. This chapter explores
a few implications of the argument, specifically regarding
the use of sources. It also points to the need for additional
inquiry.

 ## Who Speaks for Whom?: The Use of "White" Sources in Black Theology

An early critique that was leveled by some Black thinkers
against those who were engaged in the project of Black
theology, was that the latter group of scholars relied too
heavily on "White" sources. This criticism was made, for
example, of Cone's highly influential first and second
books, *Black Theology and Black Power*, and *A Black
Theology of Liberation*. Critics of Cone argued that what
he was doing in these texts was not Black theology, but
was instead some kind of White theology painted Black.
Charles Long, for example, doubted that "Black theology"

was even possible, since theology itself was a European task, imperialistic by its very nature, and not interested in the exigencies of Black religion.[7] Gayraud Wilmore and Cecil Cone contended that "Black theology must not be identified primarily, if at all, with biblical Christianity, but should be identified with the history and culture of Black people stretching back to African religions."[8] Wilmore and Cecil Cone argued that neither the Bible nor Jesus Christ should be considered a theological source or norm for Black theology.

James Cone responded to these early critiques with disbelief and amazement. He tried to understand what it was that his critics were maintaining:

> [These critics] claimed that both *Black Theology and Black Power* and *A Black Theology of Liberation* used conceptual categories that came from Europe and not Africa. This meant that I had not been fully liberated from the rational structure of Western thought forms. If theology is black, they asked, must not the sources used for its articulation also be black? Where are the black sources in James Cone? To be sure, he refers to a few black preachers of the nineteenth century, but they are not essential to the content of his theological message or the form that the argument takes. They are simply used as tokens in a theological system derived from white theology.[9]

Dismayed by his colleagues' reactions, Cone wrote several works that were intended to reshape the content of Black theology and ethics in light of more explicitly "Black sources." These books included *The Spirituals and the Blues* (1972) and *God of the Oppressed* (1975). While Cone has tried to listen and learn from his critics on this point, he remains skeptical about whether or not he has answered them adequately.[10] He is convinced that none of his critics have been able to write the kind of all-and-only-Black-sources kind of Black theological study that he himself was accused of not writing.

Katie Geneva Cannon reintroduces the concern over "White" sources and frameworks of thought in her 1995 book, *Katie's Canon*.[11] As we have seen, she argues that the Black woman ethicist is expected by the "guild" of Christian ethics to "[receive] the preestablished disciplinary structures of intellectual inquiry in the field of ethics and [to try] to balance the paradigms and assumptions of this intellectual tradition with a new set of questions arising from the context of Black women's lives."[12] Yet Black women ethicists are suspicious of the requirement to master traditional theological and ethical materials, for these materials appear to exhibit no concern for the well-being of Black women; most of these materials exhibit no awareness that Black women even exist. Why should womanists spend any time with the accepted canon of western ethical thought if this canon is oblivious to Black women, and oblivious to its own overlooking, neglect, or distortion of Black women's experiences?[13] Until the advent of the civil rights and Black Power movements in the 1960s and the women's movement in the 1970s, the likelihood was slim that Blacks could study the religious dimension of their own lives without justifying such a study with reference to some system of thought or important figure in the traditional canon of theological, philosophical, and ethical thought. With the emergence of Black theology and ethics, many Black scholars abandoned all attempts to re-encounter the traditional canon to see if these sources could be of use to Black studies. They have concluded that the entire

tradition should be abandoned and an entirely new
tradition should be built purely on the basis of Black
experience and Black reflection on Black experience.

There are other Black thinkers who have regarded this
kind of exclusivism and isolationism as neither possible
nor advisable. These thinkers have sought to read
traditional sources in ways that illuminate what it means
to be Black and human. In *Prophesy Deliverance*, for
example, Cornel West develops an Afro-American religious
philosophy that focuses on the socioeconomic dimensions
of Black oppression, advocating a creative alliance between
the prophetic Afro-American Christian tradition and
progressive Marxism.[14] More specifically, West emphasizes
the ideals of egalitarianism and communally-situated
self-realization, which he associates with the prophetic
Christian tradition, and he employs elements of American
pragmatism, represented by William James, George
Mead, John Dewey, and West's mentor, Richard Rorty,
which he weaves into a constructive Christian vision
of a transformed society.[15] Throughout, his analysis
incorporates the Marxist critique of, and polemic
against, capitalist society.[16]

Black scholars like West seem, however, to be in the
minority vis-a-vis the rest of the Black intellectual
community. Most Black scholars of religious studies
have little interest in or patience for traditional
sources. These sources do not interpret the Christian
message for the African-American community; they
do not relate the gospel to the problem of race in America.[17]
Hence, they are not worthy of Black attention. Moreover,
many Black intellectuals argue that the freedom to
focus scholarly attention on Black religious history and
experience is a freedom that was hard-won within

the academy, and it should not be lost in an attempt
to resuscitate sources that are likely to be only
marginally, if at all, applicable to the ongoing struggles
in the Black community.

It is obvious from the last chapter that King saw no
obligation to employ only Black sources in the production
of a theology and an ethic that Black people (among
others) would find compelling. King was not concerned
with proving his Blackness or his loyalty to the liberation
of Black people; these were a given. King was struggling
as a Black person, among Black people for Black liberation,
and he took advantage of any resources that could
possibly help him in his efforts. If a White philosopher
or theologian proposed an conception of God or the
human being that seemed as if it might help Blacks to
understand their own relationship to God, and God's
relationship to their quest for freedom, then King embraced
it and used it. He did so, however, with no sense of
loyalty to the entire system of the thinker from whom he
appropriated ideas. As Richard Lischer points out, King
used the ideas of people like Rauschenbusch, Marx, Hegel,
Tillich, and Niebuhr selectively, carefully, and sparingly,
never in total, and with skepticism concerning the merit
of their larger systems of thought. These men were not
viewed as seers who could provide the final word on Black
life, but as thinkers whose conceptions of God and human
reality, suitably read, could illuminate various dimensions
of what it means to be Black and human.[18]

Lischer is correct in suggesting that King's use of
traditional philosophical and religious sources was not
determined by academic standards of intellectual, value-
free research and the scientific study of religious ideas.
King was a Baptist preacher, a social activist, and a

Christian humanist who encouraged the nation to engage in nonviolent direct action for the purpose of securing certain privileges and rights for Blacks, who had been systematically and historically shut out of full citizenship. His appropriation of sources was not determined by the norms of the academy, but by the needs of the sit-in, the boycott, the freedom march, and the jail house.

In my judgment, King's writings reveal the value of using traditional sources for illuminating and transforming the worlds of Black suffering, while opening the discussion up to non-Blacks who may suffer similar problems, and also to people who may be contributing to this suffering through evil actions or neglect. King's writings show the pragmatic and the ethical value of discussing Black concerns in relation to the concerns of non-Blacks, with the conviction that there is the possibility of mutual understanding between Blacks and others, and with mutual understanding can come mutual respect, and with mutual respect can come a lasting transformation of unjust social structures and relationships.

One concern that Blacks share with many other human beings, despite noticeable differences in social and historical context, is the concern to fight injustice, and to do so with dignity. In addition, Blacks share with many others a need to exercise courage in the face of obstacles that threaten to leave one feeling worthless, helpless, and hopeless. Some Black thinkers have found that Paul Tillich's conception of the courage-to-be is helpful in clarifying the significance of courage for Blacks. Let us consider Tillich's conception briefly, and then explore the way that James Cone, Katie Cannon, and Martin King make use of this conception in their own efforts to capture the meaning and value of courage.

The Courage to Be

Tillich begins his analysis of courage by suggesting that for both America and Europe the modern age could be called an "age of anxiety."[19] Believing that courage and anxiety are ontologically interdependent, Tillich offers an analysis of anxiety. The realization that our being alive is a contingent matter, and that at any moment we could simply cease to exist, generates within human beings a sense of anxiety. It causes a growing realization that we are threatened with nonbeing, and that this theat is ultimately unavoidable because nonbeing is a part of our being.[20] That is, the threat of nonbeing, and the anxiety associated with it are intrinsic to us as finite human beings. As Tillich says, "anxiety is finitude, experienced as one's own finitude. This is that natural anxiety of man as man, and in some way of all living beings. It is the anxiety of nonbeing, the awareness of one's own finitude as finitude."[21]

Anxiety is "the state in which a being is aware of its possible nonbeing" or again, "the existential awareness of nonbeing."[22] Tillich distinguishes three types of anxiety in terms of the three ways that nonbeing threatens human being. First, nonbeing threatens our most basic affirmation of ourselves as existing beings. It threatens "relatively" in the form of contingency and unpredictability. It threatens "absolutely" in terms of the possibility of death. According to Tillich, the anxiety death, of all forms of anxiety, is "most basic, most universal and inescapable. . . . [E]xistentially everybody is aware of the complete loss of self which biological extinction implies."[23]

Nonbeing also threatens our affirmation of ourselves
as spiritual beings, who "[live] creatively in the various
spheres of meaning. Creativity, in this context, has the
sense not of original creativity as performed by the genius
but of living spontaneously, in action and reaction, with
the contents of one's cultural life."[24] Nonbeing threatens
our spiritual self-affirmation "relatively," in the form of
emptiness, and "absolutely," in the form of utter meaninglessness. Whereas "the anxiety of emptiness is aroused
by the threat of nonbeing to the special contents of the
spiritual life," the anxiety of meaninglessness "is aroused
by the loss of a spiritual center, of an answer, however
symbolic and incorrect, to the question of the meaning
of existence."[25]

Finally, nonbeing threatens our affirmation of ourselves
as moral agents who are responsible for making something
of ourselves, for realizing our full human potential.
Nonbeing threatens "relatively," in the form of the guilt
that we experience over falling short of this potential:
"Even in what [one] considers his best deed nonbeing is
present and prevents it from being perfect."[26] Nonbeing
also threatens "absolutely," in the form of self-rejection
and self-condemnation. Human beings live anxiously
with the awareness that we have the power, not only to
slip up here and there, but to contradict our essential
being, and this awareness can tempt us toward "complete
self-rejection, to the feeling of being condemned – not to
an external punishment but to the despair of having lost
our destiny."[27]

Courage is the self's affirmation of itself, the self's attempt
to actualize itself in the face of an anxious awareness of

this threefold threat. Because the self is an individual who participates in the world, "self-affirmation has two sides which are distinguishable but not separable: one [side] is the affirmation of the self as [an individual] self; that is of a separated, self-centered, individualized, incomparable, free, self-determining self."[28] The other side is the affirmation of the self "as a part," i.e., as a being who belongs to a world from which the self remains, at the same time, separated.[29] Self and world are polar elements of the structure of being; they are correlated, ontologically. Similarly, the processes of individualization and participation are correlated.[30] Also correlated are the courage to be as oneself and the courage to be as a part. For Tillich, "It is one courage which takes a double threat of nonbeing into itself. The courage to be is essentially always the courage to be as a part and the courage to be as oneself, in interdependence."[31]

In summary, in a situation where we are confronted with the reality of our own human finitude, we experience reality partly in the form of a threat; we experience anxiety. The "courage to be" is the affirmation of ourselves as existing entities, as spiritual beings, and as responsible moral agents in spite of the threat of ontic, spiritual, and moral nonbeing, which is directed against our individual selves and our selves *qua* constituted in and through participation in communities and worlds. Finally, the ground of courage, for Tillich, is the ground of being itself:

> Courage is the self-affirmation of being in spite of the fact of nonbeing. It is the act of the individual self in taking the anxiety of nonbeing upon itself by affirming either as a part of an embracing whole or in its individual

selfhood. Courage always involves a risk, it is always threatened by nonbeing, whether the risk of losing oneself and becoming a thing within the whole of things or losing one's world in an empty self-relatedness. Courage needs the power of being, a power transcending the nonbeing which is experienced in the anxiety of fate and death, which is present in the anxiety of emptiness and meaninglessness, which is effective in the anxiety of guilt and condemnation. *The courage which takes this threefold anxiety into itself must be rooted in a power of being that is greater than the power of oneself and power of one's world.* Neither self-affirmation as a part nor self-affirmation as oneself is beyond the manifold threat of nonbeing . . . There are no exceptions to this rule; and this means that every courage to be has an open or hidden religious root. For religion is the state of being grasped by the power of being-itself.[32]

In other words, insofar as one has the courage to be, one has faith. "Faith is the state of being grasped by the power of being-itself. . . . It is the state of being grasped by the power of being which transcends everything that is and in which everything that is participates. He who is grasped by this power is able to affirm himself because he knows that he is affirmed by the power of being-itself."[33] It is he who accepts that he is accepted who is able to realize most fully the courage to be. "Absolute faith" is the act of accepting that one is accepted by the power of being-itself despite the infinite gap between the power and all existing beings.

The Courage to Be in Black Theology

If it can be shown that the insights of traditional theology
have import for the interpretation and formation of Black
experience, then a new kind of Black theological discourse
can emerge: traditional sources, rather than simply being
dismissed as the products of patriarchal or imperialistic
personages who had no interest in or sympathy for Black
life, can be seen as possibilities for re-reading Black life,
even as Black life can be seen as a possibility for re-reading
traditional texts in ways that are likely to make a difference
to people who are suffering and are most in need of a
liberating Word.

James Cone, the progenitor of the modern Black theology
movement, employed White sources of theology from the
beginning of his career in order to make sense of the Black
struggle for freedom in America. From the start, Cone
acknowledged specifically the importance of courage in
the ongoing Black effort to achieve self-affirmation and
self-determination, and he made reference to the contribution of Paul Tillich's work in understanding the meaning
of courage for Blacks. Cone employed Tillich's concept of
courage in order to illuminate, for example, the locus of
God's self-revelation in America. God is revealed, for Cone,
where Blacks find the courage to affirm their human
dignity in the face of the injustice and violence of a racist
society:

> Revelation is a historical liberation of an oppressed
> people from slavery. When an oppressed people come to

know who it is, it will not tolerate oppression. This is the
key to self-understanding. This is what Paul Tillich calls
the courage to be – that is, the courage to affirm one's
being in spite of those elements of existence which
threaten being. It is the courage to be black in spite of
white racists. *This is what revelation means in our times*
(emphasis mine).[34]

Cone appealed to Tillich's conception of courage also in an
effort to clarify the meaning of Black Power.

A further clarification of the meaning of Black Power may
be found in Paul Tillich's analysis of "the courage to be,"
which is "the ethical act in which man affirms his being
in spite of those elements of his existence which conflict
with his essential self-affirmation." Black Power, then, is
a humanizing force because it is the black man's attempt
to affirm his being, his attempt to be recognized as
"Thou" in spite of "the other," the white power which
dehumanizes him. The structure of white society
attempts to make "black being" into "nonbeing" or
"nothingness." In existential philosophy, nonbeing
is usually identified as that which threatens being; it
is that ever-present possibility of the inability to affirm
one's own existence. The courage to be, then, is the
courage to affirm one's being by striking out at the
dehumanizing forces which threaten being. And, as
Tillich goes on to say, "He who is not capable of a
powerful self-affirmation in spite of the anxiety of nonbeing is forced into a weak, reduced self-affirmation.[35]

It is interesting to note that no extensive scholarship has
been done on the relationship between Tillich's notion of
courage and Black Power. Cone implies that the connection

between the two is clear enough to warrant the further
study of Tillich by Black theologians and ethicists, who
would appropriately bring to a re-reading of Tillich a
particular concern for the well-being of Black people and
the Black community.

Along similar lines, Cone employed Tillich's view of
courage in seeking to clarify the meaning of divine
providence. God is present to Black people as the ground
of their being, as the infinite source of the courage
to affirm themselves as Blacks. For Cone, this means
(problematically, I have argued) that God is present
as the source of the power of Blacks to affirm themselves
vis-a-vis Whites, "in spite of whiteness," and "against
whites." In spite of the contingencies of circumstance that
force Blacks into the role of second-class citizens, and
in spite of the deeper threat of meaninglessness, Blacks
can affirm themselves as spiritual beings because God is
present to them as the power of Black self-affirmation.[36]

While the use of Tillich's view of courage is not extensive
in Cone's writings, it is clear that Cone perceives a
resonance between Tillich's view and the experiences
of millions of Black people who have been personally
abused and institutionally excluded within the American
context, but have nevertheless sought and found the
power to affirm themselves as dignified human beings.
The effort to understand and affirm themselves, and
the effort to eschew all definitions of themselves that
thwart such efforts is, for Cone, a kind of courage to
be. This is significant, and it undermines Cone's early
vitriolic indictments of the White academy and its failure
to say anything relevant to the hopes, dreams, and life
concerns of suffering Blacks.[37]

Another Black theologian who has acknowledge the usefulness of Tillich's view of courage, even as she has also sought to turn attention away from traditional sources and toward Black women's literature as a source for theology and ethics, is Katie Cannon. In *Black Womanist Ethics*, Cannon identifies and seeks to elucidate a virtue that Black women have acquired in their attempts to exercise responsible moral agencies in spite of the devastation in their lives and their families. She calls this virtue "unshouted courage."[38] Black people, and Black women in particular, find themselves caught up in systems that demean, subjugate and exploit. Within the dynamics of such systems, Black women are threatened with the prospect of making choices, not with an eye to the promotion of their own and others' full humanity, but simply with an eye toward survival. In such a situation courage is a moral necessity.

Cannon employs the essays and creative works of Zora Neale Hurston to identify the virtue of "unshouted courage," but she reads Hurston (and Hurston's interpreters) partly in light of Tillich.

> Alice Walker, in introducing Hurston's nonfiction, asserts that the fundamental thesis that Hurston embodied and exhibited in her essays was that one "must struggle every minute of life to affirm black people's right to a healthy existence." This idea concurs with the understanding of courage in Paul Tillich's work. Tillich says that courage is an ethical act when humans affirm their own being in spite of those elements in their existence which conflict with their essential self-affirmation.[39]

This concurrence or correspondence is not, unfortunately, explicated by Cannon. Nevertheless, Cannon's realization that it exists points to the need to establish a dialogue between these two sources, so that each might benefit from mutual correction and enrichment.

Many intriguing questions emerge from the correspondence identified by Canon between the courage of Black women as moral agents in their situations of oppression and the courage to be, as outlined by Tillich. What is the relationship between the "unshouted courage" of Black women who face the triple threat of racism, sexism, and classism, and the courage of any human who must affirm herself or himself in spite of the triple threat of ontic, spiritual, and moral "death"? How much can legitimately be appropriated from Tillich, in order to illuminate the experiences of Black women, and to what extent can the insights gained through a close examination of Black women's lives deepen the insights of Tillich? These questions are eminently worth pursuing, and Black people, given their familiarity with Black experience, are in an excellent position to initiate further inquiry.

A third African-American thinker who has made use of Tillich's concept of courage in order to interpret and inspire African-American life is Dr. King. King knew that exclusion, injustice, and abuse elicit a variety of responses in human beings. One common response is a passive yielding to the powerful oppressor, which is due to a sense of inferiority and powerlessness. A second response, on the other end of the spectrum, is an active antisociality, which is fed by a pent up vindictiveness that is directed toward a generalized oppressor, but inflicted on a convenient scapegoat. A third response is the active and nonviolent affirmation of one's "somebodyness." As we have seen, King regarded this third response as the "middle way," and he devoted his life to helping Black people to become, in their own eyes, "somebodies."[40]

Becoming "somebodies" in a situation structured to convince Blacks that they are "nobodies" or mere "things" requires courage. Finding courage is the most vital step that Blacks can take to resist their "thingification" and make a positive, joyful assertion of their dignified personhood. In effect, courage is the form that the assertion of authentic personhood must take in a situation where one is threatened with death, meaninglessness, and the loss of moral agency. "With courage and fearlessness we must set out daringly to stabilize our egos. This alone will give us a confirmation of our roots and a validation of our worth."[41]

Realizing the fundamental significance of courage led King to look to a variety of portrayals of courage in search for helpful representations. The view that King alluded to most often and which he found especially compelling was Tillich's. In recounting in *The Trumpet of Conscience* the waves of doubt and discouragement that came over him during his tenure as leader of the civil rights movement, King speaks about how his dream seemed to be turning into a nightmare. As he saw many of his Black brothers and sisters displaying their frustration and outrage in the rioting in the urban ghettoes, as he watched the war in Vietnam escalate, and as he became the personal victim of "deferred dreams" and of "blasted hopes," he was tempted to despair. But he resisted this temptation.

> In any social revolution there are times when the tail winds of triumph and fulfillment favor us, and other times when strong head winds of disappointment and setbacks beat against us relentlessly. We must not permit

adverse winds to overwhelm us as we journey across life's mighty Atlantic; we must be sustained by our engines of courage in spite of the winds. This refusal to be stopped, this "courage-to-be," this determination to go on "in spite of" is the hallmark of any great movement.[42]

Tillich's conception of courage serves as a powerful tool for naming the power to go on in the face of almost impossible odds.

Blacks are called to be as resourceful, responsible, and productive as their White societal counterparts, who have not experienced the same constraints. This call, unfair as it is, is the Black person's dilemma. Having started behind in the race of life, the Black person must run faster than the ones in front; given the difficult of winning the race, it is perpetually tempting to give up in cynicism and despair. The only remedy for this temptation is courage. The dilemma is serious and the handicaps are real, "but equally real is the power of a creative will and its ability to give us the courage to go on 'in spite of.'"[43]

King tended to refer to a broad stream of thinkers as he sought to make meaningful the reality of fear and the response of courage.[44] Still, it is Tillich who seems to be most helpful in conceiving the relationship between courage and self-affirmation:

Courage, therefore, is the power of the mind to overcome fear. Unlike anxiety, fear has a definite object which may be faced, analyzed, attacked, and if need be, endured. How often the object of our fear is fear itself: In his *Journal*, Henry David Thoreau wrote, "Nothing is so much to be feared as fear." Centuries earlier, Epictetus

wrote, "For it is not death or hardship that is a fearful
thing, but the fear of hardship and death." Courage
takes the fear produced by a definite object into itself
and thereby conquers the fear involved. Paul Tillich has
written, "Courage is self-affirmation 'in spite of' . . . that
which tends to hinder the self from affirming itself.' It is
self-affirmation in spite of death and nonbeing, and he
who is courageous takes the fear of death into his
self-affirmation and acts upon it. This courageous self-
affirmation, which is surely a remedy for fear, is not
selfishness, for self-affirmation includes both a proper
self-love and properly positioned love of others.[45]

The correspondence between King's definition of courage
and Tillich's is striking, even though Tillich distinguishes
between fear and anxiety and is more interested in courage
as a response to various forms of anxiety.

What King adds to Tillich, I think, is the suggestion that
courageous self-affirmation is not only a remedy for fear,
but it is also an antidote to selfishness, since authentic
self-affirmation includes a "proper self-love," and a proper
self-love frees a person to affirm the being and dignity of
others. Another way of saying the same thing is to invoke
King's teachings about the beloved community, which were
examined in chapter four. As we saw, King encouraged
people to expand the boundaries of their separate selves to
include others and the interests of others within the self.
The courage of self-affirmation is thus intrinsically related
to the courage to affirm the other as part of the self, as
an equally valuable child of God who is worth suffering
and even dying for. This is an important qualification,
in my view, for it provides a decidedly altruistic cast to the
determination not to allow crippling fear or anxiety to

paralyze one's efforts to uphold human dignity. The
courage to be cannot be merely a courage-to-be-for-oneself,
on one's own behalf; it must also be a courage-to-be-
fundamentally-for-others (who are experienced to be part
of the self).[46]

During the Montgomery boycott, one reporter asked King
if his role in the protest made him fear for his own life.
King's reply captures well the importance in his mind of
the "courage-to-be-for-others":

> No, I'm not. My attitude is that this is a great cause.
> This is a great issue that we are confronted with and the
> consequences for my personal life are not particularly
> important. It is that triumph for the cause that I am
> concerned about, and I have always felt that ultimately
> along the way of life an individual must stand up and
> be counted and be willing to face the consequences,
> whatever they are. If he is filled with fear, he cannot do
> it. And my great prayer is always that God will save me
> from the paralysis of crippling fear, because I think when
> a person lives with the fear of the consequences for his
> personal life, he can never do anything in terms of lifting
> the whole of humanity and solving many of the social
> problems that we confront.[47]

King draws a strong connection between the courage to
be and the commitment to sacrifice one's own interests and
even one's life, for the sake of those who are suffering
and will continue to suffer if nothing changes. There is a
fascinating irony in this: it is precisely the courage of self-
affirmation that enables a self freely to sacrifice itself for
others. When the act of self-sacrifice is grounded in

courage, it is a consummate act of a dignified spirit and a
responsible moral agent.

King embodied this kind of courageous self-affirmation,
which was rooted in the experience of an open and
extensive self, at many junctures of his public life. Vincent
Harding has described how King responded to the
courage that he saw in protestors with an intensification
of his own courage. The ability to affirm the self appeared,
in Harding's estimation, to multiply itself and to flow
freely between selves in the encounter between King and
those with whom he marched and suffered.[48] For instance,
in *Why We Can't Wait*, King rehearsed the crisis that he
faced when he learned during the Birmingham march that
the bondsmen of the movement were financially unable to
post bail for the demonstrators:

> Suppose I went to jail? What would happen to the three
> hundred [already in Birmingham jails]? Where would the
> money come from to assure their release? What would
> happen to our campaign? Who would be willing to
> follow us into jail, not knowing when or whether he
> would ever walk out once more into the Birmingham
> sunshine? I sat in the midst of the deepest quiet I have
> ever felt, with two dozen others in the room. There
> comes a time in the atmosphere of leadership when
> a man surrounded by loyal friends and allies realizes he
> has come face to face with himself. I was alone in that
> crowded room. I walked to another room in the back of
> the suite, and stood in the center of the floor. I think I
> was standing also at the center of all that my life had
> brought me to. I thought of the twenty four people,
> waiting in the next room. I thought of the three hundred,
> waiting in prison. I thought of the Birmingham Negro

community, waiting. Then my mind leaped beyond the
Gaston Motel, past the city jail, past the city lines and state
lines, and I thought of twenty million black people who
dreamed that someday they might be able to cross the
Red Sea of injustice and find their way to the promised
land of integration and freedom. There was no more
room for doubt. I pulled off my shirt and pants, got into
work clothes and went back to the other room to tell
them I had decided to go to jail. "I don't know what will
happen; I don't know where the money will come from.
But I have to make a faith act.[49]

This extended quotation reveals that King exercised a kind
of courage that was rooted in a sense of self so expansive
that, in some hard-to-define sense, it included the whole
of humanity.

It is not my intention to explore further the implications
of such a conception of the self for the meaning of courage
as self-affirmation. I want simply to raise the issue as one
that is worth exploring, in light of reciprocal investigations
into Tillich, King, and any other thinkers who might shed
some light on the matter.

 ## Conclusion

The future of the Black theological and ethical project
is contingent upon its ability to affirm two critical values
simultaneously and with equal vigor: first, the value of
investigating the particularity of Black experiences of
oppression and liberation (in open and honest conversation with simultaneous investigations into other people's

experiences of the ongoing struggle to live well); and
second, the value of interpreting the broad human import
of these experiences, in light of the best available resources
of critical thought. As a discourse that is devoted to a clear
appraisal of the life choices of Black people, it seems
important that future projects recognize the great fund of
resources that traditional sources offer to make more plain
the struggles of Blacks in America. As a discourse devoted
to the affirmation of human dignity, it is important also
that traditional resources be called to task to speak about
the human in a way that has relevance to those on the
margins, who struggle to resist messages that they are not,
in fact, human. To do less than open up this reciprocal
inquiry is to fail, not only Blacks, but also other human
beings who could benefit from a dialogue with Blacks.

The richness of a Tillichian-King dialogue on the meaning
of courage calls for further study, especially in reference to
King's expansion of courageous self-affirmation to include
the courage-to-be-for-others. While it has been noted by
many that much of King's ethical and theological vision
is presented in a sporadic and unsystematic way,[50] it has
also been recognized that many dimensions of his thought
warrant further consideration, and clearer delineation,
augmented by contemporary concerns and insights.[51] It
would be possible for someone to develop a more
systematic theology or ethic out of his collection of
insights. Developing such a project would be intellectually
stimulating, but much more than this it would likely have
profound practical implications. It could point readers who
are hungry for meaning and a sense of belonging to a
richer, more just, and more loving approximation to King's
notion of beloved community.

Conclusion

The diverse experiences of Black Americans constitute a rich resource for understanding the problems and potentialities of religious and moral life. To date, this resource has yet to be tapped in a way that makes a significant difference to the disciplines of theology and ethics. Early within the development of Black theology and ethics, a tendency arose, which effected Black scholars' abilities to speak cogently to the Black Christian community and to the broader human community about what is true and good. From the beginning, Black theologians have tended to absolutize Black particularity: they overgeneralize it, romanticize it, construe it as uniquely emblematic of God's presence in the world, and construct it over against conceptions of White people and culture, in ways that make Black self-conceptions reactive, rather than truly constructive.

This propensity was exemplified especially in the early writings of James Cone. Cone's early rhetoric was vehement. He used the term "Blackness" to refer to people who were racially and ethnically African-American, but he also used it as a symbol for God's redemptive activity in the world. This equivocation generated the impression that, for Cone, Blacks really were superior to Whites. Moreover, Whites were not permitted to critique Black theological and ethical reflection. Cone made clear that it was illegitimate for Whites to interfere in any way with Black efforts to articulate a theology of liberation from a patently Black frame of reference. Blacks were to attain their own self-definition and affirmation apart from Whites, by any means necessary. Cone's early thought is prototypical of a Black absolutized particularism, and his thinking continues to be instrumental in virtually all discussions of Black theology and ethics, especially in the academy.

Some Black theologians and ethicists since the formative years have recognized the significance of this problem, and they have sought (albeit mostly indirectly) to avoid it. Three major lines of response have emerged. J. Deotis Roberts and Major Jones represent an approach that exposes the self-destructiveness of hatred and urges mutual forgiveness and reconciliation between Blacks and Whites. These authors made an important contribution, but their works are now very dated: they are locked up within a bipolar framework, and they fail to envision a future for Black theology in a context of global and multicultural concern.

Scholars who emphasize the "hermeneutics of return" seem to transcend the Black-White framework of earlier Black theology by choosing simply to focus on the religious and moral lives of African-Americans. They have done in-depth studies of the symbols and folklore of the slaves, stretching back to their pasts in Africa. While this method holds great promise for constructive

Black theological thought, its continuing challenge is to transcend the tendency to romanticize the slave religious experience, as well as the tendency to encourage Black people to construe Black liberation merely as a reaction of survival and resistance to White oppression, rather than as a way of being Black and human beyond the context of White abuse and neglect.

Womanist theology represents the most incisive and promising critique of absolutized particularism in Black theology and ethics. Womanists have shown the failure of the early Black theological project to be attentive to differences *within* Black experience; it has revealed the need to talk about race and class always with an eye toward problems of gender discrimination; and it has made its work more accessible to diverse communities other than Black communities. While womanist thought is pushing Black theological discourse in a positive direction, however, it continues for the most part to frame its arguments in terms of survival and resistance motifs, and it is deeply conditioned by the Black-White conceptual dualism of the early years.

In my mind, the problem of absolutized particularism is overcome in King's theological ethic of human dignity. For him, Black life has its origin in the Creator, who alone serves as the infinite ground and guarantor of human liberation. Blacks are not themselves God, but because Blacks, like all other human beings, reflect the image of God, they possess a profound, incalculable dignity, a fundamental "somebodyness" that can never be compromised, lost, or rescinded. By virtue of the way that this dignity reveals itself within the context of Black particularity, Black lives are worthy of attention and study. By virtue of the fact that the essential dignity of Blacks is shared by all other human beings, the study of Black particularity has the potential to inform others, including those who are not Black, about what it means to be human and to flourish as human beings. Since all human groupings possess the same connection to God, our destinies and legacies are fundamentally intertwined. True liberation involves working toward the realization of beloved community.

King explicates Black life and human life simultaneously, refusing to neglect either pole. His integrative and universalist approach allows for a wider range of sources to be used to support Black theological and ethical inquiry. Rather than relying on Black sources alone, King encourages critical re-readings of the classics of the Christian tradition; he appeals to whatever sources might be of help in making plain the relationships between Black life, human life, and God; in so doing, he reveals that traditional sources can benefit, in turn, from such an inquiry. That is to say, new dimensions of their contemporary relevance can be revealed. King shows us that we may retain our own unique heritage in terms of our cultural legacies, yet learn from others who also are members of the extended human family.

My deepest desire is that these reflections on the problems and promises of Black theology and ethics will point the way to an approach that makes manifest the important contributions that particularistic inquiries into Black lives and cultures can make to the common human endeavor to live meaningfully and well.

End Notes

Chapter 1 Notes

1   Cornell West has outlined four stages in the evolution of
    Black theology and ethics. The first stage he describes as "Black
    Theology of Liberation as Critique of Slavery" (mid-1600s-1863),
    the second as "Black Theology of Liberation as Critique of
    Institutional Racism" (1864-1969), the third as "Black Theology
    of Liberation as Critique of White North American Theology"
    (1969-1977), and the fourth as "Black Theology of Liberation as
    Critique of U.S. Capitalism" (1977-present) (C. West, *Prophesy
    Deliverance! An Afro-American Revolutionary Christianity.*
    [Philadelphia: Westminster, 1982], pp. 101-108). While much
    could be learned from a thorough rendering of all four stages,
    for the purposes of this project I will focus only on the key
    arguments and figures in the latter two.

2   W.E.B. DuBois, *The Souls of Black Folk* (New York: Bantam,
    1989), p. 5. Cornel West has added a third dimension to the
    "twoness" articulated by Dubois; he writes of a "triple crisis"
    of Black self-recognition: "Their cultural predicament was
    comprised of African appearance and unconscious cultural mores,
    involuntary displacement to America without American status,

and American alienation from European ethos complicated through domination by incompletely European Americans (cf. Cornel West, *Prophesy Deliverance: An Afro-American Revolutionary Christianity* [Philadelphia: Westminster Press, 1992], p. 30-31). West argues that DuBois overlooked the broader dialectic of "being American yet feeling European, of being provincial but yearning for British cosmopolitans, of being at once incompletely civilized and materially prosperous" (*Ibid.*).

3   Cf. Henry Young, *Hope in Process: A Theology of Social Pluralism* (Minneapolis: Fortress Press, 1990), p. 85. Cornel West has rightly said that the notion that Black people are human beings is, comparatively speaking, a relatively new discovery in the West. The notion that African-Americans have the potential of other human groups for beauty, culture, and intellectual capacity is still a questioned and debated claim, even in many academic and intellectual circles (cf. Cornel West, *Ibid.* p. 47).

4   Gayraud Wilmore, *Black Religion and Black Radicalism.* 2d rev. ed., (Maryknoll, New York: Orbis Books, 1983), p. 4. A similar and more thorough treatment of the nature of the slaves' transformation of Christianity to fit their own peculiar experience of slavery can also be seen in Albert J. Raboteau's *Slave Religion: The "Invisible Institution" in the Antebellum South.* (New York: Oxford University Press, 1978).

5   Wilmore, *Ibid.*, p. 5. See also James Cone, "Black Theology and the Imperative and Dilemma of Solidarity." in *Struggles for Solidarity: Liberation Theologies in Tension.* Lorine M. Getz and Ruy O. Costa, eds. (Minneapolis: Fortress Press, 1992), p. 45.

6   Benjamin Mays' classic book *The Negro's God as Reflected in His Literature* (Boston: Chapman & Grimes, 1938) documents the significance of the Christian faith in the experience of Blacks. He surveys poems from the mid-1700s to Black literature of the 1930s. Cornel West has rightly suggested that evangelical and

pietistic Christianity is "the most influential and enduring intellectual tradition" in African-American thought. From the moment African slaves were brought to this continent, they attempted to make sense of their oppression in light of biblical texts, Protestant hymns and Christian testimonies (See Cornel West, *Ibid.*, p. 15).

7   Mays, *Ibid.*

8   Poet Phyllis Wheatley is a prime example of an African-American who saw the Christian religion as a defining vision for Black freedom. Many African-Americans saw the enslavement of African-Americans as a providential blessing of God to rescue the so-called Black, heathen hoards from the darkness of idols and iniquity of the so-called "Dark Continent." James Cone affirms this distinction when he suggests that "The faith of African-Americans is deeply embedded in our African and slave past. It has sustained our identity amid wretched circumstances, extending our spiritual and political vision far beyond the alternatives provided by the Whites who enslaved us," (cf. James Cone, "Black Theology and the Imperative and Dilemma of Solidarity." in *Struggles for Solidarity: Liberation Theologies in Tension.* Lorine M. Getz and Ruy O. Costa, eds. [Minneapolis: Fortress Press, 1992]), p. 45.

9   Frederick Douglass is an example of an African-American who expressed great ambivalence regarding the discrepancy between the faith displayed in the life and teaching of Jesus Christ and the mean-spirited religion which was often forced upon the slave population. For instance, he stated in 1846 that "I hate the slaveholding, the mind-darkening, the soul-destroying religion that exists in America. Loving the one [i.e., the faith shown through Christ and his teaching] I must hate the other [i.e., the faith shown by the slave holders with which Douglass was familiar]." Virginia Fabella and Sergio Torress, eds., *The Emergent Gospel* (Maryknoll, New York: Orbis Books, 1976), p. 79.

10 Hans Baer and Merril Singer recognize explicitly this critical role of Christianity to shape and influence the ongoing life of the Black community. "African-American religion has acted as a form of self-expression and resistance to a white dominated society. Indeed, one scholar goes so far as to argue that African-American churches constitute the "most activist sector of American religion" . . . During various periods, Black ministers served as federal and state officials, state legislators, and U.S. congresspeople, and one was even elected a U.S. Senator. Recently, the Rev. Jesse Jackson has run for the U.S. presidency and garnered a notable number of votes in primary elections. Further, many Black churches have sponsored political debates held in their sanctuaries and served as rallying centers for political and economic reform." (Cf. Hans A. Baer and Merrill Singer, *African-American Religion in the Twentieth Century*. (Knoxville: University of Tennessee Press, 1984), p. x.

11 West, *Prophesy Deliverance*, p. 36. See also Baer and Singer, *Ibid*.

12 West, *Ibid*. The centrality of the role of Black religion as a form of self-expression and resistance within White dominated society is thoroughly documented in the work edited by Milton Sernett, *Afro-American Religious History: A Documentary Witness* (Durham: Duke University Press, 1985).

13 A number of excellent works document the mood and the history of this high time of social change. See August Meier, Elliot Rudwick, and Francis L. Broderick, *Black Protest Thought in the Twentieth Century* (Indianapolis: Bobbs-Merrill Publishing, 1971); Lawrence W. Levine, *Black Culture and Black Consciousness* (New York: Oxford University Press, 1977); Herbert Aptheker, *A Documentary History of the Negro People in the United States*, Vol. 7 (New York: Carol Publishing Group, 1994); Taylor Branch, *Parting the Waters: America In the King Years 1954-63* (New York: Simon and Schuster, 1988); John H. Bracey, Jr., August Meier, and Elliott Rudwick, ed. *Black Nationalism in America* (Indianapolis: Bobbs-Merrill Educational Publishing, 1970).

14 I am indebted here to James Cone's persuasive analysis that
    Black theological discourse emerged in the late twentieth century
    because of these three intertwining and important influences. See
    James Cone, "Black Theology and the Imperative and Dilemma
    of Solidarity" in *Struggles for Solidarity: Liberation Theologies in
    Tension.* Lorine M. Getz, Ruy O Costa, eds. (Minneapolis:
    Fortress Press, 1992), p. 37.

15 James Cone, "Black Theology: Its Origin, Method, and Relation
    to Third World Theologies" in *Churches in Struggle.* William K.
    Tabb, ed. (New York: Monthly Review Press, 1986), pp. 32-33.
    Cone suggests that this period of history was known for the denial
    and dismissing of Black theology by almost all White theologians,
    largely because "since White theologians control the seminaries
    and the university departments of religion, they try to make Black
    people feel that only Europeans (and people who think like them)
    can define theology. To challenge the White monopoly on the
    definition of theology, many young Black scholars realized that
    they had to carry the fight [for Black freedom] to the seminaries
    and the universities where theology was being written and taught"
    (cf. Cone, "Black Theology . . . and Solidarity," pp. 39-40).

16 *Ibid.* Cone notes that the conservative White Christian church,
    on the one hand, sought to decry the claim that both religion and
    politics might mix well for the sake of social liberation, and the
    liberal White Christian churches, on the other hand, tended to
    either keep quiet on the theme or advocated a kind of gradualism
    that denounced the validity and effectiveness of the boycotts,
    freedom rides and marches, and the sit-ins.

17 One of the most important and excellent introductions to
    Malcolm X and his personal philosophy vis-a-vis religion and
    Christianity is the collaborative text of Alex Haley and Malcolm
    X on his life story and journey (cf. *The Autobiography of
    Malcolm X*, with the assistance of Alex Haley. (New York: Grove
    Press, 1965). See also Malcolm X, *By Any Means Necessary*.
    (New York: Pathfinder Press, 1970).

18   William H. Grier and Price M. Cobbs, in speaking of King, suggest that he was not slain by a single man alone; for them, his murder grew out of that large body of violent bigotry that America nurtured from its inception, that diseased psychology which "screams for the blood of the radical, or the conservative, or the villain, or the saint." Their words on the inevitable ineffectiveness of King's approach is telling: "To the extent that he was Black and was calling America to account, his days were numbered by the nation he sought to save" (William H. Grier and Price M. Cobbs, *Black Rage.* (New York: Basic Books, Inc., 1968), p. 206.

19   Grier and Cobbs suggest that "history may well show that of all the men who lived during our fateful century none illustrated the breadth or the grand potential of man so magnificently as did Malcolm X. If, in future chronicles, America is regarded as the major nation of our day, and the rise of darker people from bondage as the major event, then no figure has appeared thus far who captures the spirit of our times as does Malcolm. Malcolm is an authentic hero, indeed the only universal black hero. In his relenting opposition to the viciousness in America, he fired the imagination of black men all over the world" (*Black Rage*, p. 200.). While some might argue with them against such a univocal view of Malcolm X, there can be no doubt that his ideas and concepts were important in the formation of early Black theological and ethical thought.

20   Malcolm X, *By Any Means Necessary*, p. 115.

21   Malcolm X, *The Autobiography*, p. 222.

22   See Edwin S. Redkey, ed. *Respect Black: The Writings and Speeches of Henry McNeal Turner.* (New York: Arno Press, 1971).

23   See Amy Jacques-Garvey, ed. *Philosophy and Opinions of Marcus Garvey.* Two Volumes in one. (New York: Arno Press, 1968).

24 Redkey, *Respect Black*, p. 176.

25 Jacques-Garvey, *Philosophy*, p. 44.

26 Joseph Washington, *Black Religion: The Negro and Christianity in the United States* (Boston: Beacon Press, 1964), p. 144. According to Washington, King's contribution was little more than a kind of syncretistic Black Baptist emotionalism, which was expected to generate more heat than light (p. 10).

27 Washington, *Black Religion,* p. 271.

28 Joseph R. Washington, Jr. "Are American Negro Churches Christian?" in *Black Theology: A Documentary History. Vol. One: 1966-1979.* eds. James H. Cone and Gayraud S. Wilmore. 2ⁿᵈ ed. (Maryknoll: Orbis Press, 1993), pp. 92-100.

29 Washington, *Ibid.,* p. 100.

30 Cone, "Black Theology: Its Origin," pp. 34-35.

31 Joseph R. Washington, *The Politics of God.* (Boston: Beacon Press, 1967).

32 Cone, "Black Theology . . . and Solidarity", p. 39. The statement by the National Committee of Negro Churchmen was, in one sense, an apology for the validity of the language shift from the "Freedom Now!" emphasis of King and the other civil rights leaders, to the controversial "Black Power!" cry of Stokely Carmichael. It critiqued the then "gross imbalance of power and conscience between Negroes and White Americans," and deplored the overt violence of the riots, but asserted uncompromisingly the belief that the actual situation of social upheaval was due to a deliberate neglect of power sharing by America's political leaders and the complicit neglect of White churchmen. Their answer was not to call for the isolationism of racial bigotry, or for the

abandonment of the gains already made through the civil rights
movement, but to appeal to a future of America in which Whites
and Blacks, with a real sense of shared power – economically,
politically, socially – work together to rebuild the cities and society
(cf. "Statement by the National Committee of Negro Churchmen,
July 31, 1966" in *Black Theology: A Documentary History,
Volume One: 1966-1979*. James H. Cone and Gayraud S.
Wilmore, eds. Maryknoll: Orbis Books, 1993), pp. 19-26.

33 James H. Cone, *Black Theology and Black Power*. (New York:
Seabury Press, 1969), p. 5.

34 Cone, *Black Theology*, p. 6.

35 Albert Cleage. *The Black Messiah*. (New York: Sheed and
Ward, 1969).

36 *Ibid.*, p 3.

37 *Ibid.*, pp. 98-99. Cleage's passionate militancy can be understood
only in the light of the upheaval that was occurring at the end
of the 1960s. For Blacks, who had endured centuries of unjust
discrimination, violence, abuse, and exploitation purely on the
basis of specious arguments regarding the inferiority and illegitimacy
of Blacks per se, the argument of Cleage is seen as a radical
redefinition of the value and self-worth of Blacks. While it appears
to be overstated in terms of color, it must be understood that
color (and its corollary concepts of culture, race, and personhood)
had been the basis of the discrimination that was demonstrated
so blatantly both de facto and de jure since the arrival of Blacks in
America. Cleage went on to write *Black Christian Nationalism*,
where he offered his own exegetical, theological, and philosophical
vision of how the Black church might restructure itself to become
relevant to the Black revolution then taking place (cf. *Black
Christian Nationalism: New Directions for the Black Church*.
[New York: Morrow Quill Publishing, 1972]).

38 James Forman. "The Black Manifesto." in *Black Theology: A Documentary Witness: Volume One: 1966-1979*. James H. Cone and Gayraud Wilmore, eds. (Maryknoll: Orbis Books, 1993), p. 31. Previously this Manifesto had been the product of a conference assembled in Detroit, Michigan for the National Black Economic Development Conference, and had a tremendous impact on the churches because of his indictment of the nation as the most vicious, racist system on earth, and its revelation of the nature of the chasm that existed between Whites and Blacks and their religious institutions.

39 *Ibid.*, p. 1.

40 *Ibid.*, p. 6.

41 *Ibid.*, p. 31.

42 *Ibid.*, pp. 39-40.

43 What is critical to understand in Cone's thought, not only in this first groundbreaking work, but, I believe, throughout his abundant scholarship is that the association of Christ with Black experience is directly related to its ability to best describe where evil is most prevalent, where suffering is most unjust, and therefore where Christ is most present. This is what leads Cone to suggest that "in twentieth century America, *Christ means Black Power!*" (*Ibid.*, p. 112.). This rhetoric, however strident or direct, is not empty; it is based on his theological judgment that within any given society, you will find God most present among those who are least loved, most unjustly abused, and most undeservingly brutalized. In Cone's judgment, this can easily be found in the American experience in the ghettos and streets of the Black poor and oppressed.

44 James Cone, *A Black Theology of Liberation*. 2nd ed. (Maryknoll: Orbis Books, 1989), p. 31.

45 Cone, *Black Theology and Black Power*, p. 68.

46 *Ibid.*

47 *Ibid.*, p. 122.

48 *Ibid.*, p. 25.

49 James Cone, *A Black Theology of Liberation*. 2nd ed. (Maryknoll: Orbis Books, 1989), p. 70.

50 *BTL*, p. 66.

51 Cone's initial theological vision became the yardstick by which others interested in Black theology and ethics measured themselves and their own visions. Some offered moderate rejoinders to Cone's proposal for Black theology (e.g., Columbus Salley and Roland Behm, *Your God is Too White*. [Downers Grove, Ill.: InterVarsity Press, 1971]), while others continued to stress universalizability as imperative for Black theology (e.g., Warner Traynham, *Christian Faith in Black and White*. [Wakefield, MA: Paramter Press, 1973]; J. Deotis Roberts, *A Black Political Theology*. [Philadelphia: Westminster, 1974]; Major Jones, *Christian Ethics for Black Theology: The Politics of Liberation*. [Nashville: Abingdon, 1974]). Most of the initial reactions of the commentators criticized Cone and Cleage for their dependence on Black Power concepts to construct Black theologies, and the destructive power of hatred within Black communities.

52 Cecil Cone, *The Identity Crisis in Black Theology*. (Nashville: African Methodist Episcopal Church, 1975), p. 90.

53 *Ibid.*, p. 122.

54 *Ibid.*, p. 141. Cecil Cone's critique opened the flood gates of
different trajectories of Black theological and ethical thought,
which have emerged since 1975. In 1978 a compilation of
essays was published entitled, *Black Theology II: Essays on the
Formation and Outreach of Contemporary Black Theology,*
which focuses on the need for Black theology to broaden its
dialogical dimension, among Black theologians and ethicists,
and among certain White theologians as well. "Black theology
[must] reach out to embrace other vanguards of the human
liberation movement" (cf. Calvin Bruce and William R. Jones,
eds., *Black Theology II: Essays on the Formation and Outreach
of Contemporary Black Theology.* [Lewisburg, PA: Bucknell
University Press, 1978], p. 21.). It was about this time that Black
theology began its ongoing dialogue with Third World theologies
and other kinds of liberation theologies seeking to address more
broadly the connection between the religious dimension of life and
socio-political liberation (cf. Kofi Appiah-Kubi and Sergio Torres,
eds., *African Theology En Route.* [Maryknoll: Orbis Books,
1979]).

55 Gayraud Wilmore, *Black Religion and Black Radicalism.* (New
York: Doubleday, 1972), p. 304. The challenge of both Cecil Cone
and Gayraud Wilmore for Black theology to try to come to better
terms with the (primarily West) African roots of the Black religious
experience has been taken up by many Black theologians since
the time of their challenge and into the present. See Dwight N.
Hopkins, *Shoes that Fit Our Feet.* (Maryknoll: Orbis Books,
1993); Henry Mitchell, *Black Belief: Folk Beliefs of Blacks in
America and West Africa.* (New York: Harper and Row, 1975);
Nicholas Cooper-Lewter and Henry H. Mitchell, *Soul Theology:
The Heart of American Black Culture.* (Nashville: Abingdon, 1986).

56 Cone, *A Black Theology of Liberation,* p. 17ff.

Chapter 2 Notes

1   Cone has acknowledged that his first book *Black Theology and Black Power* (Seabury, 1969) [*BTBP*] was written out of rage and anger in the midst of the turbulent social unrest of the late 1960's. Its fiery and passionate rhetoric brought a storm of response, and his second work *A Black Theology of Liberation* (1970) [*BTL*] was written to answer his critics. It gives the first systematic account of the views of Black theology. These two books represent the most provocative works within Cone's developing corpus. Many of his later books including such titles as *The God of the Oppressed* (1975) [*GO*], *For My People* (1984) [*FMP*], *Speaking the Truth* (1986), and his autobiography *My Soul Looks Back* (1982) [*SLB*] do not contain the attacking rhetoric of the first two accounts. These latter books, while not speaking as directly to anthropological issues, show a less polemical, more careful explication of his basic commitment to liberation as the organizing principle of theology. Over the years, Cone shows himself to be one who adjusts his thought as he dialogues with others. He has de-emphasized some themes (e.g., the emphasis on violence in his first book), and incorporated new ideas and analyses as his experience and judgment broadened. Cone, however, has not repudiated the polemical rhetoric or argumentation in his first, important works. This is especially significant, as in the second edition of *A Black Theology of Liberation* Cone acknowledges its defects concerning sexism, classicism, and Third World conditions, but does not repudiate, for example, its polarizing construction of Blackness and Whiteness. It is in this book his most explicit statement of human nature is given, and thus this book will command a major part of this chapter's analysis. For Cone's own excellent analysis of the development of his thought, in response to critics, see James H. Cone, *My Soul Looks Back* (Nashville: Abingdon, 1982) [*SLB*], and James Cone, "The Gospel and the Liberation of the Poor," in *Christian Century* 98/5 (1981), pp. 162-166.

2   My intent is not to rehash the wide variety of criticisms that
      were offered and partially answered by Cone in the early and
      mid 1970s, but to address what I hold to be a fundamental,
      uncorrected fissure in his thinking, namely, absolutized
      particularism.

3   Cone suggests that the two most important realities that have
      shaped his consciousness are the Black church experience and the
      perceived socio-political significance of White people. The Black
      church introduced him to the "essence of life" of the Black people
      of his hometown, Bearden, Arkansas, and his perception of the
      socio-political significance of Whites revealed, in Cone's words,
      the potent fact that "White people did everything within their
      power to define Black reality" (cf. *God of the Oppressed* [New
      York: Seabury Press, 1975], pp. 1-3) [GO].

4   Carlyle Fielding Stewart III, *God, Being and Liberation:
      A Comparative Analysis of the Theologies and Ethics of James
      H. Cone and Howard Thurman* (New York: University Press
      of America, 1989), pp.13-14.

5   This is a key tenet of liberation theology in general, and Black
      Theology in particular. Cone reflects on the impact of his own
      experiences in Arkansas, with his parents and the Macedonia
      A.M.E. Church, as well as his difficult experiences in college,
      especially at Garrett-Northwestern: "When people ask me about
      the decisive influences on my theological and political perspectives,
      my response always includes something about my mother and
      father, and what it meant for a Black person to grow up in Bearden,
      Arkansas, during the 1940s and 50s.... The more I reflect on
      who I am, and what is important to me, the more the Bearden
      experience looms large in my consciousness." *SLB*, p.17. (See
      also *GO*, pp. 3ff., p. 52).

6   *BTL*, p. 86.

7   *BTL, Ibid.* The purpose of theological discourse, in Cone's vision,
    is to provide a simultaneous exegesis of Scripture and existence.
    On the one hand, the theologian recognizes that the Scripture as
    a witness to God's own word, ought to be viewed as a primary
    source of theological discourse. On the other hand, this exegesis
    ought not be viewed purely in a rational or abstract manner, but
    as a word "to those who are oppressed and humiliated in the
    world" (*GO*, p. 8). Therefore, in doing Black theology, the Black
    perspective must be given its due importance as one dimension
    of this theological hermeneutic grid.

8   *BTL*, p. 87.

9   *BTL*, p. 84.

10 Cone expresses in many contexts his original conception of the
    hegemonic character of White theologians to control the language
    regarding what it means to be human, and thereby to eclipse
    Black experience as human. See James H. Cone, "Black Theology
    and the Imperative and Dilemma of Solidarity." in *Struggles for
    Solidarity: Liberation Theologies in Tension.* Lorine M. Getz and
    Ruy O. Costa, eds. (Minneapolis: Fortress Press, 1992), p. 37-48.
    For an excellent critique of Cone's adaptation of Tillich's idea of
    correlation in theological method see Carlyle Fielding Stewart, III's
    "The Method of Correlation in the Theology of James H. Cone."
    The Journal of Religious Thought. Vol. 40, (Fall-Winter 1983-84),
    p. 27-38.

11 *BTL*, p. 121.

12 James Cone, "Black Theology and the Black Church: Where Do
    We Go From Here?" in *Black Theology: A Documentary History,
    1966-1979* (Maryknoll: Orbis, 1979), p. 353.

13 *BTL*, p. 66.

14 *BTL*, p. 151. Cone states that while in some sense all human
    beings are oppressed, Whites ought not equate "suburban

loneliness" with the "physical oppression derived from unjust social structures." "Of course, everyone has problems, but those problems can be understood only from one social perspective, namely the social perspective of the poor in the struggle of freedom" (*GO*, pp. 148-49).

15 *BTL*, p. 66.

16 James Cone, "The Gospel and the Liberation of the Poor," *Christian Century* 98/5 (1981), p. 165. "Since the writing of my first essay 'Christianity and Black Power,' it had become very clear to me that the gospel was identical with the liberation of the poor from oppression. That is why I identified the gospel with Black Power and the White church with the Anti-Christ. Although I would express each identification a little differently today, I still stand by the theological truth that gave rise to that conviction."

17 *BTL*, p. 108.

18 *Ibid.*, p. 66ff.

19 These designations of "Blackness" were not meant, according to Cone, to exclude other racial or cultural groups from defining God, Jesus and redemption in terms of their own social realities, i.e. God can be red, brown, yellow, or have some other trait that characterizes the poor either in America or around the world. Nor is there any sense of the superiority, in Cone's later thought, of Black culture over other oppressed cultures in the world. The central issue is that theology, including its anthropology, can only be defined in terms of the group doing the theologizing. For Blacks, therefore, God, Jesus, and salvation itself is Black (cf. *BTL*, pp. 66ff.). See also, *FMP*, p. 67; James Cone, "A Dream or Nightmare? Martin Luther King, Jr. and Malcolm X: Speaking the Truth," *Sojourners*, 15/1 (1986), p. 30.

20 *BTL*, p. 89.

21 *BTL*, p. 120.

22 *BTL*, p. 32.

23 *BTL*, p. 89.

24 *BTL*, p. 88.

25 *Ibid.*, p. 94.

26 *BTL*, p. 88.

27 *BTL*, pp. 94-97. For Cone, "conversion" involves the conscious, deliberate act of associating oneself with a community of oppressed individuals. To change community is to change one's being. "It is not possible to transcend the community; it frames our being because being is always being in relation to others. Is it possible to change communities? To change communities involves a change of being. It is a radical movement, a radical reorientation of one's existence in the world. Christianity calls this experience conversion," p. 97.

28 "Whatever else Christian theology might be, it must take sides with the victims who are economically and politically oppressed. If theology does not side with the victims of economic injustice, it cannot represent the Victim, Jesus of Nazareth, who was crucified, because he was a threat to the political and religious structures of his time." Cone, "Christian Faith and Political Praxis," p. 132.

29 See *Cone*, "Toward the Morning," p. 16.

30 *Cone*, "Christian Faith and Political Praxis," p. 134.

31 *BTL*, pp. 104-106.

32 *BTL*, p. 106.

33 Cone makes this point explicitly in a later article which speaks of
    the nature of Christian theology ("What is Christian Theology?"
    in *Encounter* 43/2, [Spring 1982], p. 122). "When the oppressed
    are inclined to use their position as a privilege, as an immunity
    from error, they do well to remember the scripture's witness to
    God's righteousness as other than anything human." The oppressed
    are not more sanctified or God-like purely on the basis of their
    oppression and helplessness, but since God has chosen to disclose
    the divine righteousness in their liberation, they are in a favored
    position to discern the nature of good and evil.

34 *BTL*, p. 108.

35 Cone, "Black Theology on Revolution, Violence, and
    Reconciliation," p. 11.

36 *Ibid.*

37 *BTL*, p. 107.

38 *BTL*, p. 98.

39 Cone, "Toward the Morning," p. 15.

40 *Ibid.*, p. 16.

41 North American liberation theologian Robert McAfee Brown
    in his *Theology In A New Key* (Philadelphia: Eastminster, 1978)
    argues cogently for our need to be suspicious of our own
    hermeneutical and ideological biases in order to be open to
    views radically different from our own, (*Ibid.*, see pp. 80-85).

42 On this point Cone has written more recently: "Christian theology
    can be written from the perspective of red, brown, and yellow
    peoples. It can also be written in the light of feminine experience...
    Christian theology can also be written from the perspective of
    class as has been profoundly disclosed in the writings of Latin

American Liberation theologians. It is also possible to combine the
issues of class, sex, and color as was recently attempted in Letty
Russell's *Human Liberation in a Feminist Perspective*. The
possibilities are many and varied. *There is not one Christian
theology, but many Christian theologies which are valid
expressions of the gospel of Jesus* [italics mine], cf. Cone,
"What is Christian Theology?", pp.121f.

43 Remarkably, Cone says that he was never exposed to even one
book written by a Black person (as a required reading) during his
six years of graduate study at Garrett-Northwestern (Cone, "The
Gospel and the Liberation of the Poor," p. 164).

44 James Cone, *For My People* (Maryknoll: Orbis, 1984), pp.
147-48.

45 Cone sees the lack of focus on liberation as a heretic strand
within the history of the Western church: "By failing to explicate
the connection between word and action, the church tended to
identify the gospel with right speech and thus became the chief
heretic. The church became so preoccupied with its own spoken
word about God that it failed to hear and thus live according
to God's Word of freedom for the poor. From Augustine to
Schleiermacher, it is hard to find a theologian in the western
church who defines the gospel in terms of God's liberation of
the oppressed" (cf. Cone, "What is Christian Theology?",
pp. 123-124).

46 For a sampling of the kinds of critiques Cone received in
connection to his early conceptions of Black theology, see J. Deotis
Roberts's "Black Theological Ethics: A Bibliographical Essay."
Journal of Religious Education. Vol. 3. (March 1, 1975); "A
Critique of James Cones's God of the Oppressed." *Journal of ITC*.
(Fall 1975); William Jones, "Theodicy and Methodology in Black
Theology: A Critique of Washington, Cone, and Cleage." *Harvard
Theological Review*. Vol. 64. (1971); Frederick Sontag "Coconut
Theology: Is James Cone the Uncle Tom of Black Theology?" *The
Journal of Religious Thought* (Fall-Winter 1979-80). Aubrey

Boesak, *Farewell to Innocence* (New York: Orbis Books, 1977);
Preston N. Williams, "James Cone and the Problem of a Black
Ethic." *Harvard Theological Review*. 65 (1972). Warren
McWilliams, "Theodicy According to James Cone." *The Journal
of Religious Thought*. Vol. 36, No. 2. (Fall-Winter 1979-80); An
entire Union Seminary Quarterly Review is dedicated to dialogue
with Cone's view with contributions from C. Eric Lincoln,
Jurgen Moltmann, Herbert O. Edwards, Paul L. Lehman, Helmut
Collwitzer, Frederick Herzog, and a response from Cone (*Union
Seminary Quarterly Review*. Vol. 31, No. 1. [Fall 1975]).

47 BTL, p. 108.

48 Practically speaking, it seems quite clear that Cone is open to
dialogue and critique from theologians from other communities.
His theory, however, does not allow these theologians to bring to
bear a theoretical critique of his position which could lead directly
to its modification.

49 Cone, "What is Christian Theology?", p. 127.

50 In responding to William Jones, an African-American critic of
Black Theology, Cone says that a disagreement between he and
Jones on the problem of evil should not be settled by any appeal to
western theology and philosophy, but on the basis of whether the
answer helps them fight against evil in the world (*Ibid.*, p. 127).

51 Cone critiques both J. Deotis Roberts's *Liberation and
Reconciliation: A Black Theology* (Philadelphia: Westminster,
1971) and Major Jones's two works *Black Awareness: A Theology
of Hope* (Nashville: Abingdon, 1971) and *Christian Ethics for
Black Theology* (Nashville: Abingdon, 1974) for assuming that
the process of reconciliation should come before liberation.
"Sociologically and theologically, I do not think that there is any
reason to believe that oppressors can participate in the liberation
of the people they hold in bondage" (cf. James Cone, "Epilogue:
An Interpretation of the Debate Among Black Theologians," in
Black Theology: A Documentary History, 1966-1979 [Maryknoll:

Orbis, 1979], pp. 609-623). I would argue, however, that the entire process of reconciliation demands, on closer consideration, that no party involved ("oppressed" or "oppressor") can have its humanity denied or eclipsed without sabotaging the entire process of dialogue and relationship. The *participation* of all in the process of healing and reconciliation is fundamental in deepening one's recognition of the *humanity* of all involved.

52   Cone is clear that revolutionary violence may be both necessary and justified, given the evil of the system and the exigencies of the liberative situation. The Christian should not choose between violence and nonviolence, but between committing the lesser and the greater evil. If Whites respond positively to the appeals ingredient in the theory and activity of Black Power, then perhaps bloodshed can be avoided, but if they ignore the pleas of Blacks in their just impatience and outrage against their own dehumanization, violence will likely, according to Cone, manifest itself. "The decision lies with White America and White Americans who speak the name of Christ" (cf. *BTBP*, p. 143).

53   Cone highlights this lack of attention to the problem of sexual discrimination. In the preface of the twentieth anniversary addition of his first book, *Black Theology and Black Power*, Cone says "An example of the weakness of the 1960s black freedom movement, as defined in *Black Theology and Black Power*, was its complete blindness to the problem of sexism, especially in the black church community. When I read my book today, I am embarrassed by its sexist language and patriarchal perspective. There is not even one reference to a woman in the whole book! With black women playing such a dominant role in the African-American liberation struggle, past and present, how could I have been so blind?" (Cf. *BTBP*, p.x).

54   Cone has admitted, in several articles and books, some of the weaknesses and limitations of his earlier conceptions of theology, but not the ones that I have developed here (see *FMP*, pp. 86-96; *BTL*, pp. xviii-xxi; Cone, "The Gospel of Liberation," pp. 164ff).

Chapter 3 Notes

1   Dwight N. Hopkins and George Cummings in their important
     work, *Cut Loose Your Stammering Tongue*, outline what they
     perceive to be the four stages of the development of contemporary
     Black theology. Stage one began with the formation of the ad hoc
     National Committee of Negro Churchmen in the summer of 1996,
     specifically with the release of their statement on Black Power in
     the New York Times on July 31, 1966. Stage two was initiated by
     the formation of the Society for the Study of Black Religion in
     1970, which saw a growing interaction among Black religious
     scholars regarding issues of reconciliation and liberation. Stage
     three, which emerged in the mid-1970s, saw the creation of the
     Black Theology Project which explored the connection between
     African-Americans and the Third World. The final (and present)
     stage, which began during the 1980s, emphasizes the work of
     younger African-American scholars, "and most strikingly, the
     cutting edge challenge of womanists (Black female religious
     scholars), who have pressed for a holistic black theology that
     entails an integration of race, class, gender, and sexual orientation
     analyses" (*Cut Loose Your Stammering Tongue*. [New York: Orbis
     Books, 1991], pp. xiii-xiv). My own thinking on the viability of
     Black theological discourse fits most appropriately in the spirit of
     this latest phase of thought, but also seeks to press beyond it,
     as I will show.

2   The term "womanist" was coined by author and commentator
     Alice Walker to describe and differentiate Black feminist thinkers
     from their White counterparts. It was first mentioned in Walker's
     important book, *In Search of Our Mother's Gardens*, where she
     explains the need for Black women to have their own liberation
     movement. White women, in her view, are primarily concerned
     with the needs and struggles of White women; they tend to be
     ignorant of or unconcerned with the life struggles of African-

American women. Black women experience themselves to be doubly or triply oppressed – as Blacks in a society renowned for its racists ideology and practices, as women in a patriarchal society that tends to represent women as inferior and therefore unworthy of equal protection under the law, and as people who are poor or whose sisters are caught up in deadly cycles of poverty – and they need a theology and ethic that is grounded in reflection on the nexus of these related forms of oppression.

3   J. Deotis Roberts, *Liberation and Reconciliation: A Black Theology.* rev. ed. (Maryknoll: Orbis Books, 1994), p. ix. Roberts originally published this text in 1971. In the preface of the 1994 edition, Roberts suggests that since the publication of the first edition, he has developed a greater sensitivity to the need to address a larger audience than the Black dispossessed – an audience including the masses of poor and oppressed people globally. Further, he reaffirms his understanding that liberation and reconciliation must remain connected, especially in light of our growing pluralism, and the need to address the message of Black theology to the entire human family (*Ibid.*, xiii-xiv).

4   Roberts, *Liberation and Reconciliation*, p. 7.

5   *Ibid*, p. 52.

6   *Ibid*, p. 33.

7   Major Jones, *Christian Ethics for a Black Theology.* (Nashville: Abingdon, 1974), p. 37. Jones also wrote an important theological text *Black Awareness: A Theology of Hope* (Nashville: Abingdon, 1971) which offers a theology of hope that is anchored in an awareness of the reality of God, as construed from a Black perspective.

8   Jones, *Black Awareness*, p. 15.

9   Jones, *Christian Ethics for Black Theology*, pp. 73-74.

10 *Ibid.*, p. 119.

11 See Roberts, *Liberation and Reconciliation*, pp. 60-61.

12 James H. Cone in his fascinating biography *My Soul Looks Back* (Maryknoll: Orbis Books, 1992) speaks of his initial surprise at the critical assessment given from several important Black scholars (e.g., Charles Long, Carleton Lee, Cecil Cone and Gayraud Wilmore) that Cone's theology was far too dependent on White theology: "They claimed *Black Theology and Black Power* and *A Black Theology of Liberation* used conceptual categories that came from Europe and not Africa. This meant that I had not been fully liberated from the rational structure of Western thought forms. "If theology is Black," they asked, "must not the sources used for its articulation also be black? Where are the black sources in James Cone? To be sure, he refers to a few black preachers of the nineteenth century, but they are not essential to the content of his theological message or the form that the argument takes. They are simply used as tokens in a theological system derived from white theology" (cf. p. 60). As a result of a continuing dialogue with these and others, Cone shifted the direction of his research and turned to distinctively Black sources. *The Spirituals and The Blues* (1972), and *God of the Oppressed* (1975) were written to answer his early critics. Cone is personally ambivalent as to whether or not these treatments were adequate to the concerns of his critics.

13 A significant argument, which is widely held today in some circles, unfolds as follows: 1) In order to understand and appreciate the problems, challenges, and struggles of the descendants of African slaves in America, one must share their identity in some fundamental sense, either by being part of their racial lineage or by identifying wholeheartedly with, and becoming a participant in, the particular forms of their communal struggle; 2) It is self-evident that White theologians and ethicists are not racially Black, nor have they identified with the historical struggles of African-Americans in their pursuit of full citizenship and the recognition of their full

humanity; therefore 3) White theologians and ethicists can
provide no credible theological or ethical structure, foundation,
or prolegomena for Black theology and ethics. This argument,
in its various forms, has considerable power in many academic
and colloquial settings where issues of race and relationship
are seriously considered. It is flawed, however. It is a mistake to
hold that, because human beings do not share in the exact same
experiences of other human beings – because they do not have,
in particular, the same racial or ethnic origin and do not live
completely inside the experiences of other people with that racial
or ethnic identity – that they cannot understand these people or
speak some measure of truth to their human situation. An absolutized particularistic theology and ethic fails to take seriously and
elucidate the fact that there is a common ground that all human
beings share, which makes it possible for us to understand each
other, not simply in spite of our differences, but in light of them.

14 This viewpoint was widely shared by a number of Black
    thinkers who endorsed the view of absolutized particularism, or
    ontological Blackness. These thinkers were not concerned about
    the intelligibility of this construct, but only about the importance
    of attending to authentically Black sources. There continues to be
    a tendency in Black theology to adopt a "hermeneutics of return";
    many Black commentators are trying to understand the God-talk
    and life potential of Blacks vis-a-vis Black-authored sources of
    African-American history, including but not limited to the emblems,
    symbols, artifacts, and conceptions of the slaves, and the early
    Black Christian understandings of God, freedom, wholeness,
    and justice in the context of oppression within the United States.
    For a critique of this method, see Victor Anderson, *Beyond
    Ontological Blackness*. (New York: Continuum Publishing
    Company, 1995), p. 90.

15 Some of the key texts representing this "hermeneutics of return"
    include: Dwight N. Hopkins, *Shoes That Fit Our Feet: Sources for
    a Constructive Black Theology*. (Maryknoll, New York: Orbis
    Books, 1993); Dwight Hopkins and George C. L. Cummings, ed.

Cut Loose Your Stammering Tongue. (Maryknoll: Orbis Books, 1991); James H. Evans, Jr. "Keepers of the Dream: The Black Church and Martin Luther King, Jr." *American Baptist Quarterly* 5 (1) (1986), p. 75; "Towards an Afro-American Theology." *Journal of Religious Thought* 40 (1983-84), pp. 39-54; *Black Theology: A Critical assessment and Annotated Bibliography.* (New York: Greenwood Press, 1987); Riggins R. Earl, Jr. *Dark Symbols, Obscure Signs.* (Maryknoll: Orbis Books, 1993); Cain Hope Felder. *Troubling Biblical Waters: Race, Class, and Family.* (Maryknoll: Orbis Books, 1992); see also Clifton H. Johnson, ed. *God Struck Me Dead: Voices of Ex-Slaves.* (Cleveland: Pilgrim Press, 1993); Albert J. Raboteau. *A Fire in My Bones: Reflections on African-American Religious History.* (Boston: Beacon Press, 1995); *Slave Religion: The Invisible Institution in the Antebellum South.* (Oxford: Oxford University Press, 1978).

16 This is a term used by Victor Anderson in *Beyond Ontological Blackness.*

17 Hopkins and Cummings, *Cut Loose Your Stammering Tongue*, p. 13.

18 Hopkins, *Shoes that Fit Our Feet*, p. 4.

19 Anderson, *Beyond Ontological Blackness*, pp. 93-94.

20 This is critical to the entire enterprise of the hermeneutic of return, for if they cannot demonstrate the correlation between the Africanisms of slave religious experience and the Christian theological matrix, then slave religion is not a new vision of Christian religion. Anderson argues that scholars who take this tack collapse the two together, and then claim speciously that an interconnection exists (see, Anderson, *Beyond Ontological Blackness*, p. 97).

21 See, for example, the work of Audre Lorde, who identifies some of the tragic ways that Black women have internalized the racism and sexism that they have ingested as their "daily bread." "Eye to Eye: Black Women, Hatred, and Anger," in *Sister Outsider.* (Trumansburg, New York: The Crossing Press, 1984).

22 Anderson, pp. 91-92.

23 Victor Anderson recognizes three distinctive bibliographic trajectories
    which constitute the corpus of Black theological and ethical writings.
    The first represents what is called the *classical* trajectory, represented
    by the works of James H. Cone, Gayraud Wilmore, Major Jones and
    J. Deotis Roberts. The second trajectory can be classified as those
    thinkers referred to by Anderson and others as the "*hermeneutics of
    return,*" those who focus on Afrocentric, slave narratival, and
    historical sources to form a constructive Black theology and ethics.
    This is represented by thinkers such as Dwight H. Hopkins and
    George Cummings, ed., *Cut Loose the Stammering Tongue: Black
    Theology and Slave Narratives* (Maryknoll: Orbis Books, 1991), and
    Riggins R. Earl, Jr., *Dark Symbols, Obscure Signs: God, Self and the
    Community in the Slave Mind* (Maryknoll: Orbis, 1993). The final
    trajectory noted by Anderson refers to the womanist strand including
    such thinkers as Katie Cannon, *Black Womanist Ethics*; Delores
    Williams, *Sisters in the Wilderness: The Challenge of Womanist
    God-Talk* (Maryknoll: Orbis Books, 1993), Cheryl Sanders, ed.,
    Living the Intersection: Womanist and Afrocentrism in Theology
    (Minneapolis: Fortress, 1995), and Kelly Brown Douglas, *The Black
    Christ* (Maryknoll: Orbis Books, 1994), (cf. Anderson, *Beyond
    Ontological Blackness*, p. 166). A clear and comprehensive listing of
    these various trajectories is included in the two volume series edited
    by Gayraud Wilmore and James H. Cone, *Black Theology: A
    Documentary History* (Maryknoll: Orbis Books, 1993).

24 Cf. W.E.B. DuBois, *The Souls of Black Folk*, (New York: The New
    York America Library, 1969), p. 45.

25 This has been amply acknowledged by the first thinkers in Black
    theology, especially Cone, who alludes to his "blindness" in this
    area both in the preface to the 1986 edition to his *A Theology of
    Liberation* (James Cone, *A Black Theology of Liberation*.
    [Maryknoll: Orbis Books, 1989], pp. xvii-xix) as well as the
    preface in the twentieth year edition of *Black Theology and*

Black Power (James H. Cone, *Black Theology and Black Power*. [San Francisco: Harper Publishers, 1989], pp. x-xii).

26 For a solid analysis of this anomaly please see Katie Cannon's *Black Womanist Ethics*. (Atlanta: Scholars Press, 1988), pp. 59-73.

27 See Paula Giddings, *When and Where I Enter*, chapters 16-18, for a thorough analysis of the complex relationships which existed between Black men and women in both the civil rights and Black consciousness movements of the sixties and early seventies (see Paula Giddings, *When and Where I Enter*. [New York: Bantam books, 1984]).

28 For a rich and comprehensive analysis of the role of Black women in the Black church see chapter 10, "The Pulpit and the Pew: the Black church and Women," in Lincoln's and Mamiya's excellent work on the Black church (see, C. Eric Lincoln and Lawrence H. Mamiya, *The Black Church in the African American Experience*. [Durham: Duke University Press, 1990], pp. 274-308.)

29 *Ibid.*, p. 301f.

30 Jacqueline Grant, *White Woman's Christ and Black Women's Jesus: Feminist Christology and Black Women's Jesus*. (Atlanta: Scholars Press, 1989), pp. 195-197.

31 *Ibid.*, pp. 199-200. The indictment by Grant of feminist theology to participate in the racism of the larger American society is given as evidence for the "negative response which Black women have had with respects to feminism." Grant recognizes a new Black women's consciousness which emerged in the 1970s in opposition to the White women's liberation movement, sparked in no small measure by a Black women's literature which gave a different analysis of women's experience (cf. Toni Cade, *The Black Woman*. [New York: Macmillan Publishing Co., 1970]; Ntozake Shange. *For Colored Girls Only Who Have Considered Suicide When the Rainbow is*

Enuf. [New York: Macmillan Publishing Co., 1975]; Michelle Wallace. *Black Macho and the Myth of the Superwoman.* [New York: Dial Press, 1978]; Patricia Hill-Collins. *Black Feminist Thought: Knowledge, Consciousness, and the Politics of Empowerment.* [New York: Routledge, 1990]; bell hooks. *Aint I A Woman? Black Women and Feminism.* [Boston: South End Press, 1981]; Alice Walker. *The Color Purple.* [New York: Harcourt, Brace and Jovanovich Publishers, 1982]; *In Search of Our Mother's Gardens.* [New York: Harcourt, Brace, and Jovanovich, 1983]).

32 This freedom to return to a kind of universalist language marks a significant change from the early Black theological project's suspicion and disdain for universal categories or conversations about what constitutes human life, and not merely black life. For instance, J. Deotis Roberts disavowed the duty of a Black ethicist or theologian to speak on behalf of other oppressed minorities, although he encouraged them to articulate their interpretation of their experience themselves. He suggests "The White oppressor must be confronted by the scandal of particularity. He must not be allowed the escape hatch of universality" (cf. *A Black Political Theology.* [Philadelphia: Westminster, 1971], p. 16). Womanists have rejected the claim that it is legitimate to ignore concrete human experience as you seek to explicate its universal significance. One ought not seek to speak cogently to universal perspective without giving attention to all the rough contingencies of the specific context of particularization. Black women are in fact, according to the argument, human beings, and therefore deserve the full attention, protections, and rights that any other human being is afforded within a given society.

33 Alice Walker, *In Search of Our Mothers' Gardens* (New York: Harcourt, Brace, and Jovanovich, 1983), pp. xi-xii.

34 Delores Williams, "A Womanist Perspective on Sin." In *A Troubling in My Soul: Womanist Perspectives on Evil and Suffering.* Edited by Emilie M. Townes. (Maryknoll: Orbis Books, 1993), pp. 145-146.

35 Cannon, *Katie's Canon*, p. 123.

36 Cannon, *Black Womanist Ethics*, p. 75.

37 The themes of appropriation and reciprocity of one another's understanding is an important one in womanist, mujerista (Hispanic), and feminist theologies and ethics. One of the key efforts within the women's movement generically is seeking to discover ways in which the diverse experience of women may be found to both illumine and enrich each others lives (cf. Judith Plaskow, ed. "Appropriation and Reciprocity in Womanist/ Mujerista/Feminist Work." *Journal of Feminist Studies in Religion.* Vol. 8, No. 2. [Fall 1992], pp. 91-124).

38 Cf. Cheryl J. Sanders, Katie G. Cannon, Emilie M Townes, M. Shawn Copeland, bell hooks, Cheryl Townsend Gilkes. "Roundtable Discussion: Christian Ethics and Theology in Womanist Perspective." *Journal of Feminist Studies in Religion.* Vol. 5, No. 2. (Fall 1989), pp. 83-112. See also Cheryl J. Sanders, ed. *Living The Intersection: Womanism and Afrocentrism in Theology.* (Minneapolis: Fortress Press, 1995).

39 Sanders, "Roundtable Discussion: Christian Ethics and Theology in Womanist Perspective," p. 83.

40 *Ibid.*, p. 86. Sanders reflects, "Perhaps it is unrealistic to expect compliance with all of these criteria as a prerequisite for employing womanist nomenclature. But it is intellectually dishonest to label a person, movement, or idea as womanist on the basis of only one or two of these criteria to the exclusion of the others" (*Ibid.*).

Chapter 4 Notes

1   James H. Cone, "The Theology of Martin Luther King, Jr." *Union Seminary Quarterly Review* 40 (4): (1986), p. 35. Cone proclaims elsewhere that "no thinker has made a greater impact upon Black religious thought and upon American society and religion as a whole than Martin Luther King, Jr. The fact that many White theologians can write about American religion and theology with no reference to him reveals both the persistence of racism in the academy and the tendency to limit theology narrowly to the academic discourse of seminary and university professors" (James H. Cone, "Black Theology in Religion" *Journal of the American Academy of Religion.* 53 [3], pp. 758-59).

2   Some of the more significant biographical works include David J. Garrow, *Bearing the Cross: Martin Luther King, Jr., and the Southern Christian Leadership Conference.* (New York: Morrow, 1986); David J. Garrow, *The FBI and Martin Luther King, Jr.: From "Solo" to Memphis.* (New York: Norton, 1981); David J. Garrow, ed., *The Martin Luther King Jr., FBI File, Black Studies Research Sources. Microfilms from Major Archival and Manuscript Collections.* (Frederick, MD: University Publications of America, 1984); David J. Garrow, *Protest at Selma: Martin Luther King, Jr. and the Voting Rights Act of 1965.* (New Haven: Yale University Press, 1978); Coretta Scott King, *My Life with Martin Luther King, Jr.* (New York: Holt, Rinehart & Winston, 1969); C. Eric Lincoln, *Martin Luther King, Jr.: A Profile.* rev. ed. (New York: Hill & Wang, 1984); David L. Lewis, *King: A Critical Biography.* (New York: Praeger, 1970); Stephen B. Oates, *Let the Trumpet Sound: The Life of Martin Luther King, Jr.* (New York: New American Library, 1982); Kenneth L. Smith & Ira G. Zepp, *Search for the Beloved Community: The Thinking of Martin Luther King, Jr.* (Valley Forge, PA: Judson Press, 1974).

3   In addition to the Garrow texts, three excellent works that focus
    on the variety of influences on King's thought are Kenneth L.
    Smith & Ira G. Zepp, *Search for the Beloved Community: The
    Thinking of Martin Luther King, Jr.* (Valley Forge, PA: Judson
    Press, 1974); John Ansbro, *Martin Luther King, Jr.: The Making
    of a Mind.* (Maryknoll, NY: Orbis Books, 1982); and James Cone,
    "The Theology of Martin Luther King, Jr." in *Union Seminary
    Quarterly Review,* 40:4 (1986), p. 21.

4   This discussion relies much on Cone's fine analysis given in his
    article cited above ("The Theology of Martin Luther King, Jr."),
    which offers a concise overview of these sources and their
    influence on King.

5   Cone, "The Theology of Martin Luther King, Jr.", p. 23.

6   *Ibid.,* p. 24.

7   See Ervin Smith, *The Ethics of Martin Luther King, Jr.* (New York:
    Edwin Mellen Press, 1981), pp. 25-30; Noel Leo Erskine, *King
    Among the Theologians*, Cleveland: Pilgrim Press, 1994, pp.
    11-47; William D. Watley, *Roots of Resistance*, Valley Forge, Pa.:
    Judson Press, 1985, pp. 36-45.

8   See Paul Tillich, "The Problem of Theological Method," *Journal
    of Religion* 27 (1947), p. 17.

9   See Paul Tillich, *The Courage to Be.* (New Haven: Yale University
    Press, 1952).

10 Cone, "The Theology of Martin Luther King, Jr.," p. 25.

11 Martin Luther King, Jr., *Stride Toward Freedom.* (New York:
    Harper and Row Publishers, 1958), p. 217.

12 Henry David Thoreau quoted in Cone, "The Theology of Martin
    Luther King, Jr.," p. 25.

13 *Ibid.*

14 Martin Luther King, Jr., "The Un-Christian Christian," *Ebony*,
    (August 1965), p. 77. For a careful overview of the experiential
    sources which influenced King one may consult Walter E. Fluker,
    *They Looked for a City: A Comparative Analysis of the Ideal of
    Community in the Thought of Howard Thurman and Martin
    Luther King, Jr.* (New York: University Press of America, 1989),
    pp. 82ff.

15 Richard Lischer, "The Word That Moves: The Preaching of
    Martin Luther King, Jr." *Theology Today.* 46 (July 1989), p.170.

16 Richard Lischer, *The Preacher King.* (New York: Oxford
    University Press, 1995), pp. 94-95.

17 Martin Luther King, Jr., *Stride Toward Freedom.* (San Francisco:
    Harper and Row, 1986), p. 84.

18 Martin Luther King, Jr., *The Measure of a Man.* (Philadelphia:
    Fortress Press, 1988).

19 *Ibid.,* pp. 49-50.

20 *Ibid.,* pp. 55-56. See also *The Strength to Love.* (Philadelphia:
    Fortress Press, 1963), p. 97.

21 *Ibid.,* p. 55.

22 Martin Luther King, Jr., *I Have a Dream.* ed. James M.
    Washington. (San Francisco: Harper Collins, 1992), p. 23.

23 Martin Luther King, Jr., *The Trumpet of Conscience.* (New York:
    Harper and Row Publishers, 1967), p. 75.

24 See William D. Watley's treatment of the theological and
    philosophical underpinnings of King's thought in *Roots of*

Resistance: The Nonviolent Ethic of Martin Luther King, Jr.
(Valley Forge, PA: Judson Press, 1985), pp. 127-128.

25 Coretta Scott King, My Life with Martin Luther King, Jr. (New
    York: Penguin Group, 1993), p. 109.

26 King, Stride Toward Freedom, p. 69.

27 Ibid. This faith in God enables people to deal creatively with
    shattered dreams, and provides a confidence, even in the midst of
    struggle, that there is a divine Spirit who will not abandon us in
    our need. "However dismal and catastrophic may be the present
    circumstances, we know we are not alone, for God dwells with us
    in life's most confining and oppressive cells. And even if we die there
    without having received the earthly promise, he shall lead us down
    that mysterious road called death and at last to that indescribable
    city he has prepared for us" (King, Strength to Love, p. 95).

28 James P. Hannigan, Martin Luther King, Jr. and the Foundations
    of Nonviolence. (Lanham, MD: University Press of America, 1984),
    p. 75. Hannigan is careful to point out that King's God was not
    a metaphysical construction, or the product of philosophical
    investigation. Hannigan provides a fine overview of King's
    dissertation work, where he criticizes the conceptions of God
    in both Tillich and Wieman (Ibid., pp. 78-82.)

29 Melbourne S. Cummings and Lyndrey A. Niles, "King as
    Persuader: Facing the Ultimate Sacrifice." The Journal of Religious
    Thought 48 (2) (Winter-Spring 1991-92), pp. 49-56.

30 Ibid., p. 50. In a very poignant article in the Christian Century,
    King states that, although he had been nearly fatally stabbed, his
    house had been bombed, he had been arrested several times, and
    had received a threat of death virtually every day of his involvement
    in the movement, he did not consider his own personal sufferings
    an imposition. Christian Century 77 (27) (April 1960), p. 510.

31 Martin Luther King, Jr., *The Strength to Love*. (Philadelphia: Fortress Press, 1963), pp. 112-114. Cone recounts this episode in his treatment of King's theology. See Cone, "The Theology of Martin Luther King., Jr.", p. 27. See also "Thou Fool," (27 August 1967), King Center Archives.

32 King, *Strength to Love*, p. 113.

33 King's "Thou Fool" sermon quoted in Cone, "The Theology of Martin Luther King, Jr.", p. 27.

34 Martin Luther King, Jr., *Stride Toward Freedom*. (New York: Harper, 1958), p. 135.

35 *Ibid.*

36 This event was still regarded by King eleven years later as a turning point in his ministry and life. He continued to rely on the conviction that was born at that kitchen table. "I believe firmly in immortality. . . . I'm not worried about tomorrow. I get weary every now and then, the future looks difficult and dim, but I'm not worried about it ultimately because I have faith in God. . . . Sometimes I feel discouraged, and feel my work's in vain, but then the Holy Spirit revives my soul again," Martin Luther King, Jr., at a Chicago rally quoted in David J. Garrow, *Bearing the Cross*, p. 576).

37 Martin Luther King, Jr., *Why We Can't Wait*. (New York: Harper and Row, 1964), p. 97.

38 Cone, "The Theology of Martin Luther King, Jr.", p. 27.

39 King commonly uses "man" or "mankind," rather than "humankind." I replicate his use of these terms when quoting him directly, but I wish to signal my awareness of the problematic character of such terms. Their use can disguise a presumption

concerning the normativity of male experience and the male perspective, which has been shown by feminists and womanists to be a morally problematic presumption.

40 King, *The Measure of a Man*, p. 16-17.

41 Martin Luther King, Jr., *Where Do We Go From Here: Chaos or Community?*. (New York: Harper & Row, 1967), p. 97.

42 Martin Luther King, Jr. "The Ethical Demands of Integration." In James M. Washington, ed. *A Testament of Hope: The Essential Writings of Martin Luther King, Jr.* (San Francisco: Harper and Row, 1986), p. 119.

43 *Ibid.* King also recognizes the same idea of the dignity of all humans in the language of the Constitution, in Kant's Categorical Imperative, and in Martin Buber's dialogical philosophy, which articulates the difference between the "I-It" and the "I-Thou" modes of being in relation to persons.

44 Ervin Smith suggests that the idea of the sacredness of human personality, and more specifically, the sacredness of Black humanity, was significant for King, not only because it articulated his religious conviction of a personal God, but also because it asserted that human beings, who are created in the image of God, are "inviolable" in their personal beings. Of all the notions King employed within his ethical vision, Smith suggests, this one was the most important for his nonviolent strategy, and remained the center of his thought for the duration of his life and work. Ervin Smith, *The Ethics of Martin Luther King, Jr.* (New York: Edwin Mellen Press, 1981), p. 40.

45 King, *The Measure of A Man*, pp. 20-21.

46 King's "Address to New York State Civil War Centennial Commission" quoted in Garth Baker-Fletcher, "King's Late View

of Dignity, 1962-1968: Seven Motivic Concepts." *The Journal of Religious Thought*. 48 (2) (Winter-Spring 1991-1992), p. 19.

47 King is explicit that the positive response to the prolonged dilemma of Black despair must be to develop a rugged sense of "somebodyness." "The tragedy of slavery and segregation is that they instilled in the Negro a disastrous sense of his own worthlessness. To overcome this terrible feeling of being less than human, the Negro must assert for all to hear and see a majestic sense of worth. There is such a thing as a desegregated mind. We must no longer allow the outer chains of an oppressive society to shackle our minds. With courage and fearlessness we must set out daringly to stabilize our egos. This alone will give us a confirmation of our roots and a validation of our worth" (King, *Where Do We Go From Here*, pp. 122-23).

48 Coretta Scott King, *The Words of Martin Luther King, Jr.* (New York: Newmarket Press, 1984), p. 47. Ron Large argues that, "The notion of dignity is where the social significance of Martin Luther King's nonviolent theory begins; it is the realization that social change, the vision of justice, lies within the transformation of character from an abject passivity to a sense of worth. A major portion of King's involvement in the struggle for civil rights was the effort to alter the elements of character, to develop a moral character that is capable of rejecting violence" (Ron Large, "Martin Luther King, Jr.: Ethics, Nonviolence, and Character." *The Journal of Religious Thought*. 37 [2] [1980-81], p. 54).

49 King, "Interview on Merv Griffin Show, July 6, 1967" quoted in Garth Baker-Fletcher, "King's Late View on Dignity," p. 26.

50 King, *Where Do We Go From Here*, p. 53.

51 *Ibid.*

52 *Ibid.*

53 There can be little doubt the Black theology's current focus on the symbols, folklore, and experiences of Africans and the slaves would have been intriguing to King. While many contemporary critics like to point out to so-called "White" tastes and background of King, no dichotomy existed in his mind between his connection to his African and slavery roots and his enculturation in America, as a minority within the White majority culture. Integration did not mean, in any sense, the shunning of Black culture and identity, but rather full inter-group participation, open access for all to all the liberties and freedoms available to the majority, and the opportunity to grow as citizens without the stigma and unjust restriction of discrimination. See King's defense of the philosophy of integration, "The Ethical Demands for Integration," in James M Washington, *A Testament of Hope*, pp. 117-125.

54 King, *Where Do We Go From Here?*, p. 54.

55 King, *I Have A Dream*, p. 177.

56 David J. Garrow outlines King's dialogue with Stokely Carmicheal and the other SNCC leaders who, during the Meredith march in Mississippi in 1966, gave birth ot the Black Power slogan, and for all intents and purposes, weakened King's campaign and perhaps the entire civil rights movement (David J. Garrow, *Bearing the Cross*, pp. 475-490).

57 King, *Where Do We Go from Here?*, p. 36.

58 *Ibid.*, p. 41.

59 *Ibid.*, p. 36.

60 *Ibid.*, p. 45.

61 *Ibid.*, p. 46.

62 *Ibid.*, p. 48.

63 As the Black Power movement developed, so did its advocacy of
    "war" against White society, and at least in some pockets, its
    overall support of revolutionary violence. James A. Colaiaco
    relates one of Stokely Carmichael's most inflammatory speeches
    against the capitalist system, given in Cuba in the summer of
    1967, while riots were taking place in U.S. cities. Speaking to a
    group of Third World revolutionaries, Carmichael said: "We have
    a common enemy. Our enemy is white Western imperialist society.
    Our struggle is to overthrow this system. . . . We are moving into
    open guerilla warfare in the United States. We have no alternative
    but to use aggressive violence in order to own the land, houses,
    and stores inside our communities and control the politics of our
    communities" (James A. Colaiaco, *Martin Luther King, Jr.:
    Apostle of Militant Nonviolence*. [New York: St. Martin's Press,
    1988], p. 183). During this period, King and Malcolm X
    exchanged commentary on each other's several projects, and
    Stephen Oates relates that while King and Malcolm during their
    brief visit in Washington showed mutual respect for each other's
    social visions, King commented later to a Playboy reported that he
    wished Malcolm would place less emphasis on violence: "violence
    is not going to solve our problem. And in his litany of articulating
    the despair of the Negro without offering any positive creative
    alternative, I feel that Malcolm has done himself and our people
    a great disservice. Fiery, demagogic oratory in the Black ghettos,
    urging Negroes to arm themselves and prepare to engage in
    violence as he has done, can reap nothing but grief" (Stephen B.
    Oates, *Let the Trumpet Sound: The Life of Martin Luther King,
    Jr.* [New York: Penguin Books, 1982], pp. 245-46).

64 King, *The Trumpet of Conscience*, p. 15.

65 King, *Stride Toward Freedom*, pp. 212-13.

66 King, *Where Do We Go From Here?*, p. 59.

67 King, *The Strength to Love*, p. 14.

68 King, *Why We Can't Wait*, pp. 86-87.

69 King, *I Have A Dream*, p. 21.

70 King, *Why We Can't Wait*, p. 40.

71 King, *I Have A Dream*, p. 131.

72 *Ibid.*, p. 15.

73 King, *Stride Toward Freedom*, p. 217.

74 *Ibid.*, pp. 46-48.

75 Coretta Scott King, *My Life with Martin*, p. 33.

76 King, *Strength to Love*, p. 39.

77 King, *Strength to Love*, p. 143.

78 King, *Strength to Love*, pp. 48, 51, 91-92; King, *The Trumpet of Conscience*, pp. 74-75; King, *Where Do We Go From Here?*, pp. 64-65.

79 King, "The Ethical Demands for Integration", in *A Testament of Hope*, J. Washington, ed., p. 119.

80 King, *Where Do We Go From Here?*, p. 181.

81 King, *Why We Can't Wait*, p. 77.

82 James H. Cone, *The Theology of Martin Luther King, Jr.*, p. 36.

83 King, *Strength to Love*, p. 70.

84 King, *Where Do We Go From Here?*, p. 167. King carefully demonstrates that, regardless how deeply Blacks long to be secure and at peace in their "homeland," of America, they cannot ignore the larger world house in which they live. The larger world house, constituted by a "world fellowship," is emblematic of the justice, love, and peace of the kingdom of God.

85 King, *Why We Can't Wait*, p. 180.

86 King, *The Trumpet of Conscience*, p. 46. In a homily on the Good Samaritan, King makes the argument that nations or racial groups can live with pretension, as if their own nationalistic or cultural or racial concerns, status, and well-being alone were key to their prospering and fulfillment. However, "there is still something to remind us that we are interdependent, that we are all involved in a single process, that we are all somehow caught in an inescapable network of mutuality. Therefore whatever affects ones directly affects all indirectly" (see King, *Why We Can't Wait*, p. 77).

87 *Ibid.*, p. 100.

88 King, *The Trumpet of Conscience*, p. 68. See also *Where Do We Go From Here?*, p. 191.

89 In many places within King's writings he calls for a new level of compassion from Whites on behalf o the Black plight for freedom in America. He argues, among other things, that the failure of Black Power was its inability to see the Black need for White involvement in the movement. "In the final analysis the white man cannot ignore the Negro's problem, because he is a part of the Negro and the Negro is part of him. The Negro's agony diminishes the White man, and the Negro's salvation enlarges the White man" (cf. Coretta Scott King, *The Words of Martin Luther King, Jr.*, p. 22).

90 King, *The Trumpet of Conscience*, p. 69.

Chapter 5 Notes

1   Richard Lischer, *The Preacher King: Martin Luther King, Jr. and the Word that Moved America.* (New York: Oxford Press), p. 218.

2   *Ibid.*, pp. 218-19.

3   Coretta Scott King, *My Life with Martin Luther King, Jr.* rev. ed. (New York: Penguin, 1993).

4   *Ibid.*, p. 7.

5   James H. Cone. *A Black Theology of Liberation.* (Maryknoll: Orbis Books, 1989), p. 5.

6   Paul Tillich, *The Courage to Be.* (New Haven: Yale University Press, 1952).

7   Charles Long believed the theological apologetic tradition of Black religious studies, represented by Cone and Cleage, was not sufficiently historically grounded to be an accurate description of Black religion. In his estimation, Black theology, without an appeal to a more grounded, history of religions approach, would always remain limited and unconvincing (see "Perspectives for a Study of Afro-American Religion in the United States" in Charles H. Long, *Significations.* [Philadelphia: Fortress Press, 1986], pp. 173-84).

8   *James H. Cone, My Soul Looks Back.* (Maryknoll: Orbis Books, 1992) p. 60. This work is instructive as Cone provides an intriguing and important rendering of his assessment of the Wilmore and Cecil Cone's reaction to his earlier works.

9   *Ibid.*

10 *Ibid.*, p. 61.

11 Katie Geneva Cannon, *Katie's Canon: Womanism and the Soul of the Black Community.* (New York: Continuum Press, 1995), p. 124.

12 *Ibid.*

13 *Ibid.*, p. 123.

14 Cornel West, *Prophesy Deliverance!: An Afro-American Revolutionary Christianity.* (Philadelphia: Westminster Press, 1982), pp. 15-20. See also "Philosophy and the Afro-American Experience." *Philosophical Forum* (March 1979), pp. 148-177; *Prophetic Fragments.* (Grand Rapids, Mich: Eerdmans, 1988); *Beyond Eurocentrism and Multiculturalism, Volume One: Prophetic Thought In Postmodern Times.* (Monroe, Maine: Common Courage Press, 1993a.); *Beyond Eurocentrism and Multiculturalism, Volume Two: Prophetic Reflections.* (Monroe, Maine: Common Courage Press, 1993b.); *Keeping Faith: Philosophy and Race in America.* (New York: Routledge, 1993c.); *Race Matters.* (Boston: Beacon Press, 1993d.); *The American Evasion of Philosophy: A Genealogy of Pragmatism.* (Madison: University of Wisconsin Press, 1989).

15 *Prophesy Deliverance,* p. 21. West affirms the pragmatist tradition as offering Afro-American revolutionary Christianity many benefits. It is historicist in orientation, precludes dogmatic analysis, promotes practical ethical action over and above inquiries into epistemological questions, and seeks to realize change in the historical here and now, in light of what is actually possible.

16 West, *Prophesy Deliverance*, p. 108. See also West, "Black Theology and Marxist Thought," in *Black Theology: A Documentary History, 1966-1979.* James H. Cone and Gayraud S. Wilmore, eds. (Maryknoll: Orbis Books, 1979), p. 559-67.

Another example of the use of traditional philosophical sources among Black scholars is Henry James Young, *Hope in Process: A Theology of Social Pluralism.* (Minneapolis: Augsburg Press, 1990). Young employs Alfred North Whitehead's process thought to construct organic models of pluralism which he hopes will allow minority groups to reconfigure traditional theological sources in a creative and liberating way.

17 James H. Cone, *Black Theology and Black Power.* (San Francisco: Harper, 1969), pp. 84-85.

18 King's formative role as an original thinker, albeit an eclectic one, is becoming more and more recognized within traditional European-American theological circles. A growing literature continues to emerge, which recognizes certain unique and important theological concepts in King that make his vision worth of study. One of the latest, and I believe most important, of these works is Noel Erskine's work, *King Among the Theologians.* (Cleveland: Pilgrim Press, 1994).

19 Paul Tillich, *The Courage to Be.* (New Haven: Yale University Press, 1952), p. 35.

20 *Ibid.*

21 *Ibid.* Tillich sees fear as being different from anxiety. "Fear, as opposed to anxiety, has a definite object which can be faced, analyzed, attacked, endured. One can act upon it, and in acting upon it, participate in it – even if in the form of struggle. . . . Courage can meet every object of fear, because it is an object and makes participation possible (*Ibid.*, p. 36). Anxiety, however, has no object as such; its source is the threat of nothingness, which is the negation of every object, including the objects of fear. White fear and anxiety are distinguished in this way, they are not separated, but "immanent" within each other. "The sting of fear is anxiety, and anxiety strives toward fear." (*Ibid.*, p. 37).

22 *Ibid.*

23 *Ibid.*, p. 42.

24 *Ibid.*, p. 46.

25 *Ibid.*, p. 47.

26 *Ibid.*, p. 52.

27 *Ibid.*, pp. 51-52.

28 *Ibid.*, pp. 86-87.

29 *Ibid.*, p. 88.

30 *Ibid.*

31 *Ibid.*, pp. 89-90.

32 *Ibid.*, pp. 155-56.

33 *Ibid.*, pp. 172-173.

34 James H. Cone, *A Black Theology of Liberation*, p. 54.

35 Cone, *Black Theology and Black Power*, p. 7. Cone suggested further that the rebelling in the cities in the late 1960s was an "affirmation of [black] being despite the ever-present possibility of death. For the black man to accept the white society's appeal to wait or to be orderly is to affirm 'something which is less than essential . . . being' (*Ibid.*).

36 Cone, *A Black Theology of Liberation*, p. 81.

37   Others also saw initially the resonance of Tillich's thought for a
     kind of Black courage to be (e.g., J. Deotis Roberts, *Liberation
     and Reconciliation*. [Maryknoll: Orbis Books, 1994], p. 64). For
     a related effort to use Tillich to understand the meaning of
     self-affirmation for Blacks, see Major Jones, *Black Awareness:
     A Theology of Hope*. (Nashville: Abingdon Press, 1971). Jones
     argues, "The black man is saying, as he has never quite said it
     before, that 'I shall affirm my being, that being is black, and that
     black being must be recognized as an authentic selfhood.' The
     courage to be black, then, is the courage to affirm one's black
     being in the face of all that would seek to deny that black being is
     also human. The most powerful self-affirmation is for a person to
     have the courage to assert a self that is human in spite of that
     which would declare it to be less because of some mere particular
     as color." (*Ibid.*, p. 72).

38   Katie Geneva Cannon, *Black Womanist Ethics*. (Atlanta: Scholars
     Press, 1988), p. 144.

39   *Ibid.*, pp. 146-47.

40   King is explicit in suggesting that only this internal affirmation
     will transform the Negro to a self-respecting being who can take
     her place in society: "With a spirit straining toward true self-
     esteem, the Negro must boldly throw off the manacles of self-
     abnegation and say to himself and the world: 'I am somebody. I
     am a person. I am a man with dignity and honor. I have a rich and
     noble history, however painful and exploited that history has
     been. I am Black and comely.' This self-affirmation is the Black
     man's need made compelling by the White man's crimes against
     him" (see, King, *Where Do We Go From Here: Chaos or
     Community?* [New York: Harper and Row, 1967], pp.122-23).

41   *Ibid.*, p. 123.

42 *Ibid.*, p. 47. This popularized, non-technical use of Tillich is common in King's work.

43 *Ibid.*, p. 120. King argues that it is incumbent on the oppressed to cultivate the courage necessary to sustain their resistance against dehumanization and injustice.

44 King, in referring to courage, alluded to Plato, Aristotle, Aquinas, Thoreau, and others (see Martin Luther King, Jr., *Strength to Love.* [Philadelphia: Fortress Press, 1963], pp. 115-126).

45 Martin Luther King, Jr., *Strength to Love.* (Philadelphia: Fortress Press, 1963), pp. 118-119.

46 It is worth investigating the extent to which Tillich's courage to be a part could capture this altruistic dimension of the courage to be.

47 King during the press conference in the midst of the Montgomery bus boycott quoted in David Garrow, *Bearing the Cross: Martin Luther King, Jr. and the Southern Christian Leadership Conference.* (New York: William and Morrow, Inc., 1986), p. 75.

48 Vincent Harding, *Martin Luther King: The Inconvenient Hero.* (Maryknoll: Orbis Books), p. 132.

49 Martin Luther King, Jr., *Why We Can't Wait.* (New York: Penguin Books, 1963), pp. 72-73.

50 Harding, *Martin Luther King: The Inconvenient Hero*, p. 66. Harding argues that, while King's prophetic vision was compelling in its general contours, King left many specifics unclear, which need now to be made clear. This represents, according to Harding, an important challenge for King scholarship.

51 See Garth Baker-Fletcher, "King's Late View of Dignity, 1962-1968: Seven Motivic Concepts." *The Journal of Religious Thought.* Vol. 48. No. 2 (1991-92), pp. 18-32.

Bibliography

Anderson, Victor. *Beyond Ontological Blackness.* New York: Continuum Publishing Company, 1995.

Andrews, William L., ed. *Sisters of the Spirit: Three Black Women's Autobiographies of the 19th Century.* Bloomington: Indiana University Press, 1986.

Ansbro, John J. *Martin Luther King, Jr.: The Making of a Mind.* Maryknoll, New York: Orbis Books, 1986.

Appiah-Kubi, Kofi and Sergio Torres eds. *African Theology En Route.* Maryknoll, New York: Orbis Books, 1979.

Aptheker, Herbert. *A Documentary History of the Negro People in the United States.* Vol.7. New York: Carol Publishing Group, 1994.

Aquinas, Thomas. *Summa Theologica (selected questions).* Vol. I-V. Translated by Fathers of the Dominican Province. Westminster, Maryland: Christian Classics, 1981.

Aristotle. *Nicomachean Ethics.* Translated by Terence Irwin. Indianapolis: Hackett Publishing Company, 1985.

Asante, Molefi Kete. *Afrocentricity.* Trenton: Africa World Press, Inc., 1992.

Baer, Hans A. *The Black Spiritual Movement: A Religious Response to Racism.* Knoxville: University of Tennessee Press, 1984.

Baer, Hans A. and Merrill Singer. *African-American Religion in the Twentieth Century.* Knoxville: The University of Tennessee Press, 1992.

Baker-Fletcher, Garth. "King's Late View of Dignity, 1962-68: Seven Motivic Concepts." *The Journal of Religious Thought* 48 (2 1991-92): 18-33.

———. "Xodus musings: Reflections on Womanist Tar Baby Theology." *Theology Today* 50 (1 1993): 38-44.

Baker-Fletcher, Karen. "An Irresistible Power Not Ourselves." *Encounter* 53 (3 1992): 279-89.

———. "A Womanist Ontology of Freedom and Equality." *The Journal of Religious Thought* 49 (2 1992-93): 60-71.

———. "*Tar Baby* and Womanist Theology." *Theology Today* 50 (1 1993): 29-37.

Baldwin, Lewis V. "The Vision of Martin Luther King, Jr. and the Apartheid System in South Africa." *Journal of Religious Studies* 16 (1-2 1990): 22-45.

Baltazar, Eulalio R. *The Dark Center: A Process Theology of Blackness*. New York: Paulist, 1973.

Banks, William L. *The Black Church in the U.S.* Chicago: Moody Press, 1972.

Baron, Marcia. "Impartiality and Friendship." *Ethics* 101 (4 1991): 836-857.

Becker, Lawrence. "The Neglect of Virtue." *Ethics* 85 (1975): 110-112.

———. "Impartiality and Ethical Theory." *Ethics* 101 (4 1991): 698-700.

Becker, William H. "The Black Church: Manhood and Mission." *Journal of the American Academy of Religion* 40 (1972): 316-333.

Bell, Derrick. *And We Are Not Saved*. New York: Basic Books, Inc., 1987.

Bennett, Robert A. "Black Experience and the Bible." *Theology Today* 27 (1971): 422-433.

Berenbaum, Michael. "Women, Blacks, and Jews: Theologians of Survival." *Religion in Life* 45 (1976): 106-118.

Boesak, Aubrey. *Farewell to Innocence*. Maryknoll: Orbis Books, 1977.

Borowitz, Eugene B. "The Dialectic of Jewish Particularity." *Journal of Ecumenical Studies* 8 (Summer 1971): 560-74.

Bracey, John H., Jr., August Meier, and Elliott Rudwick, ed. *Black Nationalism in America*. Indianapolis: Bobbs-Merrill Educational Publishing, 1970.

Branch, Taylor. *Parting the Waters: America in the King Years 1954-63*. New York: Simon and Schuster, 1988.

Brandt, Richard. "Traits of Character: A Conceptual Analysis." *American Philosophical Quarterly* 7 (1970): 23-37.

———. "W.K. Frankena and the Ethics of Virtue." *The Monist* 64 (1981): 271-292.

Brown, Charles S. "Present Trends in Black Theology." *The Journal of Religious Thought* 32 (2 1975): 60-68.

Brown, Elsa Barkely. "Trajectories of Self-Definition: Placing Contemporary Afro-American Women's Fiction." In *Conjuring: Black Women, Fiction, and Literary Tradition*, ed. Marjorie Pryse and Hortense J. Spillers. Bloomington: Indiana University Press, 1985.

Brown, Robert McAfee. "Reflections on 'Liberation Theology'." *Religion in Life* 43 (3 1974): 269-82.

———. *Theology in a New Key*. Philadelphia: Eastminster, 1978.

Bruce, Calvin E. and William R. Jones., eds. *Black Theology II: Essays on the*

Formation and Outreach of Contemporary Black Theology. Lewisburg, PA: Bucknell University Press, 1978.

Bryan, G. McLeod. "The Strength to Love Versus the Urge to Hate: A Comparison of James Baldwin and Martin Luther King, Jr. from Their Writings." *Foundations* 7 (April 1964): 145-57.

Burrow, Rufus, Jr. "Who Teaches Black Theology?" *The Journal of Religious Thought* 43 (2 1986-87): 7-18.

Cade, Toni. *The Black Woman.* New York: Macmillan Publishing Co. 1970.

Callan, Eamonn. "Patience and Courage." *Philosophy* 68 (266 1993): 523-39.

Cannon, Katie G. "Resources for a Constructive Ethic in the Life and Work of Zora Neale Hurston." *Journal of Feminist Studies in Religion* 1 (1 1985): 37-51.

———. *Black Womanist Ethics.* Atlanta: Scholars Press, 1988.

———. "Womanist Perspectival Discourse and Canon Formation." *Journal of Feminist Studies in Religion* 9 (1-2 1993): 29-38.

———. *Katie's Canon: Womanism and the Soul of the Black Community.* New York: Continuum Press, 1995.

Cannon, Katie G, Kelly Brown Douglas, Toinette M. Eugene, and Cheryl Townsend Gilkes. "Metalogues and Dialogues: Teaching the Womanist Idea." *Journal of Feminist Studies in Religion* 8 (2 1992): 125-54.

Capps, Donald. *Deadly Sins and Saving Virtues.* Philadelphia: Fortress Press, 1987.

Carey, John J. "Black Theology: An Appraisal of the Internal and External Issues." *Theological Studies* 33 (1972): 684-697.

Carmicheal, Stokely and Charles V. Hamilton. *Black Power.* New York: Vintage Books, 1967.

Carr-Hamilton, Jacqueline D. "Notes on the Black Womanist Dilemma." *Journal of Religious Thought* 45 (Summer/Fall 1988): 67-69.

Carson, Clayborne, ed. *The Papers of Martin Luther King, Jr.* Vol. 1. Louis R. Harlan. Berkeley: University of California Press, 1992.

Cashman, Sean Dennis. *African-Americans and the Quest for Civil Rights, 1900-1990.* New York: New York University Press, 1991.

Cates, Diana Fritz. *Compassion for Friends in Friendship with God: Aristotle, Thomas Aquinas and the Ethics of Shared Selfhood.* (Unpublished dissertation).

Chapman, G. Clarke. "American Theology in Black: James H. Cone." *Cross Currents* 22 (1972): 139-157.

Christian, Barbara. *Black Feminist Criticism.* New York: Pergamon Press, 1985.

———. *Black Women Novelists: The Development of a Tradition.* Westport, Conn: Greenwood Press, 1980.

Churchmen, National Committee of Black. "Black Theology." *Christian Century* 86 (1969): 1310.

Cleage, Albert. *Black Christian Nationalism: New Directions for the Black Church.* New York: William Morrow and Company, 1972.

———. *The Black Messiah.* New York: Sheed and Ward, 1969.

Colaiaco, James A. *Martin Luther King, Jr.: Apostle of Militant Nonviolence.* New York: St. Martin's Press, 1988.

Collins, Patricia Hill. *Black Feminist Thought: Knowledge, Consciousness, and the Politics of Empowerment.* Boston: Unwin Hyman, 1990.

Cone, Cecil W. "Black Religious Experience." *Journal of the Interdenominational Theological Center* 2 (1975a): 137-139.

———. *Identity Crisis in Black Theology.* Nashville: African Methodist Episcopal Church, 1975b.

———. "Toward a New Introduction to Christian Theology: Telling the Story." *Journal of the Interdenominational Theological Center* 3 (1976): 17-27.

Cone, James H. "Christianity and Black Power." In *Is Anybody Listening to Black America*, ed. C.E. Lincoln. 3-9. New York: Seabury Press, 1968.

———. *Black Theology and Black Power.* New York: Seabury Press, 1969.

———. "Black Consciousness and the Black Church." *Christianity and Crisis* 30 (244-250 1970a):

———. "Black Power, Black Theology, and the Study of Theology and Ethics." *Theological Education* 6 (1970b): 202-215.

———. *A Black Theology of Liberation.* New York: J.B. Lippincott Company, 1970c.

———. "The Black Church and Black Power." In *The Black Church in America*, ed. Hart M. Nelsen, Raytha L. Yokley, and Anne K. Nelsen. 335-54. New York: Basic Books, Inc., 1971.

———. *The Spirituals and The Blues.* Maryknoll, New York: Orbis Books, 1972.

———. "The Social Context of Theology: Freedom, History, and Hope." *Risk* 9 (1973a): 13-24.

———. "Theological Reflections on Reconciliation." *Christianity and Crisis* 32 (1973b): 303-308.

———. "Dialectic of Theology and Life or Speaking the Truth." *Union Seminary Quarterly Review* 29 (1974a): 75-89.

———. "The Sources and Norms of Black Theology." In *The Black Experience in Religion*, ed. C. Eric Lincoln. 110-126. New York: Doubleday, 1974b.

———. "Black Theology and Ideology: A Response to My Respondents." *Union Seminary Quarterly Review* 31 (1 1975a): 71-86.

———. "Black Theology on Revolution, Violence, and Reconciliation." *Union Seminary Quarterly Review* 31 (1 1975b): 5-14.

———. "The Content and Method of Black Theology." *The Journal of Religious Thought* 32 (2 1975c): 90-103.

———. "A Critique of J. Deotis Roberts, Sr.: A Black Political Theology." *Journal of the Interdenominational Theological Center* 3 (1975d): 55-57.

———. *God of the Oppressed.* New York: Seabury Press, 1975e.

———. "The Story Context of Black Theology." *Theology Today* 32 (1975f): 144-150.

———. "A Black American Perspective on the Future of African Theology." In *African Theology En Route*, ed. Kofi Appiah-Kubi and Sergio Torres. 176-86. Maryknoll, New York: Orbis Books, 1979a.

———. "Epilogue: An Interpretation of the Debate among Black Theologians." In *Black Theology: A Documentary History*, ed. G.S. Wilmore and James H. Cone. Maryknoll, New York: Orbis Books, 1979b.

———. "A Black American Perspective on the Asian
Search for a Full Humanity." In *Asia's Struggle for
Full Humanity: Towards a Relevant Theology*, ed.
Virginia Fabella. 177-90. Maryknoll, New York:
Orbis Books, 1980.

———. "Christian Faith and Political Praxis." In *The
Challenge of Liberation Theology: A First World
Response*, ed. Brian Mahan and L. Dale Richesin.
52-64. Maryknoll, New York: Orbis Books, 1981a.

———. "The Meaning of God in the Black Spirituals." In
God as Father?, ed. Johannes-Baptist Metz and Edward
Schillebeeckx. 57-60. New York: The Seabury Press,
1981b.

———. "The Gospel and the Liberation of the Poor." In
Christian Century. 98 (5 1981): 162-66.

———. *My Soul Looks Back*. Nashville: Abingdon, 1982.

———. "What Is Christian Theology?" in *Encounter.* 43/2
(Spring 1982a): 117-128.

———. "Martin Luther King: The Source for His Courage
to Face Death." In *Martyrdom Today*, ed. Johannes-
Baptist Metz and Edward Schillebeeckx. 74-79. New
York: The Seabury Press, 1983a.

———. "Reflections from the Perspective of U.S. Blacks:
Black Theology and Third World Theology." In
Irruption of the Third World, ed. Virginia Fabella and
Sergio Torres. 235-245. Maryknoll, New York: Orbis
Books, 1983c.

———. *For My People*. Maryknoll, New York: Orbis Books, 1984a.

———. "Martin Luther King, Jr.: Black Theology, Black Church." *Theology Today* 40 (January 1984b): 409-20.

———. "Black Theology in American Religion." *Journal of the American Academy of Religion* 53 (3 1985a): 755-71.

———. "Black Theology: Its Origin, Methodology, and Relationship to Third World Theologies." In *Doing Theology in a Divided World*, ed. Virginia Fabella and Sergio Torres. 93-105. Maryknoll, New York: Orbis Books, 1985b.

———. "Black Theology as Public Theology in America." In *Civil Religion and Political Theology*, ed. Leroy S. Rouner. 187-206. Notre Dame, Indiana: University of Notre Dame Press, 1986a.

———. "Black Theology: Its Origin, Method, and Relation to Third World Theologies." In *Churches in Struggle*, ed. William K. Tabb. 32-45. New York: Monthly Review Press, 1986b.

———. *Speaking the Truth*. Grand Rapids: Wm. B. Eerdmans, 1986c.

———. "The Theology of Martin Luther King, Jr." *Union Seminary Quarterly Review* 40 (4 1986d): 21-40.

———. "What Is the Church?" In *Hammering Swords into Ploughshares: Essays in Honor of Archbishop Mpilo Desmond Tutu*, ed. B. Tlhagale and I. Mosala. 141-157. Johannesburg, South Africa: Skoatville, 1986e.

———. "A Dream or Nightmare? Martin Luther King, Jr. and Malcolm X: Speaking the Truth." In *Sojourners*. 15 (1 1986f): 26-30.

———. "Theologies of Liberation among U.S. Racial-Ethnic Minorities." In *Convergences and Differences*, ed. Leonardo Boff and Virgil Elizondo. 54-64. Edinburgh: T.& T.Clark Ltd, 1988.

———. "Theological Reflection on Black Theology." In *We Are One Voice*, ed. Simon S. Maimela and Dwight N. Hopkins. Broamfontein, South Africa: Skoatville, 1989.

———. "Black Theology: Where We Have Been and a Vision for Where We Are Going." In *Yearning to Breathe Free: Liberation Theologies in the United States*, ed. Mary Peter-Raoul, Linda Rennie Forcey, and Robert Frederick Hunter Jr. 48-60. Maryknoll, New York: Orbis Books, 1990a.

———. "God Is Black." In *Lift Every Voice: Constructing Theologies from the Underside*, ed. Susan Brooks Thistlethwaite and Mary Potter Engel. 81-94. San Francisco: Harper and Row, 1990b.

———. "Black Theology and the Imperative and Dilemma of Solidarity." In *Struggles for Solidarity*, ed. Lorine M. Getz and Ruy O. Costa. 37-48. Minneapolis: Fortress Press, 1992.

———. *Malcolm and Martin in America*. Maryknoll, New York: Orbis Books, 1993.

Cone, James H. and Gayraud S. Wilmore, eds. *Black Theology, A Documentary History, Volume One: 1966-1979*. Vol. 1. 2nd ed. Maryknoll, New York: Orbis Books, 1993a.

——, eds. *Black Theology, A Documentary History, Volume Two: 1980-1992*. Maryknoll, New York: Orbis Books, 1993b.

Cottingham, John. "The Ethics of Self-Concern." *Ethics* 101 (4 1991): 798-817.

Cummings, Melbourne S. and Lyndrey A. Niles. "King as Persuader: Facing the Ultimate Sacrifice." *The Journal of Religious Thought* 48 (2 1991-92): 49-56.

Daly, Mary. "The Courage to See." *The Christian Century* 88 (September 1971): 1108-11.

Davis, Angela Y. *Women, Race, and Class*. New York: Vintage Books, 1983.

Davis, F. James. *Who Is Black?: One Nation's Definition*. University Park, PA: The Pennsylvania State University Press, 1993.

Dent, N.J. "Virtues and Actions." *The Philosophical Quarterly* 25 (1975): 313-34.

——. "The Value of Courage." *Philosophy* 56 (1981): 574-77.

DeVeaux, William P. "Immanuel Kant, Social Justice, and Martin Luther King, Jr." *The Journal of Religious Thought* 37 (Fall-Winter 1980-81): 5-15.

Devereux, Daniel T. "Protagoras on Courage and Knowledge: *Protagoras* 351 A-B." *Apeiron* 9 (2 1975): 37-39.

Dewey, Joanna, Peggy Hutaff, and Jane Schaberg. "Respondents to Clarice J. Martin's Womanist Interpretation of the New Testament." *Journal of Feminist Studies in Religion* 6 (2 1990): 63-86.

Dobbs, Darrell. "For Lack of Wisdom: Courage and Inquiry in Plato's *Laches*." *Journal of Politics* 48 (4 1988): 825-849.

Douglas, Kelly Brown. *The Black Christ*. Maryknoll: Orbis, 1994.

Du Bois, W.E.B. *The Souls of Black Folk*. New York: Bantam, 1989.

Duff, Antony. "Aristotelian Courage." *Ratio* 29 (June 1 1987): 2-15.

Duke, Robert W. "Black Theology and the Experience of Blackness." *Journal of Religious Thought* 29 (1972): 28-42.

Dyson, Michael Eric. "Martin Luther King, Jr.: The Evil of Racism and the Recovery of Moral Vision." *Union Seminary Quarterly Review* 44 (1990): 85-99.

Earl, Riggins R., Jr. *Dark Symbols, Obscure Signs: God, Self, And Community in the Slave Mind*. Maryknoll, New York: Orbis Books, 1993.

Edmonson, Lonnie and Archie Logan. "Martin Luther King, Jr.: Theology in Context." *Duke Divinity School Review* 40 (Spring 1975): 126-132.

Edwards, Herbert O. "Black Theology and the Black Revolution." *Union Seminary Quarterly Review* 31 (1975a): 23-30.

——. "Black Theology: Retrospect and Prospect." *The Journal of Religious Thought* 32 (2 1975c): 46-59.

Ellis, Carl F. Jr. *Beyond Liberation*. Downers Grove: Inter-Varsity Press, 1983.

Erskine, Noel Leo. *Decolonizing Theology: A Carribean Perspective*. Maryknoll, New York: Orbis Books, 1981.

——. "King and the Black Church." *The Journal of Religious Thought* 48 (2 1991-92): 9-17.

——. *King Among the Theologians*. Cleveland: Pilgrim Press, 1994.

Eugene, Toinette M., Ada Maria Isasi-Diaz, Kwok Pui-lan, and Judith Plaskow. "Appropriation and Reciprocity in Womanist/Mujerista/Feminist Work." *Journal of Feminist Studies in Religion* 8 (2 1992): 91-109.

Evans, Donald. *Struggle and Fulfillment: The Inner Dynamics of Religion and Morality*. Philadelphia: Fortress Press, 1979.

Evans, James H., Jr. "Towards an Afro-American Theology." *Journal of Religious Thought* 40 (1983-84): 39-54.

———. "Keepers of the Dream: The Black Church and Martin Luther King, Jr." *American Baptist Quarterly* 5 (1 1986): 75-83.

———. *Black Theology: A Critical Assessment and Annotated Bibliography*. New York: Greenwood Press, 1987.

Fabella, Virginia and Sergio Torres, ed. *The Emergent Gospel: Theology from the Underside of History*. Maryknoll, New York: Orbis Books, 1978.

Falk, W.D. "Prudence, Temperance, and Courage." In *Moral Concepts*, ed. J. Feinberg. 114-119. London: Oxford University Press, 1969 [1963].

Fancher, Robert. "Whitehead and the Courage to Be." *Encounter* 38 (Autumn 1977): 347-61.

Farmer, H. H. "The Courage of Christ." *The Expository Times* 75 (March 1964): 176-78.

Felder, Cain Hope. *Troubling Biblical Waters: Race, Class, and Family*. Maryknoll, New York: Orbis Books, 1989.

Flemming, Arthur. "Reviving the Virtues." *Ethics* 90 (1980): 587-95.

Fluker, Walter Earl. *They Looked for a City: A Comparison of the Ideal of Community in Howard Thurman and Martin Luther King, Jr*. New York: University Press of America, 1989.

Forell, George W. "Particularity, Pluralism, and World Community." *Dialog* 10 (Spring 1971): 146-49.

Fox, Douglas A. "Being and Particularity." *Religion in Life* 35 (4 1966): 587-602.

Franklin, John Hope and August Meier, ed. *Black Leaders of the Twentieth Century*. Chicago: University of Illinois Press, 1982.

Franklin, John Hope and Alfred A. Jr. Moss. *From Slavery to Freedom: A History of Negro Americans* (6th ed.). New York: Alfred A. Knopf, Inc., 1988.

Franklin, Robert Michael. "An Ethic of Hope: The Moral Thought of Martin Luther King, Jr." *Union Seminary Quarterly Review* 40 (4 1986): 41-52.

———. "In Pursuit of a Just Society: Martin Luther King, Jr., and John Rawls." *The Journal of Religious Ethics* 18 (2 1990): 57-78.

Frazier, E. Franklin. *The Negro Family in the United States*. Chicago: University of Chicago Press, 1948.

———. *The Negro Church in America*. New York: Shocken Books, Inc., 1964.

Fredickson, George M. *The Black Image in the White Mind: The Debate on Afro-American Character and Destiny, 1817-1914*. Middletown: Wesleyan University Press, 1987.

French, P., T. Uehling Jr., and H. Wettstein, ed. *Ethical Theory: Character and Virtue. Midwest Studies in Philosophy*. Vol. 13. Notre Dame: University of Notre Dame Press, 1988.

Friedman, Marilyn. "The Practice of Partiality." *Ethics* 101 (4 1991): 818-35.

Gadamer, Hans-Georg. *The Idea of the Good in Platonic-Aristotelian Philosophy*. Translated by P.C. Smith. New Haven, Conn.: Yale University Press, 1986.

Garber, Paul R. "King Was a Black Theologian." *The Journal of Religious Thought* 31 (2 1974-75): 16-32.

Garrow, David J. *Protest at Selma: Martin Luther King, Jr. and the Voting Rights Act of 1965*. New Haven: Yale University Press, 1978.

———. *The FBI and Martin Luther King, Jr.: From "Solo" to Memphis*. New York: Norton, 1981.

———, ed. *The Martin Luther King, Jr. FBI File, Black Studies Research Sources. Microfilms from Major Archival and Manuscript Collections*. Frederick, MD: University Publications of America, 1984.

———. "The Intellectual Development of Martin Luther King, Jr.: Influences and Commentaries." *Union Seminary Quarterly Review* 40 (4 1986): 5-20.

———. *Bearing the Cross: Martin Luther King, Jr., and the Southern Christian Leadership Conference*. New York: Morrow, 1986b.

————, ed. *Martin Luther King, Jr.: Civil Rights Leader, Theologian, Orator*. Vol. 1. Brooklyn, New York: Carlson, 1989.

Geffre, Claude, Gustavo Gutierrez, and Virgil Elizondo, ed. *Different Theologies, Common Responsibility: Babel or Pentecost*. Edinburgh, Scotland: T.& T. Clark Ltd., 1984.

Gelber, S. Michael. "More Than Compassion, Less Than Hate, Sensitive Courage." *Judaism* 10 (Autumn 1961): 304-309.

Geldbach, Erich. "Farewell to White Innocence." *Journal of Religious Thought* 36 (1979): 50-53.

Giddings, Paula. *When and Where I Enter: The Impact of Black Women on Race and Sex in America*. New York: Bantam Books, 1984.

Goldberg, David Theo, ed. *Anatomy of Racism*. Minneapolis: The University of Minnesota Press, 1990.

Gollwitzer, Helmut. "Why Black Theology?" *Union Seminary Quarterly Review* 31 (1 1975): 38-58.

Gould, Carol S. "Socratic Intellectualism and the Problem of Courage: An Interpretation of Plato's *Laches*." *History of Philosophy Quarterly* 4 (3 1987): 265-79.

Grant, Jacqueline. *White Woman's Christ and Black Women's Jesus: Feminist Christology and Black Women's Jesus*. Atlanta: Scholars Press, 1989.

Grier, William H. and Price M. Cobbs. *Black Rage*. New York: Basic Books, Inc., 1968.

Gustafson, James. *Can Ethics Be Christian?* Chicago: University of Chicago Press, 1975.

———. *Ethics from a Theocentric Perspective*. vol. 1 and 2. Chicago: University of Chicago Press, 1981-1984.

Haley, Alex. *The Autobiography of Malcolm X*. New York: Grove Press, 1965.

Hampton, Henry and Steve Fayer, ed. *Voices of Freedom*. New York: Bantam Books, 1990.

Hanigan, James P. *Martin Luther King, Jr. and the Foundations of Nonviolence*. New York: University Press of America, 1984.

Harding, Vincent. *There Is a River: The Black Struggle for Freedom in America*. New York: Vintage Books, 1983.

———. "Re-calling the Inconvenient Hero: Reflections on the Last Years of Martin Luther King, Jr." *Union Seminary Quarterly Review* 40 (4 1986): 53-68.

———. *Martin Luther King: The Inconvenient Hero*. Maryknoll: Orbis Books, 1997.

Haroutunian, Joseph. "Review of Paul Tillich's *The Courage to Be*." *Theology Today* 11 (January 1955): 559-60.

Harrison, Beverly. *Making the Connections*. Boston: Beacon Press, 1985.

Hatch, Roger D. "Racism and Religion: The Contrasting Views of Benjamin Mays, Malcolm X, and Martin Luther King, Jr." *The Journal of Religious Thought* 36 (2 1979-80): 26-36.

Hauerwas, Stanley. *A Community of Character: Toward a Constructive Social Ethics.* Notre Dame: University of Notre Dame Press, 1981a.

———. *Vision and Virtue: Essays in Christian Ethical Reflection.* Notre Dame, Indiana: University of Notre Dame Press, 1981b.

———. "The Difference of Virtue and the Difference It Makes: Courage Exemplified." *Modern Theology* 9 (July 3 1993): 249-64.

Hauerwas, Stanley and Alasdair MacIntyre, eds. *Revisions: Changing Perspectives in Moral Philosophy.* South Bend, Ind.: University of Notre Dame Press, 1983.

Henry, Charles P. *Culture and African American Politics.* Bloomington: Indiana University Press, 1990.

Herman, Barbara. "Agency, Attachment, and Difference." *Ethics* 101 (4 1991): 775-97.

Herskovits, Melville. *The Myth of the Negro Past.* Boston: Beacon Press, 1941.

Herzog, Frederick. "Reorientation in Theology: Listening to Black Theology." In *The Context of Contemporary Theology*, ed. A. Mickelway. 225-241. Atlanta: John Knox Press, 1974.

Heyward, Carter. "Suffering, Redemption, and Christ." *Christianity and Crisis* 49 (December 11 1989): 381-91.

Hick, John and Paul F. Knitter, ed. *The Myth of Christian Uniqueness.* Maryknoll, New York: Orbis Books, 1987.

Hodgson, Peter C. *Children of Freedom.* Philadelphia: Fortress Press, 1974.

Holloway, Joseph E., ed. *Africanisms in American Culture.* Bloomington: Indiana University Press, 1990.

Hood, Robert. *Must God Remain Greek?* Minneapolis: Fortress Press, 1990.

hooks, bell. *Ain't I a Woman? Black Women and Feminism.* Boston: South End Press, 1981.

———. *Talking Back: Thinking Feminist, Thinking Black.* Boston: South End Press, 1989.

———. *Black Looks.* Boston: South End Press, 1992.

Hopkins, Dwight N. *Shoes That Fit Our Feet: Sources for a Constructive Black Theology.* Maryknoll, New York: Orbis Books, 1993.

Hopkins, Dwight N. and George C. L. Cummings, ed. *Cut Loose Your Stammering Tongue.* Maryknoll: Orbis, 1991.

Hudson, Stephen. "Character Traits and Desires." *Ethics* 90 (1980): 539-549.

Hunt, Lester. "Courage and Principle." *Canadian Journal of Philosophy* 10 (1980): 281-293.

Hunt, Mary E., Emilie M. Townes, and Ellen M. Umansky. "Respondents to 'Appropriation and Reciprocity in Womanist/Mujerista/Feminist Work'." *Journal of Feminist Studies in Religion* 8 (2 1992): 110-122.

Hurston, Zora Neale. *Their Eyes Were Watching God.* Urbana: University of Illinois Press, 1991.

Jacques-Garvey, Amy. ed. *Philosophy and Opinions of Marcus Garvey.* Two volumes in one. New York: Arno Press, 1968.

James, Robinson B. "A Tillichian Analysis of James Cone's Black Theology." *Perspective in Religious Studies* 1 (1974): 15-28.

Jaynes, Gerald David and Robin M. Jr. Williams, ed. *A Common Destiny: Blacks and American Society.* Washington, D.C.: National Academy Press, 1989.

Jenkins, John. "Yearley, Aquinas, and Comparative Method." *Journal of Religious Ethics* 21 (2 1993): 377-384.

Johnson, Clifton H., ed. *God Struck Me Dead: Voices of Ex-Slaves.* 2nd ed., Cleveland: Pilgrim Press, 1993.

Jones, Major. *Black Awareness: A Theology of Hope.* Nashville: Abingdon, 1971.

———. *Christian Ethics for Black Theology.* Nashville: Abingdon Press, 1974.

———. *The Color of God: The Concept of God in Afro-American Thought.* Macon, GA: Mercer University Press, 1987.

Jones, Miles J. "Toward a Theology of the Black Experience." *Christian Century* 87 (1970): 1088-1091.

Jones, William. "Theodicy and Methodology in Black Theology: A Critique of Washington, Cone, and Cleage." *Harvard Theological Review* 64 (1971b): 541-57.

———. "Theodicy and Methodology in Black Theology: A Critique of Washington, Cone, and Cleage." *Harvard Theological Review* 64 (1971c): 541-57.

———. "Reconciliation and Liberation in Black Theology: Some Implications for Religious Education." *Religious Education* (1972): 383-389.

———. *Is God a White Racist?: A Preamble to Black Theology.* Garden City, New York: Doubleday Publishing Company, Inc., 1973.

Kean, Charles D. "Review of Paul Tillich's, *The Courage to Be.*" *Anglican Theological Review* 35 (October 1953): 270-74.

Kelsey, George D. *Racism and the Christian Understanding of Man.* New York: Charles Scribner's Sons, 1965.

Kierkegaard, Søren. *Works of Love.* Translated by Howard Hong and Edna Hong. New York: Harper and Row Publishers, 1962.

———. *Christian Discourses*. Translated by Walter Lowrie. Princeton: Princeton University Press, 1974.

King, Coretta Scott. *My Life with Martin Luther King, Jr.* New York: Holt, Rinehart, and Winston, Inc., 1969.

———. "The Legacy of Martin Luther King, Jr.: The Church in Action." *Theology Today* 27 (July 1970): 129-39.

———. *The Words of Martin Luther King, Jr.* New York: Newmarket Press, 1984.

King, Deborah K. "Multiple Jeopardy, Multiple Consciousness: The Context of a Black Feminist Ideology." *Signs* 1 (1988): 42-72.

King, Martin Luther, Jr. *Stride Towards Freedom: The Montgomery Story*. New York: Harper and Row, 1958.

———. *Strength to Love*. Philadelphia: Fortress Press, 1963.

———. *Why We Can't Wait*. New York: Harper and Row, 1963b.

———. "The Un-christian Christian." In *Ebony*. (August 1965): 77.

———. *Where Do We Go from Here: Chaos or Community?* New York: Harper and Row, 1967.

———. *The Trumpet of Conscience*. New York: Harper and Row, 1968.

———. "Paul's Letter to American Christians: Dr. King's Address to the Fiftieth Meeting of the American Baptist Convention." *American Baptist Quarterly* 5 (1 1986): 4-11.

———. *The Measure of a Man*. Philadelphia: Fortress Press, 1988.

———. *I Have a Dream*. James M. Washington, ed. San Francisco: Harper Collins, 1992.

Kohl, Helmut. "Painful Questions." *Society* 26 (March-April 1989): 7-9.

Krieger, David J. "Conversion: On the Possibility of Global Thinking in an Age of Particularism." *Journal of the American Academy of Religion* 58 (2 1990): 223-243.

Kruschwitz, Robert B. and Robert C. Roberts, ed. *The Virtues: Contemporary Essays on Moral Character*. 1987.

Lake, Frank. "Review of Paul Tillich's *The Courage to Be*." *Scottish Journal of Theology* 6 (December 1953): 418-21.

Large, Ron. "Martin Luther King, Jr.: Ethics, Nonviolence, and Moral Character." *The Journal of Religious Thought* 46 (1 1989): 51-63.

Lecky, Robert S. and H. Elliott Wright. *Black Manifesto: Religion, Racism, and Reparations*. New York: Sheed and Ward, 1969.

Lehmann, Paul L. "Black Theology and Christian Theology." *Union Seminary Quarterly Review* 31 (1 1975): 31-37.

Lerner, Gerda, ed. *Black Women in White America: A Documentary History*. New York: Vintage Books, 1972.

Levine, Lawrence W. *Black Culture and Black Consciousness*. New York: Oxford University Press, 1977.

Lewis, David L. *King: A Critical Biography*. Baltimore: Penguin, 1970.

Lincoln, C. Eric, ed. *Martin Luther King, Jr.: A Profile*. New York: Hill and Wang, Inc., 1970.

———. "A Perspective on James H. Cone's Black Theology." *Union Seminary Quarterly Review* 31 (1 1975): 15-22.

Lincoln, C. Eric and Lawrence H. Mamiya. *The Black Church in the African American Experience*. Durham, N.C.: Duke University Press, 1990.

Lischer, Richard. "The Word That Moves: The Preaching of Martin Luther King, Jr." *Theology Today* 46 (July 1989): 169-82.

———. *The Preacher King*. New York: Oxford University Press, 1995.

Long, Charles H. "The Black Reality: Toward a Theology of Freedom." *Criterion* 8 (1969): 2-7.

———. "Perspectives for a Study of Afro-American Religion in the U.S." *History of Religions* 2 (1971): 54-66.

———. *Significations: Signs, Symbols, and Images in the Interpretation of Religion.* Philadelphia: Fortress, 1986.

Lorde, Audre. *Sister Outsider.* Trumansburg, New York: Crossing Press, 1984.

Louden, Robert. "On Some Vices of Virtue Ethics." *American Philosophical Quarterly* 21 (1984): 227-36.

———. "Kant's Virtue Ethics." *Philosophy* 61 (1986): 473-489.

MacIntyre, Alasdair. *After Virtue.* Notre Dame, Indiana: University of Notre Dame Press, 1981.

———. *Whose Justice, Which Rationality?* Notre Dame, Indiana: University of Notre Dame Press, 1988.

MacIntyre, Alasdair and Stanley Hauerwas, eds. *Revisions: Changing Conceptions in Moral Philosophy.* South Bend: Indiana, 1983.

Mackenzie, Compton. *On Moral Courage.* London: Collins Press, 1962.

Martin, Clarice J. "Womanist Interpretation of the New Testament: The Quest for Holistic and Inclusive Translation and Interpretation." *Journal of Feminist Studies in Religion* 6 (2 1990): 41-62.

Martin, Joan M. "The Notion of Difference for Emerging Womanist Ethics: The Writings of Audre Lorde and bell hooks." *Journal of Feminist Studies in Religion* 9 (1-2 1993): 39-52.

Martin, Sandy D. "King and Interfaith Dialogue, 1955-68." *The Journal of Religious Thought* 48 (2 1991-92): 34-48.

Mays, Benjamin E. *The Negro's God*. New York: Chapman and Grimes, 1938.

Mbon, Friday M. "James Cone and the Question of What It Means to Be Really Human." *Journal of Religious Studies* 18 (1-2 1992): 34-49.

McCall, Emmanuel L. *The Black Christian Experience*. Nashville: Broadman Press, 1972.

McCandless, David. "Beckett and Tillich: Courage and Existence in *Waiting for Godot*." *Philosophy and Literature* 12 (1 1988): 48-57.

McClain, William B. "The Black Religious Experience in the United States." In *This Far By Faith: American Black Worship and Its African Roots*, ed. R.W. Hovda. 28-37. Washington, D.C.: National Office of Black Catholics, 1977.

McClendon, James, Jr. "M.L.King: Politician or American Church Father?" *Journal of Ecumenical Studies* 8 (Winter 1971): 115-121.

McKinney, Richard I. "Reflections on the Concept of Black Theology." *Journal of Religious Thought* 26 (1969): 10-14.

McWilliams, Warren. "Theodicy According to James Cone." *The Journal of Religious Thought* 36 (2 1979-80): 45-54.

Meier, August. *Negro Thought in America, 1880-1915.* Ann Arbor: The University of Michigan Press, 1966.

Meier, August and Elliott Rudwick. *From Plantation to Ghetto (3rd ed.).* New York: Hill and Wang, 1976.

Meier, August, Elliott Rudwick, and Francis L. Broderick, ed. *Black Protest Thought in the Twentieth Century.* Indianapolis: Bobbs-Merrill Company, Inc., 1983.

Meilaender, Gilbert. *The Theory and Practice of Virtue.* Notre Dame: University of Notre Dame Press, 1984.

Mikelson, Thomas J. S. "Cosmic Companionship: The Place of God in the Moral Reasoning of Martin Luther King, Jr." *The Journal of Religious Ethics* 18 (2 1990): 1-14.

Miller, Keith D. *Voice of Deliverance: The Language of Martin Luther King, Jr., and Its Sources.* New York: The Free Press, 1992.

Miller, Samuel H. "Critical Review of Paul Tillich's *The Courage to Be.*" *Journal of Religion* 46 (January 1966): 200-03.

Mills, M. J. "The Discussions of andreia in the Eudemian and Nicomachean Ethics." *Phronesis* 25 (2 1980): 198-218.

Mitchell, Henry H. *Black Belief: Folk Beliefs of Blacks in America and West Africa*. New York: Harper and Row, 1975.

Mitchell, Henry H. and Nicholas Cooper Lewter, eds. *Soul Theology: The Heart of American Black Culture*. San Franciso: Harper & Row, 1986.

Mollegen, Albert T. "Review of Paul Tillich's *The Courage to Be.*" *Journal of Religious Thought* 11 (1 1953-54): 68-69.

Moltmann, Jurgen. et. al. Select articles on James Cone. ed. *Union Seminary Quarterly Review:* 31/1 (Fall 1975): 3-86.

More, Henry. *An Account of the Virtues*. New York: Facsimile Text Society, 1930.

Morrison, Roy D. "Theology and Ethics: The Perspectives of Black Philosophy." In *Philosophy of Religion and Philosophy: 1975*, ed. J. McClendon. 123-138. Missoula, Montana: Scholars Press, 1975.

Morrison, Toni. *The Bluest Eye*. New York: Washington Square Press, 1972.

——, ed. *Race-ing, Justice, En-gendering Power*. New York: Pantheon Books, 1992.

Murray, Pauli. "Black Theology and Feminist Theology: A Comparative View." *Anglican Theological Review* 60 (1 1978): 3-24.

——. "Black, Feminist Theologies: Links, Parallels and Tensions." *Christianity and Crisis* 40 (6 1980): 86-95.

Naveh, Eyal. "Dialectical Redemption: Reinhold Niebuhr, Martin Luther King, Jr., and the Kingdom of God in America." *The Journal of Religious Thought* 48 (2 1991-92): 57-76.

Neuhaus, Richard J., ed. *Virtue: Public and Private.* Grand Rapids, Mich.: William B. Eerdmans Publishing Company, 1986.

Niebuhr, H.R. *The Responsible Self.* New York: Harper and Row, 1963.

Norden, Bryan W. Van. "Yearley on Mencius." *Journal of Religious Ethics* 21 (2 1993): 369-376.

Nussbaum, Martha C. *The Fragility of Goodness.* New York: Cambridge University Press, 1986.

——. "Comparing Virtues." *Journal of Religious Ethics* 21 (2 1993): 345-368.

Oates, Stephen B. *Let the Trumpet Sound: The Life of Martin Luther King, Jr.* New York: Harper and Row, 1982.

Oglesby, Enoch H. *Ethics and Theology from the Other Side: Sounds of Moral Struggle.* Washington, D.C.: University Press of America, 1979.

Olds, Mason. "Humanism and Liberation Theology." *Religious Humanism* 21 (3 1987): 98-109.

Outka, Gene. *Agape: An Ethical Analysis.* New Haven: Yale University Press, 1972.

Panikkar, Raimundo. "The Crux of Christian Ecumenism: Can Universality and Chosenness Be Held Simultaneously?" *Journal of Ecumenical Studies* 26 (1 1989): 82-99.

Paris, Peter J. *The Social Teaching of the Black Churches.* Philadelphia: Fortress Press, 1985.

———. *Black Religious Leaders: Conflict in Unity.* 2nd. ed., Louisville: Westminster/John Knox Press, 1991.

———. "From Womanist Thought to Womanist Action." *Journal of Feminist Studies in Religion* 9 (1-2 1993): 115-126.

Pears, David. "Aristotle's Analysis of Courage." In *Midwest Studies in Philosophy,*

Volume III – Studies in Ethical Theory, ed. Peter French, Theodore Uehling, and Howard Wettstein. 1978.

———. "Courage as a Mean." In *Essays on Aristotle's Ethics,* ed. A. Rorty. 171-87. 1980.

Pence, Gregory E. "Recent Work on Virtue." *American Philosophical Quarterly* 21 (4 1984): 281-298.

Penner, Terry. "What Laches and Nicias Miss – And Whether Socrates Thinks Courage Merely a Part of Virtue." *Ancient Philosophy* 12 (1992): 1-27.

Pieper, Josef. *Fortitude and Temperance.* Translated by Daniel F. Coogan. New York: Pantheon Books, 1954.

Piper, Adrian M.S. "Impartiality, Compassion, and Modal Imagination." *Ethics* 101 (4 1991): 726-57.

Plaskow, Judith. ed. "Appropriation and Reciprocity in Womanist/Mujerista/Feminist Work." In *The Journal of Feminist Studies in Religion.* 8, No.2 (Fall 1992): 91-124.

Pohier, Jacques and Dietmar Mieth, ed. *Christian Ethics: Uniformity, Universality, Pluralism.* New York: The Seabury Press, 1981.

Potter, Nelson T. and Mark Timmons, ed. *Morality and Universality: Essays on Ethical Universalizability.* Vol. 45. Theory and Decision Library. Boston: D. Reidel Publishing Company, 1985.

Pybus, Elizabeth. *Human Goodness: Generosity and Courage.* Toronto: University of Toronto Press, 1991.

Raboteau, Albert J. *Slave Religion: The Invisible Institution in the Antebellum South.* New York: Oxford University Press, 1978.

———. "Martin Luther King, Jr., and the Tradition of Black Religious Protest." In *Religion and the Life of the Nation*, ed. Rowland A. Sherrill. 46-63. Urbana: University of Illinois Press, 1990.

———. *A Fire in My Bones: Reflections on African-American Religious History.* Boston: Beacon Press, 1995.

Rawls, John. *A Theory of Justice.* Cambridge, Mass: Belknap Press of Harvard, 1971.

Ray, Benjamin C. *African Religions: Symbol, Ritual, and Community.* Englewood Cliffs: Prentice-Hall, Inc., 1976.

Redkey, Edwin S., ed. *Respect Black: The Writings and Speeches of Henry McNeal Turner.* New York: Arno Press, 1971.

Reist, Benjamin. *Theology in Red, White, and Black.* Philadelphia: Westminster, 1975.

Roberts, J. Deotis. "Folklore and Religion: The Black Experience." *Journal of Religious Thought* 27 (Summer Supplement 1970): 5-15.

———. *Liberation and Reconciliation: A Black Theology.* Philadelphia: Westminster Press, 1971a.

———. *A Black Political Theology.* Philadelphia: Westminster Press, 1974.

———. "Contextual Theology: Liberation and Indigenization." *Christian Century* 93 (January 28 1976): 64-68.

———. "Christian Liberation Ethics: The Black Experience." *Religion in Life* 158 (Summer 1979): 227-235.

———. *The Roots of a Black Future*. Philadelphia: Westminster Press, 1980.

———. *Black Theology Today*. New York: Edwin Mellen Press, 1983.

———. *Black Theology in Dialogue*. Philadelphia: Westminster Press, 1987.

Roberts, J. Deotis and James Gardner, eds. *Quest for a Black Theology*. Philadelphia: Pilgrim Press, 1971b.

Rorty, Amelie, ed. *Explaining Emotions*. 1980a.

———, ed. *Essays on Aristotle's Ethics*. Berkley: University of California, 1980b.

———. "The Two Faces of Courage." *Philosophy* 61 (236 1986): 151-171.

Roth, Guenther. "Remembrance and Responsibility." *Society* 26 (March-April 1989): 4-5.

Ruether, Rosemary R. "Black Theology and the Black Church." *Journal of Religious Thought* 26 (Summer Supplement 1969): 26-33.

———. "The Foundations of Liberation Languages: Christianity and Revolutionary Movements." *The Journal of Religious Thought* 32 (1 1975): 74-85.

——. "Courage as a Christian Virtue." *Cross Currents* 33 (1 1983): 8-16.

Runzo, Joseph, ed. *Ethics, Religion, and the Good Society: New Directions in a Pluralistic World.* Louisville: Westminster/John Knox Press, 1992.

Salley, Columbus and Ronald Behm. *Your God Is Too White.* Downers Grove, Illinois: InterVarsity, 1970.

——. *What Color Is Your God?* Downers Grove, Illinois: InterVarsity Press, 1981.

Sanders, Cheryl J. "Black Women: Moral Agents." *Christianity and Crisis* 49 (December 11 1989a): 391-92.

——. "Religious Conversion, Ethics, and the Afro-American Slave: Evaluating Alternative Approaches." *The Journal of Religious Thought* 45 (2 1989b): 7-20.

——. Katie G. Cannon, Emilie M. Townes, M. Shawn Copeland, bell hooks, and Cheryl Townsend Gilkes. "Christian Ethics and Theology in Womanist Perspective." *Journal of Feminist Studies in Religion* 5 (2 1989): 83-112.

——. *Living the Intersection: Womanist and Afrocentrism inTheology.* Minneapolis: Fortress, 1995.

Sanneh, Lamin. "Particularity, Pluralism, and Commitment." *Christian Century* 107 (1990): 103-108.

Schmid, W. Thomas. "The Socratic Conception of Courage." *History of Philosophy Quarterly* 2 (2 1985): 113-129.

———. *On Manly Courage: A Study of Plato's "Laches"*. Carbondale and Edwardsville, IL: Southern Illinois University Press, 1992.

Schneewind, J.B. "Virtue, Narrative, and the Community." *Journal of Philosophy* 79 (1982): 653-663.

Seeskin, Kenneth. "Courage and Knowledge: A Perspective on the Socratic Paradox." *Southern Journal of Philosophy* 14 (1974): 511-21.

Sernett, Milton C., ed. *Afro-American Religious History: A Documentary Witness*. Durham: Duke University Press, 1985.

Shange, Ntozake. *For Colored Girls Only Who Have Considered Suicide When the Rainbow is Enuf*. New York: Macmillan Publishing Co., 1975.

Shaw, Talbert. "Religion and Afroamericans: A Propaedeutic." *The Journal of Religious Thought* 32 (1 1975): 65-73.

Sherman, Nancy. *The Fabric of Character*. New York: Oxford University Press, 1989.

Smith, Archie, Jr. "A Black Response to Sontag's *Coconut Theology*." *The Journal of Religious Thought* 36 (2 1979-80): 13-25.

Smith, Ervin. *The Ethics of Martin Luther King, Jr.* Vol. 2. Studies in American Religion, New York: Edwin Mellen Press, 1981.

Smith, Kenneth L. "The Radicalization of Martin Luther King, Jr.: The Last Three Years." *Journal of Ecumenical Studies* 26 (2 1989): 270-88.

Smith, Kenneth L. and Ira G. Zepp Jr. *Search for The Beloved Community: The Thinking of Martin Luther King, Jr.* Valley Forge, PA: Judson Press, 1974.

Smith, Steven G. "Metaphorical Courage and the Identification of God." *Soundings* 69 (Fall 1986): 241-55.

Smylie, James H. "On Jesus, Pharoahs, and the Chosen People: Martin Luther King as Biblical Interpreter and Humanist." *Interpretation* 24 (January 1970): 74-91.

Sontag, Frederick. "Coconut Theology: Is James Cone the 'Uncle Tom' of Black Theology?" *The Journal of Religious Thought* 36 (2 1979-80): 5-12.

Starkloff, Carl. "A Note on Religious 'Particularism'." *Journal of Ecumenical Studies* 9 (Fall 1972): 870-74.

Steinkraus, Warren E. "The Dangerous Ideas of Martin Luther King." *Scottish Journal of Religious Studies* 6 (1 1985): 16-25.

Stewart, Carlyle Fielding, III. "The Method of Correlation in the Theology of James H. Cone." *The Journal of Religious Thought* 40 (2 1983-84): 27-38.

———. *God, Being, and Liberation: A Comparative Analysis of the Theologies and Ethics of James H. Cone and Howard Thurman*. New York: University Press of America, 1989.

Stocker, Michael. "The Schizophrenia of Modern Ethical Theories." *Journal of Philosophy* 63 (4 1976): 453-466.

Sturm, Douglas. "Martin Luther King, Jr., as Democratic Socialist." *The Journal of Religious Ethics* 18 (2 1990): 79-106.

Sulzbach, Maria Fuerth. "Review of Paul Tillich's *The Courage to Be*." *Religion in Life* 22 (3 1953): 462-64.

Tessitore, Aristide. "Courage and Comedy in Plato's *Laches*." *The Journal of Politics* 56 (February 1994): 115-33.

Tillich, Paul. *The Courage to Be*. New Haven: Yale University Press, 1952.

Townes, Emilie M. *A Troubling in My Soul: Womanist Perspectives on Evil and Suffering*. Maryknoll: Orbis Books, 1993.

Tracy, David. "The Particularity and Universality of Christian Revelation." In *Revelation and Experience*, ed. Edward Schillebeeckx and Bas van Iersel. New York: The Seabury Press, 1979.

Trayham, Warner. *Christian Faith in Black and White*. Wakefield, MA: Parameter Press, 1973.

Urquhart, W. S. "Review of Paul Tillich's *The Courage to Be.*" *The Expository Times* 64 (July 1953): 298.

Walker, Alice. *The Color Purple.* New York: Harcourt, Brace, and Jovanovich Publishers, 1982.

———. *In Search of Our Mother's Gardens: Womanist Prose.* San Diego: Harcourt, Brace Jovanovich Press, 1983.

Walker, Margaret Urban. "Partial Consideration." *Ethics* 101 (4 1991): 758-74.

Walker, Theodore, Jr. "Theological Resources for a Black Neoclassical Social Ethics." *The Journal of Religious Thought* 45 (2 1989): 21-39.

———. *Empower the People: Social Ethics for the African-America Church.* Maryknoll: Orbis Books, 1991.

Wallace, James. "Cowardice and Courage." *American Philosophical Quarterly* (Monograph Number 7 1973):

———. *Virtues and Vices.* Ithaca: Cornell University Press, 1978.

Wallace, Michele. *Invisibility Blues: From Pop to Theory.* London: Verso Publishing, 1990.

Wallace, Michelle. *Black Macho and the Myth of the Superwoman.* New York: Dial Press, 1978.

Walton, Douglas. *Courage: A Philosophical Investigation.* Berkeley: University of California, 1986.

——. "Courage, Relativism, and Practical Reasoning." *Philosophia* 20 (3 1990): 227-40.

Walzer, Michael. "A Particularism of My Own." *Religious Studies Review* 16 (3 1990): 193-197.

Washington, Joseph. *Black Religion: The Negro and Christianity in the United States*. Boston: Beacon Press, 1964.

——. *Black and White Power Subreption*. Boston: Beacon Press, 1969.

——. "The Religion of Anti-Blackness." *Theology Today* 38 (July 1981): 146-151.

Washington, James M., ed. *A Testament of Hope: The Essential Writings of Martin Luther King, Jr.* San Francisco: Harper and Row, 1986.

Washington, Joseph R. "Are American Negro Churches Christian." *Theology Today* 20 (April 1963): 76-86.

——. *Black Religion: The Negro and Christianity in the United States*. Boston: Beacon Press, 1964.

——. *The Politics of God*. Boston: Beacon Press, 1967.

——. "The Roots and Fruits of Black Theology." *Theology Today* 30 (July 1973): 121-129.

——. "Black Religious Crisis." *Christian Century* 91 (May 1 1974): 472-475.

——. *Anti-Blackness in English Religion.* Lewiston, New York: Edwin Mellen Press, 1984.

Watley, William D. *Roots of Resistance: The Nonviolent Ethic of Martin Luther King, Jr.* Valley Forge, PA: Judson Press, 1985.

Watts, Leon W. "The National Committee of Black Churchmen." *Christianity and Crisis* 30 (November 2 & 16 1970): 237-243.

Weddle, David L. "The Liberator as Exorcist: James Cone and the Classic Doctrine of Atonement." *Religion in Life* 49 (1980): 477-87.

Weisbrot, Robert. *Father Divine and the Struggle for Racial Equality.* Chicago: The University of Illinois Press, 1983.

Weiss, Roslyn. "Courage, Confidence, and Wisdom in the 'Protagoras'." *Ancient Philosophy* 5: 11-24.

Weizsacker, Richard von. "Looking into the Mirror of History." *Society* 26 (March-April 1989): 6-7.

Welch, Sharon D. *A Feminist Ethic of Risk.* Minneapolis: Fortress Press, 1990.

West, Cornel. "Philosophy and the Afro-American Experience." *Philosophical Forum.* (March 1979) 148-77.

——. *Prophetic Fragments.* Grand Rapids, Mich: Eerdmans, 1988.

————. *The American Evasion of Philosophy: A Genealogy of Pragmatism.* Madison: University of Wisconsin Press, 1989.

————. *Prophesy Deliverance!: An Afro-American Revolutionary Christianity.* Philadelphia: Westminster Press, 1992.

————. *Beyond Eurocentrism and Multiculturalism, Volume One: Prophetic Thought in Postmodern Times.* Monroe, Maine: Common Courage Press, 1993a.

————. *Beyond Eurocentrism and Multiculturalism, Volume Two: Prophetic Reflections.* Monroe, Maine: Common Courage Press, 1993b.

————. *Keeping Faith: Philosophy and Race in America.* New York: Routledge, 1993c.

————. *Race Matters.* Boston: Beacon Press, 1993d.

Will, James E. "The Universality of God and the Particularity of Peace." In *Theology, Politics, and Peace,* ed. Theodore Runyon. 181-190. Maryknoll, New York: Orbis Books, 1989.

Williams, Delores S. "Womanist Theology: Black Women's Voices." *Christianity and Crisis* 47 (March 2 1987): 66-70.

————. *Sisters in the Wilderness: The Challenge of Womanist God-Talk.* Maryknoll: Orbis Books, 1993a.

———. "Womanist/Feminist Dialogue: Problems and Possibilities." *Journal of Feminist Studies in Religion* 9 (1-2 1993b): 67-74.

Williams, Preston N. "The Ethical Aspects of the Black Church/Black Theology Phenomenon." *Journal of Religious Thought* 26 (Summer Supplement 1969): 34-35.

———. "The Black Experience and Black Religion." In *New Theology No. 8*, ed. M.E. Marty and D.G. Peerman. 212-229. New York: Macmillan Publishing Company, Inc., 1971a.

———. "The Ethics of Black Power." In *Quest for a Black Theology*, ed. J.D. Roberts and J. Gardiner. 82-96. Philadelphia: Pilgrim Press, 1971b.

———. "James Cone and the Problem of a Black Ethic." *Harvard Theological Review* 65 (1972): 483-94.

———. "Contextualizing the Faith: The African-American Tradition and Martin Luther King, Jr." In *One Faith, Many Cultures*, ed. Ruy O. Costa. 2. Cambridge, MA: Boston Theological Institute, 1988.

———. "An Analysis of the Conception of Love and Its Influence on Justice in the Thought of Martin Luther King, Jr." *The Journal of Religious Ethics* 18 (2 1990): 15-32.

Williamson, Clark M. "In Memoriam: Martin Luther King, Jr." *Encounter* 29 (Autumn 1968): 370-74.

Wilmore, Gayraud. "The New Context of Black Theology in the United States." In *Mission Trends No.4: Liberation Theologies*, ed. G.H. Anderson and T.F. Stansky. 113-122. New York: Paulist Press, 1979.

———. "TTe Church and Theology in North America." In *Theology in the Americas*, ed. C. West, C. Guidote, and M. Coakley. Maryknoll, New York: Orbis Books, 1982a.

———. "The New Need for Intergroup Coalitions." *Christian Century* 99 (February 17 1982b): 170-173.

———. *Black Religion and Black Radicalism*. 2d rev. ed. ed., Maryknoll, New York: Orbis Books, 1983.

———, ed. *African-American Religious Studies: An Interdisciplinary Anthology*. Durham, N.C.: Duke University Press, 1989.

Wilson, William Julius. *The Declining Significance of Race*. Chicago: University of Chicago Press, 1980.

Wood, Forrest G. *The Arrogance of Faith: Christianity and Race in America from the Colonial Era to the Twentieth Century*. New York: Alfred A. Knopf, 1990.

Wright, Leon E. "Black Theology or Black Experience?" *Journal of Religious Thought* 26 (Summer Supplement 1969): 46-56.

Yearley, Lee H. *Mencius and Aquinas: Theories of Virtue and Conceptions of Courage*. Albany: State University of New York, 1990a.

———. "Recent Work on Virtue." *Religious Studies Review* 16 (no.1 1990b): 1-9.

———. "The Author Replies [to respondents of his book, Mencius and Aquinas]." *Journal of Religious Ethics* 21 (2 1993): 385-396.

Yoder, John Howard. "But Do We See Jesus: The Particularity of the Incarnation and the Universality of Truth." In *Foundations of Ethics*, ed. Leroy S. Rouner. Notre Dame, Indiana: University of Notre Dame Press, 1983.

———. "On Not Being Ashamed of the Gospel: Particularity, Pluralism, and Validation." *Faith and Philosophy* 9 (3 1992): 285-300.

Young, Andrew. "Martin Luther King as a Political Theologian." In *Theology, Politics, and Peace*, ed. Theodore Runyan. 79-85. Maryknoll, New York: Orbis Books, 1989.

Young, Henry J. *Hope in Process: A Theology of Social Pluralism*. Minneapolis: Fortress Press, 1990.

Zepp, Ira G., Jr. *The Social Vision of Martin Luther King, Jr.* Brooklyn, New York: Carlson Publishing Inc., 1989.

Rev. Dr. Don L. Davis:
A Theological Appreciation

Introduction

Dr. Don Davis is a true prodigy; a person of vast talents, interests, and gifts maximized by dedication, discipline, and hard work. No short description that I could write would do justice to the scope of his life. I cannot, I confess, even write something that would summarize the entirety of his theological and philosophical work. I suspect that Don is something like the elephant approached by the blind men in the fable; every person who speaks about him would have their own stories, their own summary of what is most important to them and about him. So all I can hope to do is to share those theological truths (taught and lived out by Don) that have left the deepest imprint on me in the more than thirty years that I have had the opportunity to call him a co-worker and a friend.

Dr. Davis' Theological Virtues

1. A **Christocentric** Approach to Theology

For I decided to know nothing among you except
Jesus Christ and him crucified (1 Cor. 2:2 ESV)

This should not be misunderstood. Anyone who knows
Don understands that he is a devout Nicene Trinitarian.
They also know that his theological inquiry is not narrow
but broad. One of his favorite Scripture quotations is
"For *all things* are yours. . . .[since] you are Christ's, and
Christ is God's" (1 Cor. 2:21 & 23). His Christocentricity
is an open door to the freedom that the theologian has
in Christ. Nonetheless, it disciplines his approach to truth.

Johann von Staupitz (the mentor of Martin Luther when
he was still a Catholic monk) could speak about theological
precepts being found and understood "in the wounds
of Christ . . . and nowhere else." That kind of thinking
captures what I mean by Dr. Davis' Christocentricity.
Theology is not an abstraction. It is an activity rooted in
the incarnation, life, works, teachings, miracles, suffering,
death, and resurrection of Jesus Christ. All theological
reflection must pass through the One who said "I am the
gate" (John 10:9).

From that starting point flows the emphasis that Don
places on the role of *Christus Victor* and the advancement
of the Kingdom of God. In a world filled with struggle,
injustice, and true moral evil, the hope of the poor is found
in a Messiah about whom St. Paul writes: He disarmed the
rulers and authorities and put them to open shame, by

triumphing over them in [the cross][1] (Col. 2:15). Dr. Davis' experience as a black man growing up in the inner-city who goes on to become a Dr. Martin Luther King, Jr. scholar gives him a clear vantage point from which to proclaim an evangelical message of a Messiah who comes to "bring justice to victory" (Matt. 12:20). Don's reflection on, and experience with, this Christ who brings the victory of God over sin, death, hell, and the grave is the wellspring from which all of his theology flows.

2. A Commitment to **Community**

> *For the body does not consist of one member but of many. . . .*
> *The eye cannot say to the hand, "I have no need of you," nor*
> *again the head to the feet, "I have no need of you". . . If one*
> *member suffers, all suffer together; if one member is honored,*
> *all rejoice together (1 Cor. 12:14, 21, 16 ESV)*

There is nothing quite so difficult as being the smartest and most capable person in a room (as Don often is) and yet deferring to others for the good of the community. In a hyper-individualistic society, this deference is often not even seen as a virtue. I think that there is nothing that I admire more about Don's character than I do his willingness to listen to all viewpoints, engage in genuine respectful dialogue with all members of a community, to defer to others when it is in the community's best interest, and to look not for the lion's share of the attention and honor but instead for ways to take the bulk of the work and difficulty of any project on his own shoulders. I say this with some authority as a person who has repeatedly benefited from Don's selflessness.

---

1   Alternate reading- see English Standard Version *Colossians* Chapter 2, footnote b.

Don's commitment to community is rooted in his understanding of the Scriptures, is strengthened by his King scholarship, and is lived out at the level of day-to-day decision-making. Dr. Davis not only talks the talk of authentic community; he puts into practice its implications.

3. An Understanding of Leadership as Representation

Therefore, we are ambassadors for Christ, God making his appeal through us. We implore you on behalf of Christ, be reconciled to God (2 Cor. 5:20 ESV)

The idea of leadership as representation is an ancient one in the church finding expression in the description of the ideal Bishop as "the icon [or image] of Christ." In Scripture, the Christian leader is meant to be a concrete exemplar of Christ, a person whose decision-making, speech, and actions reflect the will and actions of Jesus, just as the actions of Jesus were in complete conformity to the will of His Father.

In a time where Christian leadership manuals are all too often only baptized versions of the latest management research, Don has done the church a great service by reflecting and writing about the unique role of the Christian leader as a representative. Dr. Davis defines representation as "being selected to stand in the place of another, and thereby fulfill the assigned duties, exercise the rights and serve as deputy for, as well as to speak and act with another's authority on behalf of their interests and reputation." Again, Jesus is the model of this type of leadership and He clearly intends for his disciples to represent Him in the same way that He represented the Father (see Luke 10:16, John 20:21). I am genuinely grateful for the many opportunities I have had to dialogue with Dr. Davis about his understanding of leadership. His charts, particularly, express the wisdom of Scripture and the church fathers, contextualized in clear modern language. In recent years, I have more and more defaulted to Don's diagrams and writings on this subject when someone asked me to give an instruction about the nature and means of Christian leadership.

4. A Passion to Recognize **the Poor and Oppressed as God's Chosen Leaders**

Listen, my beloved brothers, has not God chosen those who are poor in the world to be rich in faith and heirs of the kingdom, which he has promised to those who love him? (James 2:5 ESV)

I think it is fair to say that this is the single most important reason that Don founded The Urban Ministry Institute (TUMI). Dr. Davis could teach at virtually any university in the country. He has been a guest lecturer at many of them and every year receives unsolicited offers from a variety of colleges to come and join their faculty. I'm sure that some of the offers have been tempting. At the end of the day, however, no American university (even those that are founded in the Christian tradition) is set up to prioritize the poor and oppressed as the most significant group to be trained for leadership of the church.

The thing I appreciate most about Don is that the belief in the poor and oppressed is rooted in his theology. Yes, his personal experience shows that a person can grow up in a community of poverty and go on to achieve at the highest level. But that is not what grounds and sustains his belief. The belief in the poor as leaders for the faith is rooted in the theological proposition that God has elected the poor for this task, that Jesus exemplified it in His own ministry, and that the Spirit of God is able to empower the least likely of people for the work of the Kingdom of God.

It is one thing, however, to espouse a theological belief. It is another, not only to practice it in your life, but to see it grow rather than diminish in importance. Don's belief in God's choice of the poor and oppressed can rightly be described as unwavering. He believed it when I first met him. He believed through the thirty plus years of our friendship. And, if anything, he believes it more firmly now than at any time that I have known him. Best of all, he has inspired thousands of other people to adopt that belief in their own life and to be living out its implications in practical ways. Thanks be to God!

 Conclusion

It has been one of the great privileges of my life to know Don and to work alongside him. We have spent countless hours in dialogue, discussion, argument, and prayer. The writer of the scriptural book of Proverbs said that "Iron sharpens iron, and one man sharpens another (27:17). I hope I have had that effect on him. I *know* that he has had that effect on me, and on countless others. He is a man, a theologian, a scholar, and a leader worthy of honor and I am grateful that I have had the chance to acknowledge that in this short reflection. Blessings to you, brother Don, today and always.

Terry G. Cornett, M.A., M.A.R.
Academic Dean Emeritus of The Urban Ministry Institute

A Celebration of Twenty Years of The Urban Ministry Institute

Rev. Dr. Don L. Davis was born November 16, 1954 into a large family in Wichita, Kansas. An outstanding athlete, he also excelled in debate, and was Student Body President in high school.

In 1975 Don married Beth, and joined World Impact, later serving as City Director. In 1976, Matthew was born, and then later came Joanna (1980), and Daniel (1984).

During these years Don became burdened by the need for affordable and accessible Bible training for the urban poor. In 1986, the Davis family moved to Wheaton College and Graduate School where Don earned a BA in Biblical Studies and MA in Systematic Theology, graduating summa cum laude while also working as a pastor and adjunct professor.

In 1989, Don began a PhD in Religion at the University of Iowa, emerging as an expert in urban church planting and cross-cultural mission. After completing his course work in 1995, he turned down a number of university teaching opportunities in order to return to the inner city

and launch *The Urban Ministry Institute* (TUMI). This
fulfilled Don's dream to offer excellent, affordable, and
culturally conducive theological education for the urban
poor. Along with Rev. Terry Cornett, Don taught dozens
of courses, which formed the formed the basis for TUMI's
premiere education resource, *The Capstone Curriculum* –
a colossal work ten years in the making.

In 1996 Don championed *Operation Jericho*, a conference
that transformed World Impact into a church-planting
organization. In 1999 Don developed the *Evangel School
for Cross-Cultural Church Planting*, which went on to
equip over forty church plant teams. Don spoke at Promise
Keeper stadium events, lectured at universities and
preached in many churches.

In 2000 Don received his PhD, graduating again with
honors. His dissertation, *Black and Human*, is among the
finest treatments on the universal struggle to form one's
identity independent of the predominant views of those in
power. Don's design of TUMI's satellite distance program,
articulated in *Multiplying Laborers for the Urban Harvest:
Changing the Paradigm of Formal Theological Education,*
could go down in history as one of the most innovative works
in world mission. It laid the foundation for indigenous
leadership training beyond urban America, including
prisons, suburban and rural churches, and foreign
countries. His blending of solid pedagogy and ingenious
administrative structure has yielded 191 TUMI satellite
campuses with over two thousand active students in
fourteen countries by mid 2015.

Don's *Let God Arise* prayer guide launched a prayer movement that has continued to this day. His commitment to prayer sustained him during the loss of many cherished family members, most poignantly his and Beth's son Matt (2003). Despite these tragedies, Don was a constant source of hope and comfort to grieving friends and family.

He has authored many books including *Fight the Good Fight of Faith* and his groundbreaking *Sacred Roots: A Primer on Retrieving the Great Tradition*. Among his dozens of courses, some of the most treasured are *Winning the World*, *Nurturing an Apostolic Heart* and *A Compelling Testimony*.

Don is a prolific song-writer and accomplished musician. Among his hundreds of songs, *The Fight Is On*, *Mo' Power*, and *Spirit of God* are especially beloved. Don's passion for worship led to the development of *TUMI Productions*, and another of his recent innovations is the *SIAFU* Chapter network – discipleship groups connected to urban churches for mentoring and service.

Despite all these accomplishments, what sets Don apart is his consistent and genuine Christlike character. In public and private, he has maintained a humble and gracious disposition. His deep love for Jesus of Nazareth has endeared him to close friends and to thousands around the world.

Rev. Don Allsman

A Select Bibliography of Works by Rev. Dr. Don L. Davis

Compiled by Dr. Hank Voss

Published Books

Don L. Davis. *Black and Human: Rediscovering King as a Resource for Black Theology and Ethics* (Martin Luther King, Jr.) (Ph.D., The University of Iowa, 2000).

———. *Let God Arise!: A Sober Call to Prevailing Prayer for a Dynamic Spiritual Awakening and the Aggressive Advancement of the Kingdom in America's Inner Cities.* Wichita, KS: The Urban Ministry Institute Press, 2000.

———. *Manual for Urban Church Planting*, 3rd ed. Wichita, KS: The Urban Ministry Institute Press, 2006.

———. *Leading and Feeding Urban Church Plant Teams*, 2nd ed. Wichita, KS: The Urban Ministry Institute Press, 2007.

———. *For the Next Generation: The Urban Ministry Institute Mentor Manual*, 2nd ed. Wichita, KS: The Urban Ministry Institute Press, 2008.

———. *Sacred Roots: A Primer on Retrieving the Great Tradition*. Wichita, KS: The Urban Ministry Institute Press, 2010.

———. *Multiplying Laborers for the Urban Harvest: Shifting the Paradigm for Servant Leadership Education*, 15th ed. Wichita, KS: The Urban Ministry Institute Press, 2013.

———. *The SIAFU Network Guidebook: Standing Together for Christ in the City*. Wichita, KS: The Urban Ministry Institute Press, 2013.

———. *Taking Ground: A Manual for Intra-Cultural Church Planting* (Wichita, KS: The Urban Ministry Institute Press, 2015).

———. *Ripe for the Harvest: A Manual for Cross-Cultural Church Planting* (Wichita, KS: The Urban Ministry Institute Press, 2015).

Dr. Don L. Davis. Ed. *Planting Healthy Churches Among the City's Poor: An Anthology of Urban Church Planting Resources*. Wichita, KS: The Urban Ministry Institute Press, 2015.

Rev. Don Allsman and Dr. Don L. Davis, *Fight the Good Fight of Faith: Playing Your Part in God's Unfolding Drama*. Wichita, KS: The Urban Ministry Institute Press, 2015.

Published Courses and Curriculum Resources

Dr. Davis is committed to theological education for the urban poor. Much of his scholarly work has focused on producing resources easily accessible to urban leaders with a low level of literacy. Nearly all of the resources in this section of the bibliography include audio or video instructional content representing hundreds of hours of lectures designed to equip urban church leaders for ministry in their own context.

Don L. Davis, *Nurturing an Apostolic Heart (Foundations for Ministry Series)*. Wichita, KS: The Urban Ministry Institute Press, 2000.

———. *The Gospel of John (Foundations for Ministry Series)*. Wichita, KS: The Urban Ministry Institute Press, 2002.

———. *The Kingdom of God*, vol. 2, 16 vols. (*The Capstone Curriculum*). Wichita, KS: The Urban Ministry Institute Press, 2004.

———. *Bible Interpretation*, vol. 5, 16 vols. (*The Capstone Curriculum*). Wichita, KS: The Urban Ministry Institute Press, 2005.

———. *Conversion and Calling*, vol. 1, 16 vols. (*The Capstone Curriculum*). Wichita, KS: The Urban Ministry Institute Press, 2005.

———. *Doing Justice and Loving Mercy*, vol. 16, 16 vols. (*The Capstone Curriculum*). Wichita, KS: The Urban Ministry Institute Press, 2005.

———. *Evangelism and Spiritual Warfare*, vol. 8, 16 vols. (*The Capstone Curriculum*). Wichita, KS: The Urban Ministry Institute Press, 2005.

———. *Focus on Reproduction*, vol. 12, 16 vols. (*The Capstone Curriculum*). Wichita, KS: The Urban Ministry Institute Press, 2005.

———. *Foundations for Christian Mission*, vol. 4, 16 vols. (*The Capstone Curriculum*). Wichita, KS: The Urban Ministry Institute Press, 2005.

———. *Foundations of Christian Leadership*, vol. 7, 16 vols. (*The Capstone Curriculum*). Wichita, KS: The Urban Ministry Institute Press, 2005.

———. *God the Father*, vol. 6, 16 vols. (*The Capstone Curriculum*). Wichita, KS: The Urban Ministry Institute Press, 2005.

———. *God the Son*, vol. 10, 16 vols. (*The Capstone Curriculum*). Wichita, KS: The Urban Ministry Institute Press, 2005.

———. *New Testament Witness to Christ and His Kingdom*, vol. 13, 16 vols. (*The Capstone Curriculum*). Wichita, KS: The Urban Ministry Institute Press, 2005.

———. *Old Testament Witness to Christ and His Kingdom*, vol. 9, 16 vols. (*The Capstone Curriculum*). Wichita, KS: The Urban Ministry Institute Press, 2005.

———. *Practicing Christian Leadership*, vol. 11, 16 vols. (*The Capstone Curriculum*). Wichita, KS: The Urban Ministry Institute Press, 2005.

————. *The Equipping Ministry*, vol. 15, 16 vols. (*The Capstone Curriculum*). Wichita, KS: The Urban Ministry Institute Press, 2005.

————. *A Compelling Testimony: Maintaining a Disciplined Walk, Christlike Character, and Godly Relationships as God's Servant (Foundations for Ministry Series)*. Wichita, KS: The Urban Ministry Institute Press, 2006.

————. *A Biblical Vision, Part I: Mastering the Old Testament Witness to Christ and His Kingdom (Foundations for Ministry Series)*. Wichita, KS: The Urban Ministry Institute Press, 2006.

————. *A Biblical Vision, Part II: Mastering the New Testament Witness to Christ and His Kingdom (Foundations for Ministry Series)*. Wichita, KS: The Urban Ministry Institute Press, 2006.

————. *Winning the World: Facilitating Urban Church Planting Movements (Foundations for Ministry Series)*. Wichita, KS: The Urban Ministry Institute Press, 2007.

————. *Church Matters: Retrieving the Great Tradition (Foundations for Ministry Series)*. Wichita, KS: The Urban Ministry Institute Press, 2007.

————. *An Authentic Calling: Representing Christ and His Kingdom through the Church (Foundations for Ministry Series)*. Wichita, KS: The Urban Ministry Institute Press, 2008.

————. *Master the Bible: How to Get and Keep the Big Picture of the Bible's Story (Foundations for Ministry Series)*. Wichita, KS: The Urban Ministry Institute Press, 2008.

——. *Marking Time: Forming Spirituality through the Church Year (Foundations for Ministry Series)*. Wichita, KS: The Urban Ministry Institute Press, 2009.

——. *Sacred Roots Workshop: Retrieving the Great Tradition in the Contemporary Church (Foundations for Ministry Series)*. Wichita, KS: The Urban Ministry Institute Press, 2010.

——. *Ministry in a Multicultural and Unchurched Society (Foundations for Ministry Series)*. Wichita, KS: The Urban Ministry Institute Press, 2012.

Don L. Davis and Terry G. Cornett, *Theology of the Church*, vol. 3, 16 vols. (*The Capstone Curriculum*). Wichita, KS: The Urban Ministry Institute Press, 2005.

Don L. Davis and Lorna Rasmussen, *Managing Projects for Ministry (Foundations for Ministry Series)*. Wichita, KS: The Urban Ministry Institute Press, 2012.

Don Davis L., *Church Resource CD*. Wichita, KS: The Urban Ministry Institute Press, 1999.

Don Davis and Don Allsman, eds., *The John Mark Curriculum*. Los Angeles: World Impact, 2000.

 Chapters, Articles, Shorter Works

Don L. Davis, "An Interview with Cornel West." *Iowa Journal of Cultural Studies* 12 (1993): 8–17.

———. "Overview and Framework for Church Planting Activity". Wichita, KS: The Urban Ministry Institute Press, 2000.

———. *Making Joyful Noises: Mastering the Fundamentals of Music.* Wichita, KS: The Urban Ministry Institute Press, 2000.

———. "Creedal Theology: A Blueprint for Urban Leadership Momentum," in *Gaining Momentum: The Urban Ministry Institute Satellite Summit Workbook.* Wichita, KS: The Urban Ministry Institute Press, 2006, 77–94.

———. "Fleshing out the Universal Priesthood: Recommended Order for Morning and Evening Sacrifices to God," in *The Wondrous Cross: TUMI Annual 2009-2010.* Wichita, KS: The Urban Ministry Institute Press, 2009, 425–36.

———. *The Most Amazing Story Ever Told.* Wichita, KS: The Urban Ministry Institute Press, 2011.

———. *The SIAFU Network Chapter Meeting Guide: How to Inspire Souls and Transform Hearts through Your SIAFU Gathering.* Wichita, KS: The Urban Ministry Institute Press, 2013.

Terry Cornett and Don Davis. *Empowering People for Freedom, Wholeness, and Justice: Theological and Ethical Foundations for World Impact's Development Ministries.* Wichita, KS: The Urban Ministry Institute Press, 1996.

Carl Ellis, ed. with Don Davis and Pastor R. C. Smith. *Saving Our Sons: Confronting the Lure of Islam With Truth, Faith & Courage.* Chicago, IMANI Books, 2007.

Published Conference Materials

Don L. Davis, *The Timothy Conference: Building Church Plant Teams*. Wichita, KS: The Urban Ministry Institute Press, 2004.

———. *Powerful in Battle Behind Men's Conference*, SIAFU Conferences. Wichita, KS: The Urban Ministry Institute Press, 2009.

———. *No Man Left Behind Men's Conference*, SIAFU Conferences. Wichita, KS: The Urban Ministry Institute Press, 2011.

———. *Fit to Represent: Vision for Discipleship Seminar*. Wichita, KS: The Urban Ministry Institute Press, 2012.

———. *War of the Worlds Men's Conference*, SIAFU Conferences. Wichita, KS: The Urban Ministry Institute Press, 2012.

———. *Mo' Power Men's Conference*, SIAFU Conferences. Wichita, KS: The Urban Ministry Institute Press, 2013.

———. *Band of Brothers: Why We Fight*, SIAFU Conferences. Wichita, KS: The Urban Ministry Institute Press, 2014.

Don L. Davis, ed., *Gaining Momentum: The Urban Ministry Institute Satellite Summit 2006 Workbook*. Wichita, KS: The Urban Ministry Institute Press, 2006.

——. ed., *The Battle Belongs to the Lord: TUMI Satellite Summit 2007 Workbook*. Wichita, KS: The Urban Ministry Institute Press, 2007.

——. ed., *Like a Master Builder: TUMI Satellite Summit 2009 Workbook*. Wichita, KS: The Urban Ministry Institute Press, 2009.

——. ed., *The Good Shepherd: TUMI Satellite Summit 2010 Workbook*. Wichita, KS: The Urban Ministry Institute Press, 2010.

——. ed., *Back to the Future: Renewing the Urban Church through the Great Tradition: TUMI Satellite Summit 2012 Workbook*. Wichita, KS: The Urban Ministry Institute Press, 2012.

——. ed., *Mission: Impossible: Adapt to Win: TUMI Satellite Summit 2013 Workbook*. Wichita, KS: The Urban Ministry Institute Press, 2013.

——. ed., *The Fight for the Future Begins: TUMI Satellite Summit 2014 Workbook*. Wichita, KS: The Urban Ministry Institute Press, 2014.

——. ed., *The Power of Team: TUMI Satellite Summit 2015 Workbook*. Wichita, KS: The Urban Ministry Institute Press, 2015.

Public Lectures

Dr. Davis has lectured at numerous educational institutions around the country as illustrated by selections below.

Don L. Davis, "Three Things I Wish I Was Taught at Wheaton" (Morris Inch Lectureship, Wheaton College, Wheaton, IL, 1991).

——. "The Erotic Prophets: The Intrigue of Divine Romance" (Staley Lecture Series, Milligan College, TN, 2000).

——. "The Ecstatic Prophets: The Hope of the Ages" (Staley Lecture Series, Milligan College, TN, 2000).

——. "The Evangelistic Prophets: Living the Examined Life" (Staley Lecture Series, Milligan College, TN, 2000).

——. "'Who Cares about King?'" (Lived Theology and Community Building Workgroup, Duke University, Durham, NC, 2001).

——. "The Making of a Prophet: The Dignity and Interconnectedness of Humankind" (Martin Luther King Celebration, Fresno, CA, 2004).

——. "Taking King Seriously: Risking Cosmic Companionship With God" (Martin Luther King Celebration, Barclay College, KS, 2004).